THE GROVE:
Recipes and History of Virginia Tech's Presidential Residence

Clara B. Cox, Editor/Author

Featuring Recipes by Chef Michael Arrington, Chef Josef R. Schelch, and Seven First Ladies of the University

and a History of The Grove by the Editor

Published by the Virginia Tech Foundation

Printed by Interstate Graphics, Inc.
Johnson City, Tennessee

ISBN 978-0-615-64928-3

First Edition Printed in the United States of America

Book Design by Barbara Corbett

Cover Photograph by John McCormick

Photography by Jim Stroup, Kelsey Kradel, Logan Wallace, Michael Kiernan, John McCormick, and Ryan Stone

Printed with private funds

The use of brand-name ingredients in this book does not necessarily imply an endorsement of those brands by the Virginia Tech Foundation.

Every effort has been made to ensure that ingredient listings and preparation directions for recipes are correct, but the Virginia Tech Foundation can assume no liability for food preparation based on recipes herein.

Dedicated to the faculty and staff of Virginia Tech
and all supporters of the Employees' Spouse
and Dependent Scholarship Program

and in grateful appreciation to Tom McAvoy
for his work on the scholarship committee
since its inception

Acknowledgments

When Kim O'Rourke, chief of staff for the Office of the President at Virginia Tech, asked me in 2010 if I would be interested in editing a cookbook of recipes from The Grove and agreed to let me write a history of the president's home, I was intrigued by the project and thrilled by the possibilities it provided—and I liked the idea of President Charles W. Steger Jr. to use it to raise money for a most worthy cause in the process. Although I had worked on other books, little did I know of the complexities involved in such a venture as this one: merging the history of a house with recipes from executive chefs and the university's first ladies.

By its very nature, the project has required the assistance of numerous people, without whose help this book could not have come to fruition. Many of them deserve particular mention.

The contributions of Janet Steger, current first lady, are wide ranging, and the ones that particularly stand out are the teas she scheduled in The Grove with individuals, including two former first ladies, to provide me with information about life in the historic home; opening files about entertaining at the house over the past two decades; providing copies of history-related materials she had collected; and guiding me through the house so I could better understand its layout and the renovations it has undergone. She also submitted recipes for the chapter on first ladies' recipes and reviewed the book.

Former first ladies who should be recognized are Adele McComas White, Dot Torgersen, and Peggy Lavery. These women provided their personal recipes and/or directed me to cookbooks in which some of their recipes appear, and they furnished information for the history section. Additionally, Adele graciously took time to review sections related to the McComas administration.

Former and present top executives deserving appreciation are President Emeritus Paul Torgersen, who reviewed the sections about him and his administration and provided photographs; President Emeritus T. Marshall Hahn Jr., who reviewed the section on his administration; and President Steger, who conceived and reviewed the book.

Several members of first families and relatives of first families gave significant assistance, from providing recipes to filling in gaps in the history and from loaning photographs to writing about their experiences in The Grove: Ann Hahn Hurst and Betty Hahn, the daughters of President Emeritus and the late Mrs. Hahn; Alice Dekker, a great niece of first lady "LizOtey" Newman; Larry McBryde, great-grandson of President and Mrs. John M. McBryde; Ivis Hutcheson, daughter-in-law of President and Mrs. John R. Hutcheson; Jack Hutcheson, grandson of President and Mrs. Hutcheson; and Lori L. Mitchell, daughter of President and Mrs. William E. Lavery.

Assistance also came from several special friends. Debbie Lawrence, Mary Grace Theodore, Kim O'Rourke, and Tom Brown aided in various ways, from supplying much-needed information to setting up contacts with key people.

Other individuals provided recollections, leads, and contact information; helped with research; reviewed various parts of the book; loaned photographs; arranged photo shoots; scheduled meetings; and/or gave other forms of special help: Lynn Eichhorn, Natalie Hart, Larry Hincker, Martha Holmes, Tamara Kennelly and other members of the university's Special Collections staff, Michael Kiernan, Duke Perry, Frances Russell, Ray Smoot, Tom Tillar, David Venné, and the helpful people in Records Management. Additionally, the Faculty Women's Club generously gave permission to reprint recipes of first ladies that appeared in two of the organization's cookbooks.

The photographers were superb, especially Jim Stroup, the principal photographer on the project, and John McCormick, who shot the cover photograph. All of them—Jim, John, Michael Kiernan, Kelsey Kradel, Logan Wallace, and Ryan Stone—are talented, creative people who brought the book to life with their work.

As for the designer, Barbara Corbett, readers can see what an exceptional job she did since her skills are evident on every page.

The executive chefs, of course, made the book what it is. Michael "Mike" Arrington, current chef, and Josef R. Schelch, a former chef with the university, submitted their personally developed recipes. Additionally, Chef Josef researched and modernized early recipes, and Chef Michael reviewed recipes after they were edited and tested many of them to the delight of photographer Jim Stroup, who not only had prime material for his shots but also enjoyed eating the "models."

Finally—but not last in appreciation—a person who helped me more than anyone, other than I, will ever know is my husband, William E. Cox, whose help was varied, unlimited, and incomparable.

The words seem inadequate considering all that these many people have done, but thank you, each and every one of you, for your significant role in the creation of this book.

Clara B. Cox
Editor/Author

Contents

Foreword

The Oxford World Dictionary defines art as "the expression or application of human creative skill and imagination." In looking at the various aspects that comprise art, such forms as music, painting, acting, sculpting, and creative writing come quickly to mind. Cooking generally does not.

In more than a decade of living in The Grove, Virginia Tech's presidential residence, I have admired and enjoyed the artistic creations of Chef Michael "Mike" Arrington, our executive chef, and, on occasion, Chef Josef R. Schelch, who has now retired from the university. As a result of these experiences, I am inclined to add cooking to my concept of the arts.

You have only to look at the photographs of their dishes in this book to see how much attention they pay to the presentation of their food. Their emphasis on texture and color and visual appeal is reminiscent of a painter applying oils to a canvas. These chefs develop their own recipes, adapt classic favorites, and then ensure that the resulting dishes are not just aesthetically pleasing but also provide epicurean enjoyment to the thousands of guests we entertain at The Grove each year.

On the pages that follow, you will find their recipes for appetizers, salads, breads, cereals, soups, sauces, entrées, vegetables, fruit dishes, and desserts. You will also find a few other "ingredients" that help make this publication a little different from the traditional cookbook: a history of The Grove, biographical sketches of the presidents who have lived in the stately home, and recipes from seven first ladies.

But this book goes beyond providing recipes and information about The Grove and its occupants. It also helps build the endowment to support the Employees' Spouse and Dependent Scholarship Program, a feature of the Staff and Faculty Annual Fund. Former university presidents joined me in starting the endowment because we want to ensure that spouses and dependent children of the university's employees will always have access to scholarships if they attend Virginia Tech. An endowment is the way to ensure a solid, long-term scholarship program.

More than a year ago, when I was considering ways to increase the endowment, it occurred to me that many of our alumni and other friends would enjoy having access to the recipes developed by executive chefs of The Grove. Why not, I reasoned, produce a book of The Grove's recipes, with the profits from selling it going directly into the endowment?

The Grove: Recipes and History of Virginia Tech's Presidential Residence is the result. Thank you for purchasing it and, thus, making a contribution to the scholarship endowment. By doing so, you are helping us to ensure that the spouses and dependent children of our outstanding faculty and staff have the financial means to study, like many of you have, at this great university.

Charles W. Steger Jr.
President

"A Dramatic Piece of Architecture up on the Hill": A History of The Grove, Virginia Tech's Presidential Residence

If not for a rotten porch and too many sick cadets on the campus of Virginia Agricultural and Mechanical College and Polytechnic Institute (today's Virginia Tech) in the late nineteenth century, the landmark presidential residence known today as The Grove probably would not exist. But in 1899, the college's board of visitors heeded President John M. McBryde when he recommended converting his home into an infirmary and building a new one for the school's chief executive. Although erected to house the college's presidents, current and future, the residence has not always served that purpose, counting a chancellor and a few ducks among its inhabitants, becoming the headquarters for university offices and office space for graduate students, and losing its pre-eminent status to other houses—twice—since its construction more than a century ago.

❖ Laying the Groundwork for a New Executive Residence

By the end of the 1800s, the college with the long name, popularly called Virginia Polytechnic Institute or simply VPI until it became a university in 1970, was renting a facility off campus to serve as an infirmary for the all-male, all-cadet student body, a facility that became intertwined with a proposal for a new home for the school's presidents. Outbreaks of contagious diseases within the corps of cadets in the 1898-1899 session forced VPI to allow many of the sick to remain in their dormitories since the infirmary lacked adequate room for them. Additionally, the facility was badly out of repair, and for financial reasons, the owner could not make the improvements it needed. Thus, in June 1899, McBryde started urging the VPI Board of Visitors to approve construction of a well-planned and well-equipped infirmary on campus. The president wanted a healthcare facility that would be well managed and commodious—large enough to meet the demands forced by any disease outbreaks. Perhaps with an eye to state funding, he also reported the need for an on-campus infirmary to Joseph W. Southall, state superintendent of public instruction:

[W]e greatly need a well-planned and thoroughly equipped infirmary. Having no suitable building of our own, we have for years been forced to rent a building outside of our grounds, which far from answers our requirements. It is, however, the best we can obtain. . . .

Local contractor William Wesley "Wes" Gray (his name is sometimes listed as Wesley W. Gray) submitted a proposal to build the facility for no more than $4,000 and offered a payment plan: the college could pay him over a period of 10 years at 5 percent interest on the deferred payments. But after presenting this information to the board in his June 20, 1899, president's report, McBryde added that a "new house for the president could be built for a few thousand dollars and his present house, with a few changes, would make an admirable infirmary." A rotten porch at his residence may have spurred McBryde's broader thinking about the infirmary project. Since assuming the chief executive position at the small Blacksburg college in 1891 and moving into the president's home, now part of Henderson Hall and located between Alumni Mall and College Avenue, he had asked the board for nothing other than the minor repairs necessary to preserve the official president's residence. But a porch, which the McBryde family found too small to be serviceable, had nearly rotted away. "If it is decided to build a new infirmary, I feel that I must ask that a new porch be added to the president's house," McBryde told the board before it made its final decision on the larger project. He added that a new porch extending along the front of the house would cost a maximum of $500.

McBryde secured the services of Lingan S. Randolph, a professor of mechanical engineering and later dean of engineering at the college, to develop plans for a new infirmary and alternate plans for converting the president's home into an infirmary and building a new executive residence. Randolph's work was examined and witnessed by Major Channing Moore Bolton, former chief engineer of the Southern Railroad, and Henry Hartwell Huggins (listed variously as Harrie Huggins and Harry Hartwell Huggins), a well-known Roanoke, Va., architect. The president used the plans to solicit bids from a number of contractors, but only three responded: Gray, who had earlier submitted a proposal to construct the infirmary; a builder named Parrish; and a builder named Barber.

In executive session on June 13, 1900, with the bids in hand, board member J. F. Ryan made the motion and it was resolved that

the house now occupied by the president be converted into an infirmary, according to the plans submitted with the several bids, and that a president's house be erected, to be of brick and in such plans as the president and executive committee may adopt, at a cost not exceeding $10,000 complete.

The board reviewed—and promptly rejected—the three bids and then instructed McBryde to solicit bids again for the converted infirmary, a new president's house, and several other facilities on campus: a science hall, a dormitory, and additions to the shops. They grouped these other projects into a package with the new presidential residence and conversion of the existing president's home into an infirmary but set the maximum for the house conversion at $2,787 and the new residence construction at $10,000. McBryde wasted no time in soliciting the bids, sending the specifications and drawings out that same month.

Unless Huggins was a fast worker, he had been retained to design or to draw up the plans for the house at some point prior to that time—possibly when he examined and witnessed Randolph's work on the project. Regardless, Huggins's drawings of the Southern Colonial Revival style residence accompanied the project specifications that McBryde mailed to a number of builders on June 29. It is not known what influence—if any—Randolph had on the design or whether the architect received any input from McBryde, although it has been reported that the house was built as the president wanted it. Because Huggins's name is on the drawings, it is assumed that he designed the home, but the boastful, self-promoting architect did not advertise that fact as he did many of the other structures he designed, especially those for colleges. Regardless, the information packet distributed by McBryde solicited bids by July 3, 1900, on

the labor and materials required in the erection and completion of a two-story, brick dwelling house to be erected for Dr. J. M. McBryde in Blacksburg, Virginia, agreeably to the specification and the accompanying drawings . . . furnished by H. H. Huggins, architect, and under the supervision of the owner, and to his entire satisfaction, or under the supervision of the architect or any person appointed by the owner to act in his stead and referred to generally herein as the superintendent.

Whether it was to design the house or execute the drawings, Huggins was, most likely, selected for the job because of his experience and reputation. Over the course of his architectural career, he designed buildings for Hollins Institute (now University) and the Virginia College for Young Ladies, which was located in

1891 - 1907

The Father of VPI

The president who spurred construction of The Grove, John McLaren McBryde, was a dynamic leader who significantly altered Virginia Agricultural and Mechanical College (VAMC, today's Virginia Tech).

McBryde transformed the often-struggling, three-year-degree-granting, vocational-type institution into an undergraduate- and graduate-degree-granting college. His foresight and ability to execute his vision laid the groundwork for today's university and resulted in a new name for the school: Virginia Agricultural and Mechanical College and Polytechnic Institute, popularly known as VPI.

A native of South Carolina, McBryde was born in 1841 and enrolled in South Carolina College (today's University of South Carolina) at age 17. He matriculated at the University of Virginia in 1860, leaving the next year to join the First South Carolina Volunteer Infantry. When typhus ended his military life, he worked for the Confederate States' Treasury Department in Richmond, Va.

McBryde married Cora Bolton of Richmond in 1863, and the couple had eight children.

After the war, he became a farmer, then a lawyer, in Buckingham County, Va., before leaving in 1879 to teach agriculture and botany at the University of Tennessee (UT). He accepted a chair at South Carolina College in 1882 and became the college's president the following year. He earned a Ph.D. at UT before his administration ended in 1891, the year he became president of VAMC.

During his lifetime, he was named a Fellow in both the American Geographical Society and the American Statistical Association.

When he retired from VPI in 1907, he was named the college's first president emeritus and received the institution's first honorary degree, a doctor of science, which he added to the honorary doctor of laws he had received from the Southern Presbyterian University.

Much loved and highly revered, the "Father of VPI" died in 1923.

Roanoke. Other projects he designed during 21 years of practice included churches; schools; residences; buildings for various businesses; and courthouses, including, according to one of his own advertisements, the Montgomery County Courthouse in nearby Christiansburg. His 1900 advertisement in a directory reports that he also "designed the immense barns, stables, and silos for the State Agricultural Experiment Station at Blacksburg." In 1908, Huggins designed a Roanoke residence, Mountain View, that is also in the Southern Colonial Revival style, although much larger than the VPI house, and is now on the National Register of Historic Places. A native of South Carolina, he had studied civil engineering at South Carolina College and had worked as a surveyor and civil engineer in South Carolina and Alabama before moving to Roanoke in 1891 to open an architectural firm with a fellow South Carolinian, Charles C. Wilson. The partnership, which advertised a specialty in hotels and public buildings, was dissolved in 1893, and Huggins continued his design practice alone until adding W. B. Bates to the business in 1910. That partnership lasted until shortly before Huggins's death in 1912 at the age of 48. Coincidentally, McBryde had been president of South Carolina College before accepting the leadership position at VPI. Whether he and the Roanoke architect had known each other before VPI retained Huggins's services for the barns, stables, and silos or for the President's Home could not be ascertained.

At some point, the decision was made to site the president's home on a hill covered with trees, known as "the grove," that was located on the extreme western edge of the campus. The hill, once part of the historic Smithfield Plantation lands, overlooked a marshy area, which was converted into the Duck Pond in 1934, and Solitude, an historic home purchased by the college when it opened in 1872. The hill is located southwest of the lower end of the Drillfield, known at the time as Sheib Field.

After contractors submitted their bids for the VPI projects in mid-1900, the board of visitors selected Wes Gray's proposal to construct the multi-building project. While erecting the president's residence, the Blacksburg contractor was also constructing the YMCA Building, now known as the Performing Arts Building, on campus. Among other campus buildings he constructed were Barracks No. 4, today part of Shanks Hall; the first Field House, a wooden structure destroyed by fire in 1923; probably Barracks No. 2, now part of Rasche Hall, since he is known to have made the bricks on campus for that barracks; the first science hall; and barns. Gray also remodeled the YMCA Building in 1924. Called "Blacksburg's most active contractor" by architectural historian Gibson Worsham, Gray also constructed a number of houses and churches in Blacksburg and several buildings, including the Hunter's Masonic Lodge, in downtown Blacksburg. Additionally, he worked on several college buildings, other types of buildings, and residences outside Blacksburg, including part of Christiansburg Industrial Institute.

❖ Construction and Landscaping of the President's Home in the Grove

By mid-1901, the foundation of the new home for presidents was completed, and work on the brick house itself had begun. By that time, a new avenue, lined with two rows of shade trees, had been constructed that ran from the Ice Pond (located slightly above and north of today's Duck Pond), by the front of Professor David O. Nourse's house, and around the grove to some new barns. By February 1902, additional improvements to the hilltop site were under way. Two cottages, which housed farm laborers, on the crest of the hill were moved to a lower position on the same hill but on the other side of the new avenue. Fences, old barns, and stables were torn down, and a mineral spring at the foot of the hill was cleaned out and enclosed in a building with a concrete floor. The land that the old agricultural facilities had once covered was graded, sowed with grass seed, and planted with trees. "These changes will make the president's house and grove part of the campus," the student publication known as *The Gray Jacket* reported, while the president himself told the board of visitors that the appearance of the lower campus "has been greatly improved by these changes."

Construction delays apparently persisted, perhaps because Gray was involved in so many college projects and perhaps because subcontractors were having problems producing bricks on campus, first because of faulty machinery and later because of early frosts. In October 1901, *The Gray Jacket* reported that the house "is nearing completion." Two months later, the publication stated that the project would probably be completed in January 1902; however, the projected completion date was reported in January as being in February. In February, *The Gray Jacket* predicted, "Our president's house will certainly be finished by March . . . ."

The residence, which the student publication called "the magnificent new house for the president," finally was completed in April 1902, and McBryde and his family moved in later that month. Although the McBrydes had five children, all of them were grown and only one, Susie, became a resident of the new facility with her parents. It is also possible that a sister of the first lady, who had been living with the McBrydes, moved into the new house with the family.

A pleased president reported to the board of visitors in June 1902 that the westward-facing house "is a beautiful building and admirably harmonizes with its situation and surroundings," and his annual report about the college to the state superintendent of public instruction included a comment that "the president's house is an attractive brick building situated in a beautiful grove in the lower part of our large campus." The vistas from the house, according to one visitor, gave a "fine view of the college buildings and grounds, the town, and the beautiful farming country stretching out for miles in every direction." The house itself, a "building of red brick, with white verandas," the visitor added, "stands in a magnificent grove of native trees and is ideal in location and appearance."

President McBryde (left of center) and members of his family gather on the grounds of the President's Home in the Grove. Photo courtesy of Larry McBryde and Special Collections, University Libraries, Virginia Tech

This photograph of the President's Home in the Grove was taken within the first decade of its construction in 1902. Photo courtesy of Special Collections, University Libraries, Virginia Tech

When it was constructed, the imposing 15,147 sq. ft. structure—two stories with a full-size attic and basement—was dominated on the west-facing front by a large columnar portico, with two-story colossal fluted columns with Ionic capitals supporting a gabled pediment. A full-length, balustrade-enclosed 9 ft. wide veranda, whose roof was supported by smaller columns, spanned the front façade and made a right angle at each end to continue about half way down the north and south façades of the house. In their book on Virginia architecture, authors Charles E. Brownell *et al.* note that the stately portico of a Southern Colonial Revival house "signaled the fact that a person of importance dwelled there, while the one-story porch acknowledged that that person was . . . an ordinary individual who did relax comfortably in full view, rocking and greeting his neighbors."

A second-floor balcony, which sat above the first-floor entrance of the President's Home, was flanked on either side by large arched windows. Double-windowed dormers in the attic extended above the arched windows, and a Buckingham slate roof was crowned with a widow's walk. Pressed zinc ornamental finials were installed at the outside ridge of each rooftop. On the north façade, a *porte cochere* provided sheltered access for visitors arriving by carriage or car and allowed entry into the house through a vestibule leading into the library. On the back half of the south façade, a side porch provided access directly into a sitting room. The east façade, or back of the house, featured a portico, although it was smaller and less grand than the one gracing the front of the house; a recessed entry; and a second-floor balcony over the rear entry.

Inside, the front part of the first floor was planned for living and entertaining and the back portion for service areas, with the second floor reserved for bedrooms—Huggins designed seven bedrooms and three bathrooms on the second floor. The first-floor entrance led into a reception hall. To the left, or north side, of the reception hall was a library and to the right, or south side, the front parlor. Sliding pocket doors allowed both rooms to be closed off from the reception hall. A "rear" parlor on the right, just beyond the front parlor, could be accessed through the reception

hall and through the front parlor, and it, too, could be shut off from the reception hall and the front parlor by closing its pocket doors. The doors between the three rooms and the reception hall could be opened to provide an area for entertaining large numbers of guests. Directly behind the library was the dining room, which was separated from the kitchen beyond it by the scullery. Two single-leaf doors provided access from the dining room into the library and into the stair hall, which lay beyond the reception hall. On the other side of the stair hall and accessed through two separate, single-leaf doors was a sitting room. Behind the stair hall were the service areas, which included the kitchen and scullery as well as a back stairway, a pantry, and a small bedroom. High ceilings and wooden paneling with dado rails graced the reception hall and rooms, and a grand staircase extended from the stair hall to the floor above. Doorways leading from the second-floor hallways were topped with operable glass transoms to increase the circulation of air. The wood flooring on the first floor was oak, with pine flooring installed on the second floor, a typical installation for the period. According to a June 1902 treasurer's report to the board of visitors, the college's special fund disbursements for the house totaled $10,447.98.

By the winter of 1903, McBryde was feeling ill effects from at least one cost-cutting measure used in constructing his home. An old, antiquated heater had been installed in the house that had been moved from Dormitory No. 1, today's Lane Hall, which was completed in 1888. McBryde asked the board to replace it:

> It is exceedingly hard to fire, and the cinders can only be removed by a person's lying flat on the floor and tipping the grate underneath with a long iron rod. In consequence, it is very difficult to get servants to keep it properly clean or to attend to it personally. The consumption of coal is something enormous. At my other residence, I used only about 900 [bushels of coal]—this past winter more than 2.200 bushels were required. The change has increased my fuel bills upwards of $160.

He asked the board to authorize $375 for a new heater for the house, but the board did not comply with his request until its June meeting.

During the 1904-1905 college session, according to *The Bugle's Echo,* "A graceful row of lindens [also known as basswood trees] was set out from the president's house to the college barns." And the following session, the president's house received two fire extinguishers in a campus-wide distribution of fire-retarding equipment.

❖The College Gets Its Infirmary

Renovation of the college's first presidential residence to convert it into an infirmary had been delayed until the McBrydes moved out, but the work proceeded during the summer of 1902, along with the addition of a new wing. "Its new wing will contain 32 beds, and the rooms in the main building will accommodate six

In 1876, four years after Charles L. C. Minor became the first president of Virginia Agricultural and Mechanical College (today's Virginia Tech), a home for the college's top administrator was constructed on campus. The house, today part of Henderson Hall, served as the residence of four more presidents before the last one, John M. McBryde, convinced the board of visitors to convert the home into an infirmary and construct a new presidential residence. Photo courtesy of Special Collections, University Libraries, Virginia Tech

more beds. It will be well supplied with bathrooms, water closets, and offices," the president reported to the board in June 1902.

The Virginia General Assembly had appropriated funds to build the house in March 1874 during the administration of the college's first president, Charles Landon Carter Minor. The board of visitors of the college, founded in 1872 as Virginia Agricultural and Mechanical College, had followed up with plans for its location and construction, but according to *The Bugle's Echo*, "A misunderstanding between the college's authorities and a brick contractor caused a short delay in the erection of President Minor's house," and the two-story brick residence was not completed until 1876. It served for three years as Minor's home and for 23 years afterward as the home for the presidents who followed him, although Professor John Hart, acting president for the 1880-1881 session, continued to live in the faculty house provided to him. (A benefit for all members of the faculty in those days was the provision of a house on campus.) The presidents succeeding Minor as residents of the first President's Home included John L. Buchanan, who lived in the executive residence twice—he was president from March 1, 1880, until June 12, 1880, and again from August 12, 1881, until January 17, 1882—followed by Thomas Nelson Conrad, from 1882 until 1886; Lunsford Lindsay Lomax, from 1886 to 1891; and McBryde, who lived there from 1891 until he moved into the second President's Home in 1902. Scott Shipp, who was president for less than two weeks in 1880 after Buchanan's first administration ended, did not remain in office long enough to move into the home.

❖ Early Entertaining at the Mansion

Reportedly, the president found the President's Home in the Grove, as it was initially named, to be an ideal setting for gatherings of guests, and the McBrydes—particularly their daughter, Susie—wasted no time in entertaining guests there. In fact, Susie McBryde is said to have instigated much of the entertaining, inviting friends for games, charades, and parties. Miss Mary G. Lacy, hired by VPI in 1903 as its first professional librarian, was a friend of Susie's and lived in the house after she began working at the college, apparently remaining there until McBryde's successor moved in. Early, if not the first, guests may have been Virginia Governor Andrew Jackson Montague and his wife, who journeyed to the campus for the 1902 commencement—the governor was the commencement speaker—and reportedly were hosted by the president. Guests at various events held at the house included members of the faculty and students. Susie frequently held parties for groups of 20 to 30 cadets, and Miss Lacy helped decorate and assisted with the party games. The parties featured fresh ice cream from a dozen hand-crank ice cream makers on the back porch. Even when McBryde's daughter hosted the parties, he would leave his study door open so that any cadet who wished to speak to him would feel invited to do so.

Col. Harry D. Temple's book, Donning the Blue and Gray, *was published in 1992 and included 37 full-color plates of different uniforms worn by the Virginia Tech Corps of Cadets since 1872, including the plate above, which shows two cadets on the lawn of the President's Home (today known as The Grove). Print courtesy of Col. Rock Roszak*

The students were, perhaps, the president's favorite guests, and he hosted receptions for many of them, including, among others, graduating classes, members of the glee club, and cadet captains. The seniors were feted with receptions on the veranda during the spring months, and students remaining on campus during the winter holidays received invitations to celebrate Christmas with the first family. McBryde, a wise, practical, clear-sighted leader who made a point of remembering the names of each cadet in the corps, was idolized by the cadets, and they demonstrated their affection for him by planning and executing one of the more unusual events at the President's Home in the Grove—without his permission or prior knowledge. According to *The Gray Jacket,* the cadets formed into companies one night in March 1904 following a favorable appropriation from the state legislature

and marched to and [surrounded] the president's mansion. So quietly was this done that not until the band stationed near the east entrance burst forth with a crash of melody, and the tumultuous cheers from nearly a thousand throats rent the air, did any of the inmates of the mansion know what was to happen. College songs were sung, and football yells yelled, and all imaginable noise created, and with Doctor's [McBryde's] unassuming speech at the close, the serenade ended successfully, the boys departing with great love in their hearts for the institution's "grand old man."

While that occasion most likely greatly pleased the president, the most important event—certainly for the McBrydes themselves—was the marriage there on October 30, 1905, of daughter Susie to Christopher Gadson Quignard.

McBryde retired in 1907 and remained in Blacksburg, where he constructed his next home in sight of the stately one on campus for whose existence he had been responsible.

❖ Four More Presidents Live in the House

After McBryde left, four additional presidents lived in the President's Home before it was substantially renovated around 1950: Dr. Paul B. Barringer, Joseph D. Eggleston, Julian A. Burruss, and John R. Hutcheson.

Paul B. Barringer

Dr. Barringer; his wife, Nannie; and at least some of their 10 children moved into the presidential home in 1907 after Dr. Barringer, who held a medical degree and had been a practicing physician, assumed the presidency of VPI on September 1 of that year. Sociable people, the Barringers entertained frequently in their home, which, by 1910 was called "the Grove." The couple—and sometimes one or more of their children—feted professors, instructors, college seniors, senior cadet officers, members of the Alleghany Chapter of the Daughters of the American Revolution (DAR), relatives, friends, and dignitaries.

It was not unusual at that time for the student newspaper, the *Virginia Tech,* to report on events at the Grove in a personals-type

The Physician President

Dr. Paul Brandon Barringer, Virginia Tech's sixth president, worked to reorganize the college, then popularly known as VPI.

Often embroiled in controversy during his 1907 to 1913 administration—from the sale of diseased livestock to charges filed against him by disgruntled alumni and employees—Barringer still made contributions that improved the college. Among them, he placed the graduate program on the same

1907 - 1913

administrative level as other departments, increased entrance requirements, extended self-government to students, and encouraged formulation of an honor code.

The son and grandson of generals, he was born in North Carolina in 1857. He studied at Kenmore University School at Amherst Courthouse, Va., and later received two M.D. degrees, both in 1877: one from the University of Virginia (UVa) and one from the University of the City of New York.

Dr. Barringer practiced medicine in North Carolina before going to Europe to study under medical specialists. On his return, he settled on a farm near Charlotte, N.C., and practiced medicine and farmed.

He married Nannie Irene Hannah of Charlotte County, Va., in 1882. They had 10 children.

The doctor established and headed a medical preparatory school at Davidson College, leaving in 1889 to become chair of physiology at UVa, where he later became chair of the faculty and a professor of therapeutics and pharmacology. He oversaw a major revision of UVa's medical curriculum and was the driving force behind the construction and staffing of its first hospital, serving as its first superintendent. During that period of his life, he received honorary LL.D. degrees from Davidson College and the University of South Carolina. He left UVa in 1907 to head the administration at VPI.

Following his six-year presidency, Dr. Barringer returned to Charlottesville, where, except for a few years he spent in military service during World War I, he practiced medicine. He died in 1941.

column, from weekend visits of friends and family members to faculty receptions. Sometimes, the descriptions of the events were short and simple, such as the report of the Barringers' daughter, Margaret, returning home from college to spend "the Christmas holidays on campus at the home of her parents . . . ." At other times, they were longer and more detailed. For example, the newspaper included the following notice on November 4, 1908:

On last Tuesday evening from 9 until 11 o'clock, Dr. and Mrs. P. B. Barringer tendered a most delightful reception to the faculty, the instructors, and several other friends. "The Grove," Dr. and Mrs. Barringer's palatial home at the western extremity of the campus, was beautifully and artistically decorated for the occasion. The punch bowl was presided over by Miss Anna Barringer, daughter of the host and hostess. Among the guests were the 10 brides now on campus. Dainty refreshments were served.

When the Barringers held a reception for the senior class, the *Virginia Tech* reported on February 17, 1909, that the

> massive oak doors at "the Grove" were swung back for the reception tendered the seniors by Dr. and Mrs. Barringer. Miss Anna Barringer, daughter of the host and hostess, in corn-colored silk, and Miss Lucile Cassell, in blue crepe de chine, and Miss Kathleen Cassell, in a princess gown of pink satin, received at the door and ushered the guests into the beautifully decorated reception rooms where the more bashfull [sic] ones among them passed into that sub-conscious state peculiar to their kind before the dancing eyes of the laughing, rollicking girls who were present the evening before at the mid-winter german. . . . [Refreshments were] oysters, salads, ices, and fruit.

Among the Barringers' more noted guests were German pianist Richard Burmeister, who gave a concert on campus and stayed at the President's Home, and a baroness, both of whom were feted with receptions. Among other events were meetings of the local chapter of the DAR, including its organizational meeting when Nannie Barringer was elected its first regent, and various types of dances. The saddest event ever held at the Grove was the funeral on August 17, 1911, of the Barringers' son, Rufus, who had died two days earlier following surgery.

Barringer's administration was punctuated by frequent controversy, and his tenure as president was not entirely a happy one. Hearing rumors that he was being persecuted to push him out of office so that a particular person could move in and believing that the governor was going to appoint new members to the board of visitors who would get rid of him, Barringer tendered his resignation on July 12, 1912. But while he remained in office and continued living at the Grove until the end of the 1912-1913 session, his wife, a daughter, and a son moved on April 2 to the family's next home in Charlottesville, Va., and another daughter returned to Hollins College the same day. Regardless of the problems Barringer faced in his administration, the *Virginia Tech* reported that the president and his wife

> have made hosts of friends by their generous hospitality, and the closing of their home "the Grove," so far as the Barringers are concerned, is a matter of regret to those who enjoyed the friendship of President Barringer and Mrs. Barringer and the younger members of the large family.

Joseph D. Eggleston

Joseph D. Eggleston assumed the presidency of VPI on July 1, 1913, and moved with his family into the President's Home. Late in his administration, Eggleston conceived an idea for one of the more unusual—but practical—uses for the home's grounds. "There is a great deal of grass in the Grove yard that could be well utilized by the sheep," he wrote Robert E. Hunt, a professor of animal husbandry, on May 8, 1919. "We would be glad to have them mow it, provided the boys will not let the sheep eat the

flowers, ferns, etc. near and around the house, but if the boys are careless, the flowers, ferns, etc. will be ruined, and the ladies thereby greatly disturbed." The sheep became the grass mowers, at least for a time, but it is not known if they disturbed the ladies by damaging the flowers, ferns, etc.

Like his predecessors, Eggleston used the elegant President's Home as the setting for various events. Regular guests included the visiting dignitaries at graduation exercises. In 1914, Eggleston's first commencement since assuming the college's highest office, he hosted a dinner for Governor H. C. Stuart, who spoke to the graduating class, but he was not able to follow that tradition in 1918, as he explained in a letter to J. Thompson Brown, rector of the board of visitors:

> Mrs. Eggleston and I wish very much we could entertain you while you are here, but our cook has recently left us and Mrs. Eggleston's sister, Miss [Elizabeth W. "Betty"]

The Agricultural Visionary

1913 - 1919

The third resident of the Grove, Joseph Dupuy Eggleston, was a well-known educator when he took over the reins of Virginia Agricultural and Mechanical College and Polytechnic Institute (popularly called VPI, today's Virginia Tech) in 1913.

As president, Eggleston found ways for VPI to develop and expand farm demonstration work and planned demonstration-work training sessions on campus even before the Smith-Lever Act moved Extension under the auspices of land-grant colleges. He was the first president to encourage and accept women as students; they were limited to summer courses on demonstration work.

He was also responsible for changing the look of the campus. He convinced the board of visitors to hire Carneal and Johnston to develop a plan for campus structures, resulting in neo-Gothic style buildings clad in native limestone, known today as Hokie Stone.

Eggleston was born in Virginia in 1867 and earned bachelor's and master's degrees at Hampden-Sydney College.

After teaching at public schools in Virginia, Georgia, and North Carolina, he became superintendent of public schools in Asheville, N.C. He then worked for the Southern Education Board at the University of Tennessee before becoming superintendent of public schools in Prince Edward County.

In 1895, he married Julia Johnson of Farmville, Va. Two children resulted from their union.

In 1906, Eggleston was tapped as Virginia's first state superintendent of public instruction. In that position, he set up the first Virginia demonstration farms and spurred establishment of an agricultural high school in each congressional district. He then became chief of the Division of Rural Education for the U.S. Bureau of Education, a job he left when he was named as VPI's president. He remained in the position until 1919.

After leaving Blacksburg, he served Hampden-Sydney College as president for 20 years. He then conducted historical research until his death in 1953.

Johnson, who helps her in such times of trouble, has been sick all spring, and we have therefore about broken up housekeeping, having only such meals as are necessary and getting others outside. We are therefore unable to follow our usual custom of entertaining the preacher of the baccalaureate sermon, the commencement speaker, etc., but I will make arrangements for you at the hotel or elsewhere while you are here.

The Egglestons also gave a series of dinner parties for faculty members, dividing them into small, manageable groups of about 10 per party. The *Virginia Tech* gave reports on some of the parties and named the guests. Other events included teas, one of which included some 250 guests, and plays on the lawn.

Eggleston's administration came to a close on July 1, 1919, when he accepted the presidency of Hampden-Sydney College, his alma mater.

Julian A. Burruss

VPI's first alumnus president, Julian A. Burruss, assumed office in 1919. Unlike his predecessor's mere six years in office, Burruss served his alma mater for 26 years. Thus, he lived in the President's Home longer than any other chief executive. During that time, a two-car brick garage or "carriage house" with a Buckingham slate roof was erected near the house in 1922, and the Grove reportedly was remodeled in 1925. In 1935, the grounds surrounding the residence acquired a new feature: an amphitheatre near the bottom of the hill between the residence and Agricultural Hall, today's Price Hall. The following year, the board of visitors authorized construction of a servant's quarters that would be built with old and second-hand materials, but Burruss decided against the project.

Burruss is particularly remembered for convincing the board of visitors to open the college to full-time women students, which the board did in 1921. Since living space was a problem for the early women, he suggested abandoning the President's Home and converting it into a dormitory for them, and the board of visitors approved a motion to erect a new executive residence and to convert the Grove into a dormitory for these new students. But nothing came of the board's action, perhaps because some of the women already lived with their families in Blacksburg, and some found other places to live, usually rooms in the private homes of college officials and professors on campus and in private homes in town. When the board's motion was made—in September 1921—the college had only five full-time women students, and they had just begun their studies at the heretofore all-male school.

One of the more famous of Burruss's guests at the Grove was William Ashley "Billy" Sunday, a baseball outfielder during the 1880s for the Chicago White Stockings and Philadelphia Phillies in the National League who became a nationally celebrated and influential evangelist. Brought to campus by the YMCA, Sunday spoke to a packed crowd in the German Hall that included the entire corps of cadets as well as numerous townspeople. Following Sunday's address, he and his wife, as well as a man who had

The First Alumnus President

The Grove's longest occupant, Julian Ashby Burruss, was the first alumnus to head Virginia Agricultural and Mechanical College and Polytechnic Institute, popularly known as VPI. His significant—and lasting—changes during 26 years in office altered the course of Virginia Tech history.

1919 - 1945

Perhaps the most far-reaching changes were persuading the board of visitors to admit women as regular students and to shorten the mandatory four-year military requirement to two years. These actions moved VPI away from its all-military structure and set the stage for a large civilian student body.

Also under Burruss, the college was expanded to include Radford College, which became the Women's Division of VPI, and the General Assembly officially renamed the Blacksburg school Virginia Polytechnic Institute.

The Virginia native, born in 1876, attended Virginia Mechanics Institute before entering Virginia Agricultural and Mechanical College (today's Virginia Tech) and earning a bachelor's degree in 1896. He received diplomas in physics, French, and German from Richmond College (today's University of Richmond); studied at Harvard; secured a master's degree in education from Columbia and a master's degree in industrial education from Teachers College in New York City; and obtained a Ph.D. from the University of Chicago.

Burruss married Rachel Cleveland Ebbert of Covington, Ky., in 1907. The union produced two children.

Burruss taught and served as commandant of cadets at Reinhardt Normal College in Georgia; taught at the Searcy Female Institute and the Speers-Langford Military Academy, both in Arkansas; and worked as a principal and then director of manual arts in public schools in Richmond. He was named the first president of the State Normal and Industrial School (now James Madison University) in 1908, leaving there in 1919 to become president of VPI.

Burruss was named president emeritus upon his retirement in 1945. He died in 1947.

accompanied them to Blacksburg, were entertained with a luncheon at Burruss's home. The three guests then left for the State Normal and Industrial School for Women (today's Radford University). Entertaining at the Grove also included a reception and musical program for 300 guests in 1929, leading to a description of the Grove event as "the scene of one of the largest social affairs of the season." Additionally, the Burrusses opened their doors for annual receptions for freshmen, given by the YMCA, until 1925, when the class size grew too large. Among other events at the residence were commencement-related activities. In 1930, the president and his wife invited members of the faculty and their spouses to a reception on the lawn of the Grove that honored alumni, their spouses, members of the graduating class, and their parents. According to *The Bugle's Echo*, "President and Mrs. Burruss, members of the Administrative Council and their wives, along with the president of the Alumni Association and his wife constituted the receiving line."

All of the events were not happy ones, however. Unlike President McBryde, who welcomed a surprise night visit by the students, Burruss was unpleasantly surprised—and amazed—when a mass student demonstration against unsanitary conditions in the dining hall ended at his home. The corps, dressed in civilian clothes, marched in regular formation to the Grove about midnight on July 27, 1942. Once there, the students read a proclamation of protest and burned an effigy, followed by several minutes of shouting, yelling, and band playing. The corps then marched back, in formation, to the barracks. Before the demonstration, Burruss had formed a committee to look into complaints about the dining hall and assumed, incorrectly, that the committee had handled any issues since none had been brought to his attention.

For medical reasons—Burruss had been injured in an automobile accident—the board of visitors named him president emeritus in 1945, ending the longest administration in Virginia Tech history. But even though his tenure as president ended in July, Burruss remained in the executive mansion until November.

John R. Hutcheson

The board of visitors named the popular John R. "Dr. Jack" Hutcheson president to succeed Julian Burruss, effective July 1, 1945. The new chief executive's salary was set at $10,000 per year plus perks: a home, electric current, heat, telephone, water, and janitor service for attending the furnace. The board particularly specified that Hutcheson be assigned the President's Home and to have it renovated before he moved in. He was also directed to secure a proposal from a "reputable firm of interior decorators" to decorate the house with furniture and equipment—it had earlier approved expenditures of $5,000 from the Squires Fund, named for college benefactor John H. Squires, for this purpose. The board also asked Hutcheson to keep an inventory of those contents in the house that were owned by the college. In November 1945, Hutcheson reported to the board:

I have discussed the matter with the interior decoration department of Miller and Rhoads in Richmond and have been advised it will be difficult to equip the President's Home . . . for less than $5,000. It may cost more than this to get the job done as the board wants it.

Although Hutcheson gave the board a figure, he did not submit a proposal to the executive committee from the interior decorators since Burruss was still living in the house, making it difficult for them to personally access it. The president emeritus was scheduled to move out in late November, and the next meeting of the board of visitors was planned the following February. If the $5,000 authorized by the board was inadequate to purchase the necessities for the house, Hutcheson suggested that "additional funds can be allocated later." Subsequently, the board authorized $1,500 from the Squires Fund to pay for rugs, draperies, and some furniture, apparently after interior decorator Charles Farley of the Virginia Galleries had recommended that three chairs, a sofa, a complete dining suit, rugs for the dining and living rooms, curtains, and draperies be purchased.

Either the renovation work was delayed or additional work was needed on the house because on April 6, 1946, the president notified Stuart K. Cassell, the college's business manager, and J. R. Abbitt, director of buildings and grounds, that J. Frank Jones, an interior decorator, had conferred with him regarding "wall treatment, floor treatment, draperies, and furnishings for the President's Home." Jones, he said, had requested a floor plan of the house and would provide detailed recommendations regarding the floor and wall treatments once he had seen the plan. "He estimates that if the right kind of foundation work is done, this will cost around $3,000," Hutcheson said, adding,

Mr. Jones's estimate is much higher than I had figured on, but if the present papering is to be removed, plaster repaired, and floors scraped and treated, he may be correct. I am, therefore, requesting that you try to figure enough out of our repair appropriation to handle the job. . . . I have an idea that we ought to contract this job just as soon as Mr. Jones sends us the specifications.

Dr. Jack

1945 - 1947

When the popular John Redd Hutcheson, known as "Dr. Jack," assumed duties in January 1945 as executive assistant to an ailing president, he commenced his presidential administration in everything but name only. In the middle of the year, the board of visitors christened the alumnus as the new president.

Dr. Jack immediately faced the aftermath of World War II—a tidal wave of veterans enrolling in the college under the GI Bill—and he worked to prepare the campus for the influx. The college installed three trailer courts and rented dormitory and classroom space at the Radford Ordinance Works.

With Hutcheson at the helm, VPI acquired its first vice president, saw the veteran enrollees nearly double the student body, began collecting funds to build the War Memorial and Chapel, laid plans for Alumni Mall, opened an admissions office, began operating a branch college in Danville, and resumed student activities that had been suspended during the war.

Dr. Jack began working for the Virginia Agricultural Extension Service in 1914, the year it was moved to VPI, and became its director in 1919. He remained in the position until he was tapped as the president's executive assistant.

Hutcheson was born in Virginia in 1886, received a bachelor's degree from VPI, and attended field artillery officer training school during World War I. He was recognized with honorary doctor's degrees from Clemson College and North Carolina State College.

He married Eleanor Parrott of Blacksburg, Va., and the couple had three children.

Illness forced Hutcheson's retirement from the presidency in 1947, and the board of visitors named him VPI's first chancellor. He became the first president of the VPI Educational Foundation in 1948. He retired as chancellor in 1956 and served as foundation president until his death in 1962.

Cassell suggested that the repairs be funded by an emergency appropriation, which he feared would revert to the state if not used by the following June 30, and agreed that the work should be contracted out, especially since the college's Department of Buildings and Grounds was "far behind in its routine repair program." He recommended that Hutcheson proceed "immediately with trying to work out some kind of [contractual] arrangements covering this job."

Apparently the board was pleased with all of the work done on the executive residence during Hutcheson's administration because it passed a resolution in August 1947, as his term in office came to an end, that recognized "the diligence and industry manifested by Mrs. John Hutcheson in supervising the redecorating and refurbishing of the President's Home" and said that the board "wishes to take this opportunity to express its appreciation for her untiring efforts and for the splendid job that has been done."

During Hutcheson's short tenure, he and the first lady, the former Eleanor Parrott of Blacksburg, generally limited entertaining in their home to small dinners. Napkins inscribed with "The Grove," the name with which Eleanor Hutcheson christened the executive mansion, provided a special touch at those events. Guests included people important to the college and members of the faculty. One of the more elaborate events hosted by the Hutchesons at the house was the wedding in June 1948 of their eldest son, John, to Ivis Reynolds. Ivis resided at the house with her in-laws the following year, the month before and the month after her first son was born. Other long-term guests were the Hutchesons' only daughter, Eleanor Catlett, and her two children, who spent the summers at the Grove. A second son, Robert, had died in World War II.

When an ill Hutcheson was removed from office in 1947, the board named him chancellor, a first for the college, and in another unprecedented move, it allowed him to continue occupying the Grove "as his residence with the necessary space being set aside therein for his office." Hutcheson remained in the President's Home for two more years—when he received a target date to move out.

The Good Will Era President

The VPI Board of Visitors promoted Vice President Walter Stephenson Newman to the presidency in 1947, instituting an "era of good will."

Newman's administration brought tremendous growth in academic and athletic programs, enrollment, and the physical plant. The third alumnus president's expanded vision of college education laid the groundwork for VPI's later development into a major university.

1947 - 1962

Newman emphasized research and graduate work, and VPI strengthened its offerings and added more graduate and undergraduate degree programs, started new departments, created two new schools (today called "colleges"), and initiated cooperative education.

A straightforward, friendly, and earnest man, Newman created many friends for the college, and his presentations on the school led to better state financial support.

Two significant developments during Newman's term came in 1953, when VPI admitted its first black student, and in 1958, when it graduated its first black student, thereby opening the doors to a more inclusive student body.

Newman was born in Virginia in 1895. He received a bachelor's degree from Hampden-Sydney College, a master's from VPI, and a Ph.D. from Pennsylvania State College. He was recognized with honorary LL.D.s from Roanoke College and Hampden-Sydney.

In 1920, he married Liz Otey "LizOtey" Hoge of Blacksburg, Va., and the couple had one son. They also reared a niece of Mrs. Newman.

Newman worked as a vocational agriculture teacher, an associate professor at VPI, Virginia's superintendent of vocational education, assistant state superintendent of public instruction, and state administrator of the National Youth Administration before he was named vice president of VPI in 1946.

Newman's health forced his retirement in 1962, and he was named president emeritus. In 1977, the year before he died, he received Virginia Tech's Ruffner Medal, one of the first two recipients of the university's highest honor.

President and Mrs. John R. Hutcheson enjoy a night of dancing away from the Grove, where they lived for four years. Photo courtesy of Ivis Hutcheson and John R. Hutcheson III.

❖ A New Leader, a Different President's Home, and a Major Renovation

The board of visitors moved Walter S. Newman, who, as vice president, had begun handling the presidential duties when Hutcheson became ill, into the top executive position, effective September 1, 1947. With Hutcheson living in the Grove, the college president's home became the Holden House, where the Newmans lived. Their residence on Faculty Row was to retain that special status for nearly four years.

Newman was, perhaps, more aware than his predecessors had been that entertaining could benefit the college, telling the board of visitors, "The administration has recognized the need for the college to participate to a greater extent in providing entertainment for visiting dignitaries and organizations." Following a request by the president, the board authorized him to hire a maid, and in 1949, it authorized annual presidential expenditures of

$1,000 for official college entertaining. It could not be ascertained whether the Grove was the scene of any of the social activities hosted by the Newmans before the Hutchesons moved out, but at least some of the larger events were held in the Student Activities Building (SAB, today's Squires Student Center) and the University Club, and the Newmans did host various college and personal events, no doubt involving fewer guests, in the Holden House.

Board of Visitors Decides on a Major Renovation

In April 1949, the board of visitors authorized its rector, William E. Wine, to work out a plan for Hutcheson to vacate the Grove and to be moved to another suitable location, and the rector complied. Consideration had been given to remodeling the residence, a recommendation of an architect employed by the board to make suggestions for how to use the building and an issue that became intertwined with the request for Hutcheson to move out. At its August 1949 meeting, the board passed a resolution asking Hutcheson "to make all possible effort to vacate the property as of November 1, 1949," citing the need to remodel the house. At the same meeting, the board authorized $32,000 for the work and directed Newman to engage an architect to prepare final plans for the remodeling. Later, a state architect inspected the house and recommended the release of $2,000 for architectural work so that estimates on the cost of remodeling could be secured.

In December 1949, the board's executive committee learned from Newman that he had engaged the services of Louis Phillipe Smithey of Smithey & Boynton in Roanoke. Smithey had studied the house, made drawings, and made suggestions, and J. M. Turner, a Roanoke contractor, had estimated that the work would cost $58,000. Newman eliminated certain improvements to get the estimate down to approximately $45,000, a figure that had increased dramatically, certainly in the state-funding portion, by the end of the renovation. The committee decided to ask the governor to release $36,572 from the Additional Housing Facilities Fund and to approve the transfer of $11,000 from operating funds into capital outlay to cover the cost of the remodeling. In January 1950, the committee looked to the governor to transfer $13,152—rather than the originally requested $11,000—from the college's operating funds to capital outlay funds "in order that there may be sufficient funds available to meet the estimates of renovating [costs] as submitted by the architect, Mr. Smithey."

In December 1950, Newman asked the executive committee to let him use $1,500 from the Squires Fund, which then had a balance of $3,000, to purchase rugs, which could not be bought with state funds. Although the rugs were estimated to cost at least a thousand dollars more, the president expressed his belief that the sale of dining room furniture owned by the college would cover the difference. If not, he volunteered to personally make up the difference so he could buy the rugs. Later, he reported to the board that the dining room furniture had not sold and that the bill for the rugs had totaled more than $2,600. In December 1949, the executive committee approved the expenditure of $3,000 for the rugs and other items needed for the remodeling. While the extensive renovation project was under way from June 19, 1950, to mid

LizOtey Newman, first lady from 1947 to 1962, played a significant role in the first major renovation of the President's Home, leaving a lasting mark on the historic structure. Photo courtesy of Alice Dekker

1951, the Newmans continued living on Faculty Row. Hutcheson, meanwhile, asked the board if he could move into the Holden House once the Newmans vacated it. Perhaps because of the length of time involved in the renovation, the Hutchesons moved instead to a small house on Kent Street, where they remained for four to five years before purchasing a house on Draper Road.

Some of the principal changes to the Grove, most of which Smithey & Boyton included in a general description of the project on April 5, 1950, came in the form of closets added to bedrooms; two additional bathrooms added to bedrooms; a large linen closet added; the plumbing system revamped; and the downstairs bedroom converted into an office with new built-in book shelves and a bathroom, with a door added to access the sitting room. The direction of the reception hall stairwell was modified with the addition of a distinctive turned newel post. The dining room fireplace was removed, as was the brick chimney roof projection. The kitchen and serving pantry received a new layout and new heavy-duty linoleum. Alterations and additions to the then-current garage to provide servants' quarters were designed but never made. The basement was remodeled to accommodate a new one-car garage, and alterations were made to add a new fruit-storage basement room and to accommodate a new steam-heating system, which was linked to the new extension of main heating lines from the Girls' Dormitory (today's Hillcrest Hall). Doorways and other areas of the house received minor changes. The glass insets in the transoms over the doors on the second floor were painted to obscure light into the rooms. A first-floor half bath was converted into a storage room for the kitchen, and storm windows were installed. The original library was converted into a drawing room, and the wall with pocket doors between the large and small parlors was removed.

Additionally, according to a student paper written by Philip L. Pointon,

> For the drawing room, dining room, reception hall, stair hall, living room, and library, the [wallpaper], canvas walls, and ceilings were to be repapered and the dados painted. The drawing room, living room, and library were to receive new wood dado caps. The fireplace in the den was restored, and bookshelves were [built into] the office or guest room. Much of the kitchen was remodeled, and an exhaust fan and swinging double doors were added. Ceramic tile walls and floors were added to the doorway leading from the stair hall to the back of the house.

First lady LizOtey (the spelling used by her family) Newman later told a reporter that the additions of bathrooms and closets where needed were her primary achievements in remodeling the house, adding, "The earlier days, people used wardrobes and didn't have closets as part of their homes, and I felt like all the guests would appreciate having their own bathroom." One of the changes she made that has, over the years, attracted considerable attention was the addition of a Chinese hand-blocked wallpaper— the wallpaper features delicate multicolored flowers, birds, and butterflies on a beige background—in the reception hall, which received negative publicity at the time because it was quite expensive. She also decorated the house with antiques. Professional advice on the interior decorating came from Stedman Oakey of the Stedman House in Roanoke.

Outside, the house acquired a new driveway; parking area; and front brick patio, which allowed the contractor to remove some of the front steps. The grounds received new shrubbery, including boxwoods, and other plants all around the house and additional landscaping, all under the direction of the first lady. She apparently intended to make changes to the front façade later, but her husband became ill and retired before she could get the work under way.

Regardless of the many changes to the interior and exterior, LizOtey Newman said that she considered the home lovely even before the renovations had commenced. Nonetheless, she told a reporter, "I did what I thought would make the home a more comfortable, pleasant, and pretty place for the guests, family, and future generations."

In November 1951, in response to a correspondent's suggestion that the $85,000 spent on the president's house in the past year should be looked into, an editor at the *Richmond News Leader* wrote:

> The president's house at Blacksburg, a 14-room affair with seven bedrooms upstairs and seven other rooms below, was built in 1902. Last year, its deteriorating condition caused the VPI board to have an architect examine the structure and make recommendations. His first recommendation was that the entire wiring system be condemned as a fire hazard. It was found that the heating system was leaking into the walls and that the plumbing was obsolete.
>
> Instead of building from scratch (it would have cost $80,000 or more to provide a wholly new structure of comparable size and modern appointments, a Richmond architect advises us), the board approved a remodeling project instead.
>
> Expenses directly attributable to remodeling finally came to $45,634. In addition, slightly more than $5,000 was spent to provide a steam line from the central campus heating plant to serve the president's house. The work was finished last May. It is believed that nothing further will have to be spent on the house, in the way of major repairs, for another 50 years.
>
> Whether this $51,000 total should be viewed with alarm seems to us exceedingly doubtful. A smaller, and perhaps adequate house probably could have been built on state-owned land for $25,000. But hotel facilities are poor in Blacksburg, and the college president is virtually compelled to act as host for numbers of distinguished visitors. . . .
>
> The president's house at VPI appears to be, at most, a middle-sized dreamhouse [sic]. In any event, those are the facts, and we find no extravagance here.

President and Mrs. Walter S. Newman pose on the main staircase in the President's Home with their two great nieces, Kent and Alice Dekker. The wallpaper visible in the photograph, which was selected by the first lady, has attracted a considerable amount of attention over the years. Photo courtesy of Alice Dekker

But the state auditor did, following his audit of the project two years later. While the state had authorized $49,724 for the project, the college had spent $68,949. As a result, state auditor J. Gordon Bennett sought an explanation from the rector of the VPI board, William E. Wine, for the nearly 28 percent cost over-run. Wine responded:

> The board of visitors is charged with the management of the entire institution, including the building and maintenance program, and we are firm in our conviction that this was a delayed maintenance project and that we were justified in charging to our maintenance account certain of the repairs that were necessary.

Bennett then recommend that any future projects having to secure written approval, as this project had, be required to obtain supplemental authorization for any expenditures in excess of the amount allocated by the state. In a critical editorial, the prominent newspaper *Norfolk Virginian Pilot* called the rector's explanation "double-talk" that was

> a reflection on public intelligence. At a state-supported school turning out engineers and architects, it should be well known that a house is not "maintained" on a reconditioning project for which a capital outlay authorization has been made. It *was* capital outlay and not maintenance, *delayed* or otherwise. The public, we think, can see right through what, in this instance, is the president of VPI's glass house. What was wanted was a house a little sweller than the one the budget provided, so they bought it. As State Auditor Bennett said, what was required was "a supplemental authorization." That's a nice way to put it, too. *In the future,* says Auditor Bennett, such authorization should be sought "on all projects of this nature." Nothing at all harsher than the state auditor's comment will happen to anybody at VPI as a result of this little off-balance house-building.

The Newmans Move in

According to a notation made by the first lady, the Newmans moved into the Grove in July 1951; a brief report of the move in a local newspaper narrows the date to the week preceding July 26, 1951—almost four years after Newman was named president. By November, a graduate student was living in the house as well.

Some grading and landscaping work remained to be done. Shortly after the Newmans moved in, the dishwasher had to be replaced, as did a pressure-reducing valve that allowed steam to build in the basement, which was discovered by the graduate student one weekend while the Newmans were away. But even as late as five years after the renovation had been completed, the president was contacting Smithey about problems. On June 16, 1952, Newman wrote to the Roanoke architect:

> I hate to keep bothering you about minor items regarding the President's Home, but the other day when the maid was washing the tile above one of the seven tubs, seven or eight pieces of tile fell into the tub. I am at a loss to understand why the tile should have been dislodged because in this particular bath the shower has never been used.
>
> . . . Of course, we have occupied the house now for almost a year, but this appears to me to be faulty workmanship at some time. I would like your advice as to how to proceed to have this condition corrected.

Three years later, Newman complained that the temporary wire grilles for two convectors in the kitchen had never been replaced with permanent grilles. Smithey invariably turned to the contractor for resolution, and between the two of them, they ensured that the problems were corrected.

Once Again, a President Hosts Events in the Grove

In 1951, with the President's Home freshly renovated and decorated, the Newmans began using it to entertain, and probably one of the first events held there was an open house for students— on May 27, 1951—nearly two months before the first family changed residences. Other events followed after their move, among them a reception for the faculty of VPI and Radford College, which, at the time, was the Women's Division of VPI; homecoming festivities that included luncheons for classes celebrating 50th anniversaries; parties for newcomers; luncheons honoring specific guests; commencement-related events, such as luncheons and open houses; and receptions for freshmen, 1,200 of them guests in 1955.

The Newmans had help in the kitchen from Alease Cardwell, whom Alice Dekker, a great niece of LizOtey Newman, describes as "an expert cook." The first lady also received assistance from her sister-in-law, Kate Estes Hoge; from several of her personal friends; and from professors and their wives to welcome guests, introduce guests to the receiving line, help form the receiving line, and stand at various doors and on the porch to direct guests. The women who assisted LizOtey Newman with the entertaining performed a variety of tasks. They helped prepare refreshments; helped arrange flowers; and once the parties commenced, poured punch. Part-time helpers, sometimes female students from the college, were hired to assist the cook in the kitchen, and at times, college male students were engaged to serve the guests.

The Newmans continued hosting events to benefit the college throughout the president's tenure, which came to an end in mid 1962. Newman suffered a heart attack in March 1961 and presented the board of visitors with a formal retirement request because, he said, "I did not feel that I could carry on as vigorously as I had been able to do the past 15 years." The board granted his request in late 1961, effective the following June 30. Before that date, the Newmans began building a house in Blacksburg, but since it was not completed when the president's administration ended, his successor graciously allowed them to remain in the Grove until they could move directly into their new home.

❖ New President, Family Enter the Grove

T. Marshall Hahn Jr. succeeded Newman as president on July 1, 1962, at the young age of 35, and he and his family moved into the Grove about a month after he assumed his new duties. Marshall and Peggy Hahn had three children, who enjoyed the spacious attic in the house and the location near the Duck Pond. At the time, the attic was a huge space with a ladder access to the widow's walk above. A smaller room, walled off from the rest of the attic, contained blackboards and desks, providing the perfect setting for the Hahn children to play "school," with the accommodating Frank "Bush" Bannister, a member of the house staff since the Newman days, serving as their "pupil." Betty Hahn, one of the children, says that she and her siblings also played in the Amphitheatre, which is near the bottom of the hill on the Drillfield side, where they put on performances after "dragging our parents down there" to see them.

Events at the Grove were similar to those of Hahn's predecessor. Betty Hahn recalls that her father held receptions for freshmen students and luncheons on the lawn for student leaders. Among the many dignitaries entertained by the Hahns, Betty particularly remembers a visit by Vincent Price, a noted actor of the time. "I had breakfast with him," she says. "He was interesting, funny, and entertaining." Governor Mills Godwin stayed at the house on a number of occasions, and David Brinkley, an NBC news correspondent, was a guest during a trip to campus to speak at the 1972 commencement. Frequent guests included members of the board of visitors and their spouses. Betty's mother planned events and worked alongside Bush Bannister and Gustina "Gussie" Brisco, another member of the house staff, in the kitchen to prepare food for luncheons, dinners, receptions, parties, and other activities, and Betty remembers "a lot of pie making." For large events, the Hahns secured additional help, which Betty believes may have come from the dining hall on campus. Some of the more frequent menu items were beef stroganoff, congealed salads with finely chopped fruits and nuts, puff pastries with crab sauce, lemon chess pie, and chicken salad. A button under the carpet in the dining room, placed near the location where Peggy Hahn's feet would rest, allowed the first lady to summon a server to remove plates when guests had finished eating.

Hahns Move off Campus

The Hahns decided in early 1970 that they wanted to live in a neighborhood where there were young people the same ages as their children. Consequently, Hahn built a house off campus in the Blacksburg community known today as Grissom-Highland and moved into it in 1971, ending the Grove's 20 years of service as Virginia Tech's fourth home for presidents. The Hahns remained in the 4,617 sq. ft. colonial-style brick home, which was located on Rainbow Ridge Drive, until the president resigned in 1974 to accept a position with Georgia-Pacific. The Georgia-Pacific Foundation purchased the residence, which had become known as the Hahn House, and donated it to the Virginia Tech Foundation that same year. The university's next president, William E. Lavery, and his family became the second first family to live on Rainbow Ridge when Lavery took over as the university's top administrator on January 1, 1975.

President Hahn built this house on Rainbow Ridge and moved into it in 1971. The house served, in effect, as Virginia Tech's president's home until the late 1980s. Photo by William E. Cox

After President Hahn and his family moved off campus, the executive residence on campus was transformed into an office building and rechristened Building 274. A secretary's station, set up in the front hallway, is visible in the photograph. Photo courtesy of Special Collections, University Libraries, Virginia Tech

❖Former President's Home Becomes an Office Building

After Hahn moved to Rainbow Ridge, his former campus home began a marked decline and was described as a "deteriorating relic of Tech's past." By then, the porches had begun to suffer from decades of exposure to sunlight and the vagaries of weather—and from mild neglect. The mansion was remodeled in 1972 to transform it into an office building, and the once glorious facility where presidents had feted governors, actors, and other dignitaries acquired the inauspicious name Building 274.

The remodeling left the north side of the first floor with a secretarial office where the original library had been, an office where the dining room had been, a small office replacing the butlery (originally the scullery), and a lounge taking over the kitchen. On the south side, the areas that had originally been the front and rear parlors were converted into a conference room. Just beyond the conference room, a door on the right from the stair hall led into an office, and further down the hall, another door to the right led into yet another office, while a door at the end of the hall opened into a file room. The six second-floor bedrooms became offices, one of them for graduate students. A secretary's station was set up in the front hallway. Six offices, including another one for graduate students, were positioned in the basement.

Shortly thereafter, the Center for the Study of Public Choice, headed by world-class economists Gordon Tullock and James Buchanan, moved into the former president's home, remaining until 1983, when Buchanan moved the center, along with seven faculty members, to George Mason University.

After the center departed the premises, Ray Smoot, the university's associate vice president for administration at the time, went to the former executive residence to inspect it. When he unlocked the door and walked in, a mallard duck flew down the inside stairway, through the reception hall, and into the conference room (originally the front parlor). "The place had definitely gone to the ducks," Smoot says. "I don't know how it got in—I guess there was an open window upstairs." Smoot escorted the duck out the front door and continued his inspection. "The place was in pretty miserable condition at that time," he recalls.

At that point, Building 274 faced the changes typical of any building that serves one office and then is altered to serve another office. Shelves, doors, vinyl flooring in the bathrooms, curtains, shades, and carpeting were removed; leaks in the roof were repaired; a partition was added to one of the bedrooms; and some of the doorways were closed off. Walls, ceilings, and doors were painted, and the gypsum boards that were installed in most of the rooms on the second floor were painted or wallpapered. Additionally, the building was rewired, all to suit the needs of its next inhabitant, the university's Office of Development, which moved into the facility in 1984. Fifteen fundraisers, headed by F. Duke Perry, director of development, remained in Building 274—with, at times, up to six graduate students from the Department of Family and Child Development, who were also assigned office space in the facility—until they moved in 1987 to different and better facilities in a new off-campus building known as the Pack Building, constructed on the corner of Tom's Creek Road and Prices Fork Road across the street from campus.

Although Building 274 did not sustain any structural damage during the years it served as an office building, the wear and tear on the former president's home mounted, and Warren Kark, university architect, later noted that "the damage to the house was neglect." So why did the university allow the house to fall into disrepair? A local newspaper reported that needed repairs were put off in favor of other projects, but according to a fund-raising brochure, published near the end of the facility's years as an office building, "[B]adly needed repairs were deferred because of restricted state budgets."

❖New Life for Building 274

At the off-campus president's home, the Laverys had hired Aldora Ester Jones to help the first lady plan menus and prepare food for university-related events. But while first lady Peggy Lavery found the Rainbow Ridge house to be a nice family home, she also found it inadequate for entertaining dignitaries and other guests important to the university, particularly when the number of guests forced her to set up dinner tables in the basement. Some events had to be restricted because of the inadequate space, and the distance to campus made it somewhat inconvenient.

Peggy Lavery began thinking about a way to resolve the problem. In 1985, an idea occurred to her that not only would solve her space problem but also would save an historic building on campus. Why not restore Building 274, which, she says, was "in bad shape," and return it to its former position on campus as the executive residence? She approached her husband about the idea and found him receptive. They talked with Charles M. Forbes, vice president for development and university relations, about the idea and finally presented it to Jack Hancock, a major university donor. "They thought it would be a good idea," she recalls.

The idea began to gel and received a stamp of approval from the Buildings and Grounds Committee of the board of visitors, which reported to the full board in 1985 that it "enthusiastically endorses the concept of the president's residence being on campus and is convinced that the proposed move will have a positive impact on the entire university community and the Commonwealth of Virginia." The Office of the University Architect and the committee began working on plans to restore the once-elegant building.

The Virginia Tech Alumni Association Board of Directors added its support of the project, submitting a resolution to the board of visitors on May 16, 1986, expressing the directors' wholehearted endorsement and support of the "efforts to restore this historic and lovely building as the primary residence of the presidents of Virginia Tech." The board of visitors finally added its stamp of approval in 1986, and the General Assembly appropriated $195,000 for the project. In 1987, the governor included additional non-general funds in the amount of $110,000 in his 1988-1990 biennium budget, which the General Assembly endorsed during the 1988 legislative session.

After working on the plans for two years—the plans reflected the tastes and styles of the period in which the house was constructed in the early twentieth century—University Architect Kark prepared a presentation for the media, and President Lavery announced at an April 1987 news conference that a $610,000 renovation process would begin on the house that spring. Lavery explained that it would be more appropriate to renovate the traditional home than to continue to support the then-current president's home off campus, adding that he and his wife

> look forward to returning to campus and using this house as a residence and a place to host large numbers of students, faculty, alumni, and friends of the university. Such use will once again integrate the president's home into the life of the university and its daily activities.

The news conference was also used to announce a fund-raising campaign for the high-profile project. "We wanted to let [everyone] know that we were doing a campaign to help get [the house] restored," Peggy Lavery says. To make up the difference in state funding and the total projected cost of the renovation itself, the university hoped to raise $300,000 from selling the house on Rainbow Ridge and planned to supplement those proceeds with money from a reserve maintenance fund. Additional money to cover the cost would come from the special fund-raising campaign. A brochure used in that effort announced:

> [T]he university plans to renovate the once-elegant building, and gifts are being solicited to supplement public funds appropriated for the project. Those who contribute will have the satisfaction of knowing that they helped preserve a significant historic landmark and helped renew a facility that will serve the entire university community.

The brochure requested donations in the form of cash, stocks, and securities to help fund the renovation and also solicited furniture and artwork, "particularly those associated with The Grove or with presidents who resided in the house."

Knowing that the Governor's Mansion in the state capital had been restored, Virginia Tech's first lady learned the name of the woman who had worked on the project, Helen Scott Reed of Mansion Restorations in Richmond, Va. Reed was approached about overseeing appointments and furnishings in the Blacksburg house and accepted the job.

The Lavery family never enjoyed the fruits of their efforts to restore The Grove, which became the home's official name, to its pre-eminence on campus. A controversial land swap in 1986 and highly publicized problems with the athletic program created a furor across the commonwealth, even though the land trade greatly benefited the university's agricultural research and Lavery developed a reorganization plan for the Athletic Association that addressed problems in that area. But with negative publicity continuing to swirl within and around the university, he announced his resignation, effective December 31, 1987, to prevent polarization of the campus. Paul E. Torgersen, dean of engineering at the time, temporarily took over the reigns of the university as interim president until a permanent president could be hired.

❖ The Grove Enters a New Era as the Residence for Presidents

Getting The Grove Back in Shape

The board of visitors named James D. McComas as the university's next president on May 23, 1988, effective September 1, 1988. Before McComas left the University of Toledo, where he was president, his wife, Adele, journeyed to Blacksburg to accompany Forbes and Reed to an antique outlet in Boone, N. C., where, Adele McComas (now White) says, "[Reed] acquainted us with the furniture she had in mind for The Grove." White recognized Reed's name. She had seen it in *Southern Accent* magazine, where she had found a photo of a dining room that was her idea of the perfect design and color. "It was the dining room in the Governor's Mansion in Virginia, and Helen Scott Reed had worked with the home when [Governor and Mrs. Chuck Robb] lived there." White also learned that Reed had worked with the first lady of the University of Virginia, with whom she was acquainted, and the two women visited the president's home in Charlottesville to see Reed's work there. Of those experiences, White recalls:

> This all added to my comfort level in working with her. She understood how a public home is used. She would ask me to respond to fabric selections and ideas—but I was always comfortable with her plan and loved learning from her. . . . I remember her saying the fabric in the library was from England, and it was the first order to be used in the United States.

The second major renovation of the presidential residence, under way from 1987 to 1989, included repairs to exterior chimneys.
Photo courtesy of Office of University Planning-Architecture

When the McComases relocated to Blacksburg, work on The Grove was still in progress, so they moved into the home on Rainbow Ridge, where they remained for about seven months before the renovation was essentially completed and they could move to campus. With experience in remodeling the president's home at the University of Toledo, White made a few alterations in the renovation plans, including eliminating some equipment from the kitchen that she knew would add unnecessary expense.

Unlike the 1950s renovation, which required major structural changes to accommodate the addition of a garage in the basement, the 1980s project was described by Kark before the work commenced in May 1987 as "more restoration than renovation." One of the big issues he faced in the interior work, he recalls, was bringing the kitchen up to date while keeping in mind that it needed to serve the needs of a family, yet accommodate the preparation of food for big events. Under his direction, university employees tackled the entire restoration project, which a local newspaper described as cleaning, scraping paint, replacing wallpaper, and refinishing wood floors.

By the project's end, workers had restored four of the nine original fireplaces to working order; upgraded the butler's pantry to have storage for dishes and glassware and equipped it with an ice maker, a sink with a garbage disposal, and a three-minute dishwasher; enclosed the back porch to make a breakfast room for use by the first family; made adjustments to the side entrance on the south façade and the first-floor bathroom to allow easy accessibility; updated the kitchen and added a large refrigerator with shelves that could be adjusted to accommodate trays of salads and desserts, a smaller refrigerator, one large and two smaller ovens, a microwave, a conventional dishwasher, and a freezer, all designed to serve large numbers of guests; installed a dumbwaiter to facilitate deliveries from the basement garage to the kitchen; updated the president's office, located in the southeastern corner of the house, with the latest in technology; installed infrared motion detectors in the house for a security system; and abated asbestos materials from the basement.

Workers carved a kitchenette from the second-floor linen room and equipped it with a microwave oven and washer/dryer combination for use by guests, and they walled off and finished a room in the attic. The hand-painted wallpaper selected by first lady LizOtey Newman in the mid 1900s had been damaged by water and received special attention as skilled university painters painstakingly restored it, filling in the beige background by hand and touching up some of the flowers. Additionally, the Office of the University Architect designed benches for placement in the front bowed windows of the two front parlors (one had originally been the library) and added knee walls topped with columns between the original front and back parlors, reminiscent of the pocket doors that had first separated the rooms. Also, a porch was constructed under the roof of the *porte cochere*.

The three main expenditures for the project involved replacing the 85-year-old electrical system; installing an air conditioning system; and doing renovation work on the exterior, such as repairing

President and Mrs. James D. McComas pose on the front stairway of the newly renovated president's home, which was renamed The Grove during the renovation. The first lady worked closely with Helen Scott Reed of Richmond on appointments and furnishings. Photo courtesy of Special Collections, University Libraries, Virginia Tech

the veranda, constructing a new stairway onto the southern section of the veranda, putting in a new circular driveway in the front, and installing several paved walkways. An electronic lift was added to carry visitors from the lower walkway area to the first-floor veranda. The grounds were also landscaped, which included adding native trees and shrubs and planting a rose garden outside the dining room windows and numerous bulbs and wildflowers throughout the grounds. After the work was completed, then-local architectural historian Gibson Worsham told a newspaper reporter that the house was "a dramatic piece of architecture up on the hill."

Recalling her involvement in the renovation work, White says,

Establishing and carrying out a plan for The Grove was a very positive experience for me. Much was in place—the plan with Helen Scott Reed for a historical restoration and her experience with having worked with these large public homes, the expertise and skills of personnel in physical plant and [employees'] ability to repair the wallpaper in the entrance, working with Grady Pennington with the grounds plan, and especially working with Minnis [Ridenour, executive vice president] and Ann [Spencer, assistant vice president for administrative affairs].

To help with their university entertaining obligations, White worked with Ridenour and Spencer to employ Martha Holmes to be in charge of housekeeping; Jim Sexton as the university's first chef to work in the president's home to help plan menus and cook for events; and Mary Kay Warwick to help the first lady with management, planning, and record-keeping. She remembers that once the team was together in The Grove, "they had a good time. They were so supportive of each other." Warwick, she says, brought many talents to the position. "She had been working in Human Resources, and when she saw the job description said that these were all her hobbies—so she applied. She immediately became our trusted 'public relations' person with students, university personnel, political offices, and anyone else who had reason to contact The Grove."

Even after the first family moved into The Grove, the first lady continued to work closely with Reed on the interior decorating, described as an eighteenth-century Virginia restoration using eighteenth- and nineteenth-century antiques and reproductions. A university news release reported that the house was furnished with "many notable period pieces and reproductions of the highest quality." A huge crystal chandelier was added in the dining room, which also acquired an eighteenth-century, mahogany English Hepplewhite sideboard, a mahogany pedestal table, and Henkle-Harris chairs with green-striped upholstery that matched the window coverings. The first lady altered Reed's plans for the dining room, asking that it be neutral enough to tastefully incorporate the university's colors of orange and maroon. The Belgium rug in the room was a custom-made reproduction of a nineteenth-century Brussels carpet featuring muted shades of the school colors with golds and greens mixed in to coordinate with other fabrics in the room. The two front parlors (the original library, which became a drawing room during the 1950s renovation, was converted into a small parlor, and the name of the room designated a living room in that renovation was returned to its original designation as a parlor) featured navy-background oriental rugs, and the drapes and furniture in the two rooms picked up other colors in the rugs. The carpet in the small parlor was a Bakhtari oriental rug, while the one in the large parlor was a Mahal oriental rug. The library (originally the sitting room) was equipped for easy transformation into a bedroom. The area rug used in the entry hall and the stair runners were custom made by Schumacher, a manufacturer of decorative textiles. The rooms on the first floor were decorated with photographs of "university firsts," such as photographs of William Addison "Add" Caldwell, the first student to register, and the first football team. The president's private quarters—three rooms on the second floor and the new attic room, which they used as a family room—were laid with wall-to-wall green carpeting. The McComases used their own furniture in those parts of the house. Three guest bedrooms on the second floor were also refurbished. Noni Parsons was the on-campus director of interior design.

"Helen Scott Reed has been wonderful to work with," the first lady wrote to a supporter who had given a generous donation to help restore the president's home. "She has been responsive to my requests for ways we will want to use the rooms." Later, she told a *Roanoke Times* reporter about a day when Reed arrived at The Grove with a station wagon full of lampshades:

> She went through the house switching and trying lamp-shades and finding just what went well in each room. It's all in the eye of the artist. She's the person who knows what she wants the final work to look like. It's been like watching an artist painting a picture.

The renovation and refurbishment cost an estimated $1.2 million, $259,741 in repair costs, $645,874 in renovation costs, and $272,161 in furnishings. The state provided $805,615 for the repairs and renovation and $100,000 for in-house labor, and private sources gave $272,161 for furnishings and interior design consultations.

Entertaining at The Grove—Once Again

The McComases moved into the president's home, which they called the "University's Home," on April 10, 1989, even though they lacked a few items of furnishings, some drapes had not been hung, and some of the landscaping was not yet completed. Once there, they added Larry Martin, who worked in physical plant, to the staff to handle inside and outside maintenance, heavy lifting, and heavy cleaning. The chef, whom the McComases had known at the University of Toledo, hired students from the hotel management program to help serve at large dinners and receptions, spurring the McComases to set up a training program for them.

Though uninvited, one early guest to "knock" at the main entrance of The Grove was a duck, reminiscent of the mallard that had greeted Ray Smoot at the house a few years earlier. "When I first came here, I was cleaning and heard a pecking sound. I finally realized it was coming from the front door," says Holmes, who continued to work at The Grove for two decades. "I opened it, and there was a mallard duck. Someone told me that the construction workers [on the renovation] had been feeding it. They said it had come for lunch." Perhaps the earliest human guests were members of the media, who received a tour of the house two days before the McComases moved in.

Promising that The Grove would be used as the "front door" to the university, the McComases proceeded to open the mansion to numerous guests, wanting the public to see the home in its newfound glory. During the first year the McComases were in the house, they entertained more than 10,000 people there. At times, the numbers of guests were so large that events were moved to the lawn. The hardest type of entertaining, Holmes recalls, was putting "the tent up outside and moving everything outside. We had to move the grill and find level spaces to set up the tables."

Among those pouring into the newly renovated mansion to enjoy the hospitality of the McComases during their first year in the house were the university's faculty members, who attended ice cream socials set up in a tent on the front lawn. A music group performed on the upstairs front balcony, and the hosts arranged tours of the home. According to White, the faculty events were designed to mimic the first faculty receptions ever held at the president's home, which were also held on the lawn and were also ice cream socials. Other events held soon after the McComases moved in were receptions for personnel in the university's physical plant, who "had done so much of the work [on The Grove]," White recalls. "[I]t was important that they and their families come to one of the first receptions just for them." Those early receptions signaled the new president's focus on campus

At left, personnel in Virginia Tech's physical plant painstakingly repair the wallpaper in the entry hall in The Grove, restoring it to its original beauty when it was hung in the 1950s. The photo at right shows an original piece of wallpaper used in the front bedroom on the west side of the house. Photo and wallpaper sample courtesy of Janet Steger

President McComas's focus on undergraduate education led to numerous student groups visiting The Grove. Sometimes, chairs were set up in the reception hall, where the president addressed his young guests.
Photo courtesy of Special Collections, University Libraries, Virginia Tech

community and the importance of the contributions of all employees in reaching the goals of the university.

The historical renovation attracted much attention in the community, and during their initial year in the home, the first family arranged receptions for numerous groups. Guests included the Faculty Women's Club, Faculty Senate, campus secretaries, students involved in graduate and undergraduate government organizations, members of the homecoming court, various state and local historical groups, alumni groups from the civilian student body and the corps of cadets, regional and state development groups, legislators, Presidential Scholars, Student Ambassadors, and individual visitors. The McComases opened the house for the Community Christmas Home Tour, and various colleges and departments requested—and received—special tours.

At the end of their first year in the mansion, the McComases acknowledged individual supporters who had made possible the renovation and restoration of The Grove. They wrote these benefactors thank-you letters, reporting that most of the project and furnishings were complete and that "The Grove will be shared through the years with all members of the Virginia Tech family and their friends." A special photo album of The Grove accompanied each letter.

McComas entertained people important to the university, its initiatives, its research, its academics, its public service, and its funding as well as people he wanted to honor for various achievements and contributions and dignitaries visiting campus. Among the more famous visitors were Jeanne Kirkpatrick, former U.S. representative to the United Nations; U.S. Senator Chuck Robb and his wife, Lynda Bird Johnson Robb; U.S. Senator Mark Hatfield; Morton Dean, special correspondent for ABC-TV News; Bob Edwards, host of "Morning Edition" on National Public Radio; Al Hunt, Washington correspondent for the *Wall Street Journal;* Robert Novak, a syndicated columnist and journalist; K. R. Narayanan, India's ambassador to the United States and later president of India, and his wife, Usha; Jim Fallows, a political writer,

editor, and former speechwriter for President Jimmy Carter; and U.S. Senator John Warner. According to Holmes, Warner "came to the back and complimented Jim [Sexton] on the crème brûlée. Jim offered him an extra one, and he took it. He was very appreciative and always talked to the staff." The only sitting president of a foreign country ever to visit the university was a guest of the McComases. Cheddi Jagan, leader of Guyana, visited campus in 1993 when Virginia Tech made a commitment to help develop the economy of the small Caribbean country. Because of his position, Jagan was accompanied by members of the U.S. Secret Service, assigned to protect visiting heads of state as well as U.S. presidents. Holmes remembers that members of various protective services, who often accompanied higher-ranking government officials, usually set up their operations and slept in the library.

Throughout his administration, McComas focused on undergraduate education and thus was involved with numerous student groups. He made a concentrated effort to attract National Merit Scholars to the university, and he personally advised up to 16 students a year—he added four each year—on a regular basis. He invited many students, including his advisees and the merit scholars, to dinner at The Grove each year. The mansion was also used to further an increased emphasis on connecting the university's Corporate Research Center with research and development interests. The McComases offered tours followed by buffet dinners in the residence to groups important to that initiative. During his last couple of years in office, the university faced budget cuts, and McComas, who made it a priority to inform faculty, staff, and students about how the cuts were being handled, held a number of informative sessions at The Grove for that purpose. The increasingly bleak state-funding picture, as Governor Douglas Wilder began cutting the budget, also had an effect on entertaining. According to White, "[F]ood preparation was done with a budget in mind and with more receptions and fewer dinners, thus not decreasing the number of people we felt it important to reach through the president's home."

The Teaching President

1994 - 2000

In late 1993, the board of visitors asked Paul Ernest Torgersen to step in, first as acting president and soon thereafter as president, effective in January 1994.

The chaired professor had worked at Virginia Tech since 1967 as a professor, department head, engineering dean and interim dean, Corporate Research Center (CRC) president, interim vice president, and interim president (twice). He taught every semester, regardless of his position, and received the Sporn Award.

Fiscally austere times forced Torgersen to make tough restructuring decisions. He merged two colleges, thinned administrative ranks, and combined services. He worked to rebuild the university's resource base and to move Tech into position to become the model land-grant university of the 21st century.

He guided the university to numerous achievements: the first woman executive vice president and provost; first woman dean of architecture and urban studies; establishment of a Center for Leadership Development; creation of a Women's Center; completion of a successful campaign, raising $337 million; addition of a graduate student representative to join the undergraduate student representative already on the board of visitors; erection of numerous buildings; and opening of The Hotel Roanoke and Conference Center. He also supported investments in athletics, which culminated in a national football championship playoff.

Torgersen was born in New York in 1931. He received a B.S. from Lehigh University and an M.S. and Ph.D. from Ohio State University.

He married Dorothea Zuschlag from New Jersey in 1954; three children followed.

Torgersen taught at Ohio State and Oklahoma State and became a registered engineer before moving to Blacksburg.

A Fellow of the American Society of Engineering Education and of the Institute of Industrial Engineers, he held numerous state and national positions on task forces, commissions, and boards. He was elected to the National Academy of Engineering, and Lehigh awarded him an honorary doctor of engineering. The United States Tennis Association ranked him in men's doubles in 1987.

Torgersen retired in 2000 as president and continues to teach at Virginia Tech.

The McComases enjoyed living and entertaining in The Grove, and the first lady, who says they were "so grateful for this place," continues to recall their experiences in the president's home as "very good ones," thanks to

the location, the staff working with us, the support of the business office, the development office, the physical plant, the faculty, the staff [of the university], and students as we tried to make The Grove the "front door" of the university —as we interpreted the needs at that time.

In late 1993, McComas became seriously ill and resigned the presidency, effective January 1, 1994. He died the following month.

❖ The Torgersens Move in

Paul Torgersen, who had served as interim president between the administrations of Lavery and McComas, was named acting president when McComas became ill in the early fall of 1993, and on December 9, 1993, the board of visitors tapped Torgersen to be the next president, effective January 1, 1994. The Torgersens moved into the president's home, which, first lady Dorothea "Dot" Torgersen says, provided "a different type of living than we were used to." At age 62, the new president and his wife liked efficient entertaining that did not extend late into the night, so the president usually had a designated guest assigned to depart from evening events at a pre-set time, thus encouraging other guests to leave as well.

When they moved in, the Torgersens had Eric A. Wiedegreen, an assistant professor of interior design, look things over, which resulted in some of the furniture being moved to different locations in the residence, and they had cable television installed. "We were lucky because Adele [McComas White] had everything set up. . . . I just loved it. We weren't going to be here long, so we made no real changes," the first lady says.

A dedicated educator, Torgersen taught at least one class each semester regardless of his position at the university—among his jobs were department head, dean of engineering, president of the Virginia Tech Corporate Research Center, interim vice president, and interim president—and continued the practice after becoming president. The winner of the Sporn Award for Excellence in Teaching, he had an affinity for students. And a tennis player himself, he liked athletics and athletes, possibly more than any of his predecessors in the presidency. Thus, The Grove was often the scene of events for students, among them student leaders; athletic teams; students in the president's class, who were invited to dine in The Grove each semester; student media groups; graduating seniors in the Marching Virginians; student service organizations; and German Club members.

In addition to numerous students, the Torgersens opened their home to a plethora of organizations and individuals important to the university and its initiatives, people whom the university wanted to recognize, and groups involved in improving the community. From events for presidents and chief academic officers of 11 historically black colleges and universities in several states to participants in Retire Blacksburg 96, part of an annual event sponsored by Blacksburg, the Greater Blacksburg Chamber of Commerce, and Virginia Tech to attract retirees to the community, and from high school guidance counselors to various groups involved in economic development initiatives throughout the region, the number of activities held in the home is indicative of how much entertaining at The Grove had increased over the years. Over stretches of time, it was not unusual for the Torgersens to host an average of two events per week.

The first lady particularly remembers visits by the princess of Thailand and her entourage; Cokie Roberts, a well-known ABC news analyst and political commentator; James Carville Jr. and Mary Matalin, a famous couple who were national political advisors, each for a different party; Eric Schmidt, then chairman and

President and Mrs. Paul E. Torgersen lived in The Grove from 1994 to 2000. Photo courtesy of Paul Torgersen

chief executive officer of Novell Inc. and later CEO of Google; Tom Moss, speaker of the House of Delegates; members of the board of visitors; and governors. She also remembers entertaining mothers of faculty members. Before moving into The Grove, she often entertained the mothers in her Palmer Drive home, and "when we moved to The Grove, we brought them to The Grove," although, she adds, the monthly get-togethers were sometimes held in other homes. A music student played the piano in the parlor for a number of occasions.

On February 22, 1999, Torgersen, who had agreed to serve five years when he was named president, announced that he would retire. The board of visitors decided that Charles W. Steger Jr., whom the board named the next president, and Torgersen should agree on a transition date, and the two settled on December 31, 1999, as Torgersen's last day, and January 1, 2000, as Steger's first day in office. But when it was announced that the Virginia Tech football team would compete against Florida State University in the Sugar Bowl for the national championship, Torgersen contacted Steger and told him that he wanted to go to New Orleans as the president, and Steger agreed. Thus, Torgersen's last day in the presidency was extended to January 6, 2000.

❖ Another Needed Restoration

By 2000, The Grove was in need of a major mechanical renovation and extensive maintenance work. Lynn Eichhorn, a campus architect with expertise in renovating historical buildings, was assigned to manage the project for the university.

Several architecture and engineering (A/E) firms were retained to provide a study of the condition of the house and to develop plans for the work that was needed. Many of the issues they found were related to the age of the building. For example, the heating system for the house continued to rely on the steam-to-hot-water converter added in the 1950s renovation. Other problems were related to areas not addressed by the major renovations of the 1950s and 1980s. The A/E firms found badly deteriorated mortar in the brick work in the chimneys and throughout the façades and discovered that some of the original iron piping still used in the plumbing system could be contributing to discolored residue in the water. The firms' study resulted in recommendations that needed to be addressed "in the light of the age of the building and the need to maintain the integrity of the structure and the weather tightness of the construction to extend the life of this magnificent residence."

The Grove Elevations - 1999

EAST ELEVATION

WEST ELEVATION

The A/E firms compiled "The Grove's Building Assessment Report," which prioritized the renovations that needed immediate attention. Officials at the university reviewed and assessed the architects' suggested improvements, assigning work to campus employees where possible and bidding out other projects. Additionally, The Grove staff identified a number of areas and items that needed repair or replacement.

Shortly after the Torgersens moved out of The Grove, the renovation work commenced. Original pine flooring in the upstairs rooms was uncovered, repaired, and refinished. The old slate roof was replaced with a new slate roof; new copper gutters, conductor heads, and downspouts with catchment basins that matched ones from early photographs were installed; a new heating, ventilating, and air conditioning system was installed; and related electrical and plumbing work was completed. Some plumbing was upgraded, and the mechanical systems were moved from the basement to the detached "carriage house" constructed during the Burruss administration. A new, stand-alone garage was erected on the east side of the house using 100-year-old bricks and a design style appropriate for the period when the house was constructed. The widow's walk, which had been a prominent feature in the early life of The Grove and had been missing for a number of years, was replaced. All work followed historic preservation standards, and additional items may be addressed in the future.

Inside, Eichhorn converted the second-floor kitchenette into a small, efficient kitchen for the private quarters, where the first lady prepares family meals and breakfast for overnight guests, who are served at the dining table in the adjacent foyer. In the area of decorating, Eichhorn and Janet Steger visited Special Collections, a department in University Libraries, and borrowed several pieces of artwork that are displayed throughout the house. For example, a portrait of Virginia Governor J. Hoge Tyler, governor from 1898 until 1902 and rector of the board of visitors from 1887 to 1889, and his daughter, Lily, was hung in the library, while two pencil drawings of Blacksburg in the 1940s by Preston Frazer, a faculty member from 1939 to 1974, now grace the North guest room.

When the furniture was moved back into the house following the renovation work, Steger and Eichhorn, building on the foundation laid by Helen Scott Reed, were able to rearrange existing pieces and purchase additional items from local furniture and antique shops to furnish an additional guest room. They also added several small tables and decorative items to facilitate entertaining and enhance the ambiance of the public spaces.

While work progressed on The Grove, the first family hosted the university's entertaining in their Palmer Drive home, which was designed by the architect/president.

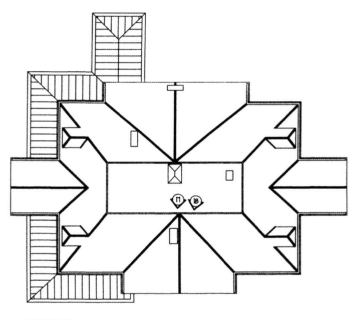

ROOF PLAN

The Visionary President

2000 - present

When the board of visitors named Charles William Steger Jr. as president, effective January 2000, it selected an alumnus and administrator who had experienced virtually all aspects of Virginia Tech life: from student, professor, and researcher to department head, dean, and vice president.

In these earlier roles, Steger helped craft the university's mission statement and strategic plan, chaired a committee that forecast and helped underpin Virginia Tech's technological future, helped develop the first core curriculum, reorganized and empowered public service, and directed a goal-exceeding campaign that raised $337.4 million.

A hallmark of his career at Virginia Tech has been to formalize a presence for the university state-wide, nationally, and internationally, most notably through the establishment of the Richmond Office in the state's capital, the construction of the Virginia Tech Research Center-Arlington in the National Capital Region, and the purchase of a villa in southern Switzerland to become the Center for European Studies and Architecture.

As president, Steger emphasizes quality, accessibility, internationalization, research, and innovation. His vision has led to a new medical college; five international centers around the globe; a top-50 national ranking in research; a massive campus building program that has added more than 2 million square feet of new space, including a Center for the Arts; completion of a successful campaign, raising $1.11 billion; and membership in the Atlantic Coast Conference.

A native Virginian, Steger was born in 1947 and earned a bachelor and master of architecture and a Ph.D. in environmental science and engineering from Virginia Tech.

He married Janet Grey Baird of Richmond, Va., in 1969. The couple has two sons.

Steger was a project planner and then managed the urban planning department for Wiley & Wilson, an architecture, engineering, and design firm. His passion for teaching brought him back to Virginia Tech as a visiting lecturer in 1973. He began working as an instructor for the College of Architecture and Urban Studies in 1974, rising through the ranks to become dean before he was named vice president for development and university relations and then president.

A Fellow in the American Institute of Architects, Steger has received numerous state and national awards and has served on state, national, and international commissions, boards, and foundations.

❖ The Stegers and The Grove

Like many of her predecessors, Janet Steger has a special appreciation for the president's home, from the staff who work there to the historic house and grounds themselves. "I love the stately image of The Grove that comes into view as I approach," says the first lady,

from the majestic, old oaks on the lawn to the massive white columns and old, red brick, to the urns at the front door and the comfortable wicker furniture on the porches. I love that it's really a home—and a warm and welcoming one—but that it also offers an experience that is not often found in today's hurried times. I love simply walking through it, and I take personal pleasure in attending to the details of furnishings and flowers and service, in assuring that every guest feels honored. It's also a joy to work with a sensitive and caring staff who take pride in doing their jobs extremely well. It is truly a privilege to live in such a beautiful, special place as The Grove and to be afforded the opportunity to share it with so many appreciative guests.

Guests and occasions at The Grove oftentimes reflect the interests of the president who lives there. Steger, who stresses the importance of the arts in educating the whole student and preparing students to live and work in a global society, has held a number of events to celebrate the arts and artists—from receptions, luncheons, and dinners featuring poetry readings, pianists, blue-grass music, and classical music to events honoring authors, orchestra conductors; violinists; leaders in the arts, and participants in the annual Vocal Arts and Music Festival. Among the guests and honorees at these events have been the author Barbara Kingsolver; poet and University Distinguished Professor

Janet Steger, current first lady, chooses flowers from The Grove gardens. She arranges many of the centerpieces that grace the home during special events. Photo by Jim Stroup

Nikki Giovanni; American operatic baritone Sherrill Milnes; Metropolitan Opera assistant conductor and operatic coach Joan Dornemann; symphonic and operatic conductor Paul Nadler; Roanoke Symphony conductor and pianist David Wiley; violinists Shmuel Ashkenasi and David Ehrlich, who played the university's prized Bergonzi violin for a board of visitors dinner; and the board of directors for Roanoke's Center in the Square, a consortium of history, art, and science museums and stage performance, opera, and ballet theatres.

Other guests have reflected the president's interest in international relations and his role in securing a permanent facility for the university's study abroad program in Riva San Vitale, Switzerland. His work on international issues has put him in close contact with a number of Swiss officials, and the Stegers have welcomed several Swiss ambassadors and other distinguished international visitors, among them ambassadors from Finland and Korea. Additionally, they have entertained a group of university presidents from Switzerland's most outstanding universities.

Guests have also included local, state, and national government officials; scientists; candidates for high-ranking university positions; campus leaders; business executives; alumni who are important friends of the university; Virginia Tech award recipients; members of the faculty and staff; and students, including the president's own students from a class he co-taught. Governors Bob McDonnell, Tim Kaine, Mark Warner, Jim Gilmore, and George Allen have all been guests of the first family, as have the late Chief Justice Leroy Hassell of the Virginia Supreme Court; U.S. Representative Eric Cantor, former House Minority Whip; and U.S. Senator John Warner. Business leaders visiting The Grove have included George Nolen and David Calhoun. Among numerous other distinguished guests have been General John Philip Abizaid, retired commander of the U.S. Central Command; General Lance L. Smith, retired commander of the U.S. Joint Forces Command and NATO Supreme Allied Commander for Transformation; Pierre Thomas, ABC News correspondent; Hoda Kotb, NBC News correspondent; Bertram R. and Diana Johnson Firestone, major owners and breeders of thoroughbred equestrian and flat-racing horses; and Jean Ellen duPont Shehan, a benefactor of the university's equine medical center.

Special members of the university community who have been frequent guests are rectors and former rectors of the board of visitors and chairs and vice chairs of the various phases of the university's Campaign for Virginia Tech. The Stegers annually hold receptions for graduate students who are recipients of prestigious fellowships and for new minority faculty members. Annual teas welcome the Faculty Women's Club, which holds the monthly meeting of its Friday Forum at The Grove. Those attending the forum enjoy annual cooking demonstrations by Executive Chef Michael Arrington. During football season, the Stegers host special receptions in the residence before home games.

Events at The Grove during quarterly meetings of the board of visitors continue a long-standing tradition started in the McComas administration and are among the busiest times at the president's home. Activities include dinners for board members

Members of the Virginia Tech Board of Visitors and university administrators enjoy dinner at The Grove, a tradition started during the McComas administration and continuing in the Steger administration. Photo by Jim Stroup

David Venné, house manager, adds a dish prepared by the chef to the buffet table. Photo by Jim Stroup

First lady Janet Steger gives Bo, the family beagle, some words of advice before an event. Bo attends special events at The Grove and, according to the first lady, "enthusiastically welcomes guests." *Photo by John McCormick*

and the university's vice presidents and other senior administrators and luncheons for spouses and guests of the board and administrators. The board-related entertaining, the first lady says, "brings these individuals together so they can become better acquainted with each other and with the university itself." When furnishings are rearranged and tables added in the large and small parlors, The Grove can accommodate 47 guests for a seated dinner.

The first lady plays a leading role in planning events and the menus for those events, personalizing them to make them special for each participant. Although she enjoys all of her visitors, she says she prefers small events that allow her to interact more easily and fully with all of her guests.

The Stegers' beagle, Bo, also attends special events, and according to the first lady, "He enthusiastically welcomes guests of The Grove. He also takes his responsibilities as a guard dog very seriously, fending off trucks of all sorts—and, in fact, anything with wheels—and informing workmen that they are most certainly not welcomed in his house!"

Thanks to the hospitality of the Stegers—and that of all first families who have lived in the president's home—that "dramatic piece of architecture up on the hill" has served the university well, establishing an enviable tradition of hospitality and standing proudly as the face of the university. As a result of the 1950-1951, 1988-1989, and 2000 renovations, the 110-year-old home may well stand another century or two, reminding all who enter of the roots and progression of Virginia Agricultural and Mechanical College and Polytechnic Institute into Virginia Tech, one of the country's leading institutions of higher learning.

President Charles W. Steger enjoys a moment with guests in the main hallway. *Photo by John McCormick*

Meet the Chefs

❧ Executive Chef Michael Arrington

The recipes of Michael "Mike" Arrington, executive chef of The Grove since 2005, comprise the major part of the recipe sections in this book.

Chef Michael's interest in food began at a young age. Even before his teenage years, he was experimenting with various concoctions, trying to recreate dishes or sauces he had enjoyed in restaurants. As an adolescent, he gained summer employment one year as a bus boy at a seafood restaurant, thanks to a connection that his father had. The following year, the restaurant needed cooks and hired young Arrington, giving him the opportunity to gain his first experience in the food and beverage industry.

"I brought one valuable lesson from that job," Arrington recalls. "I was replenishing the salad bar and was slicing watermelon. I quartered it, but instead of slicing it rind-side down, I flipped it on its side. This provided a more stable way to slice. The lead cook came in and yelled out, 'What are you doing?' I sheepishly told him I was cutting watermelon. He asked me who had shown me how to cut it that way. I said, 'No one, I just did it on my own,' thinking I had made some crucial mistake. He corrected that by saying what a good idea it was. He proceeded to race me chopping the rest of the watermelon. From this experience, I realized that no matter what your experience level is, you can learn something from anyone."

Following high school, young Mike enrolled at Virginia Tech. By his own admission, he wasn't the best student, but he did continue with his cooking, working part-time at a Mexican restaurant, his first experience with ethnic cuisine. He did not, however, continue with his college education—and he lost his job at the restaurant.

Arrington quit school and got a night job as a line cook at a Blacksburg hotel. "It was supposed to be my hiatus while I got my act together and went back to school," he says. Instead, he became increasingly aware that he liked making creations with food, and he found the lifestyle more to his liking than "a suit and

"I have been lucky to have several chefs take an interest in teaching me their philosophies. In the end, a chef's philosophy is a mix of his dining history, what he likes to eat, and philosophies he's been exposed to from others." **Photos by Jim Stroup**

a tie and a seat behind a desk." Other chefs became his mentors, and he stayed on the job for 11 years. During the last five of those years, he ran the kitchen and was free to experiment with some of his own ideas, one of the plusses of being an executive chef.

Arrington left Virginia for an Oklahoma hotel that had been bought and refurbished, but it had a reputation that new décor couldn't overcome. "After months of being in the red," he says, "management decided to go in another direction." Consequently, he lost his job—but he learned from that experience, too. "No one likes to be fired," he continues, "but having it happen to you will keep you humble—an important trait more chefs could use, in my opinion. It has been important in my work demeanor and how I approach a job in general."

After Oklahoma, the executive chef found another job—this time at a seafood restaurant in the Washington, D.C., area. The well-regarded restaurant, he says, "had stated philosophies: be true to their origin—the west coast—and that the fish is the star, not you or what you do with it. Both became important ideals for me." But Arrington tired of the long hours, always 6 a.m. to 5 p.m., but often as late as 8 p.m. "I loved what I did, but I was getting to the age where I just couldn't handle those kind of hours anymore. And I missed being in a small town."

In the year 2000, he secured a position in food service at the Donaldson Brown Hotel and Conference Center on the Virginia Tech campus. When The Inn at Virginia Tech and Skelton Conference Center replaced the hotel in 2005, he moved into the new facility. A few months later, the executive chef at The Grove left to pursue a career in academe, and Arrington successfully applied for the position.

Through all of his experiences in food service, Arrington has developed a philosophy that he follows in his cooking: "The first thing is that you must cater to your audience. You're not cooking for yourself but for the people who will eat it. Second, keep it simple. If you use great ingredients, the food should star, not you. Third, make sure you use the best ingredients. Fourth, know your subject. There are many foods I'm not fond of, but I've made a deal [with myself] that I will try them at least once. You can't use something if you have no clue as to its flavor profile. Fifth, keep your flavors balanced. Salt, sweet, bitter, acid, heat—all must balance. Know what balances what."

When Arrington creates a menu, he decides what the main ingredients will be. Then he thinks about what flavors complement those ingredients. "From a list of items, I decide what is most available at that moment. At this point, I may not decide until I get to market on where I will go [with the menu]. Then I think seasonally. Do we want a heavy demi-based sauce for beef—or even beef—on a day I know will be 90 degrees? Do we want ice cream in December?"

In the kitchen, the chef goes a step further than whistling while he cooks. "At this point in my life," he notes, "you'll find me belting out country tunes while working. I don't sing well, but I do sing loudly. Kitchens can be tense places, and I feel that it lightens the mood."

Except for a brief ice-cream course, Chef Michael has never had formal culinary training. "I have been lucky," he says, "to have several chefs take an interest in teaching me their philosophies. In the end, a chef's philosophy is a mix of his dining history, what he likes to eat, and philosophies he's been exposed to from others." Consequently, this singing chef shares his beliefs about cooking with others who want a future in the food industry, thereby perpetuating his craft.

Outside the kitchen, Chef Michael selects fresh ingredients to use in his recipes, and he is a competitive runner and triathlete who can hold his own in his age group. Photos by Jim Stroup

❧Executive Chef Josef R. Schelch

A number of recipes in the book come from Executive Chef Josef R. Schelch, who filled in at The Grove when needed, although his principal job at Virginia Tech was heading food service as the executive chef at The Inn at Virginia Tech and Skelton Conference Center. Before retiring from the university in 2010, Schelch spent many hours in Special Collections at Newman Library searching for recipes that were or might have been served at The Grove in times past.

Unlike Chef Michael, Chef Josef received his training in school—the Bad Gleichenberg Cooking School in Austria, his native country. Following his education, he worked as a chef de partie, sous chef, and chief cook aboard Holland America Line cruise ships for seven years, then spent a couple of years working at hotel restaurants in Austria as an executive chef. "I traveled a lot in my life," he says, "and I really enjoyed it, and it helped me a lot in my profession." He adds, "It's critical for chefs to travel and to study history, art, and culture with their different heritages. I feel that all cooks and chefs have an obligation—if they are inspired to borrow from another culture, they need to have some knowledge of it, some appreciation for it, and some respect for the integrity of the flavors and the ingredients." The dishes developed by Chef Josef are true to the flavors and ingredients of the cultures that inspired them.

In 1982, Chef Josef became executive sous chef at the famous Homestead Resort and Spa in Hot Springs, Va. There, he was the culinary manager of private parties, where as many as 12 courses were served for dinners; scheduled and supervised 80 employees; helped the executive chef in planning menus; and managed the resort's multiple food outlets.

He left the Homestead in 1985 to work for the Petroleum Club of Houston, Texas, as the executive chef, but after two years, he returned to his old position as executive sous chef at the Homestead. He remained in the position for five years before he was promoted to executive chef. As head of the resort's food service, he managed seven full-service outlets, including banquets attended by as many as 1,000 guests; served up to 3,000 meals per day; and scheduled and supervised a staff of 60. He recorded the best food sales in the resort's history in 2003 and 2004.

"Developing a dish," this award-winning chef says, "is not a strictly creative process—one beginning with a blank slate—but one where you've got these ingredients that you're moving around, and you're researching what works together." **Photos by Kelsey Kradel**

Chef Josef has been exposed over the years to many classic dishes, which, he notes, "typically consist of combinations—of textures, flavors, even aromas and colors—that history has been hard-pressed to offer improvements upon. Their having stood the test of time speaks to the elegance of their form, in combining flavors, not only harmoniously but, in many cases, synergistically, such that the whole is indeed greater than the sum of the individual parts."

In 1990, he was selected to promote the cookbook, *Dining at the Homestead,* a gourmet cookbook sold at Bloomingdale's in New York City. The resort also sent him to the Pinehurst Resort, twice, to work with a culinary team that catered for the U.S. Senior Open Golf Tournament. For his outstanding work at the Homestead, he received the 2003 Award of Excellence from *La Chaine des Rôtisseurs Bailliage de North Carolina.*

Developing a dish, this award-winning chef says, "is not a strictly creative process—one beginning with a blank slate—but one where you've got these ingredients that you're moving around, and you're researching what works together." He has also learned during his long career that there are three items that are quite important in the professional kitchen: "sharp knives (there is nothing worse than attempting to slice a tomato with a dull one), a vita-prep blender (it can turn a brick to sawdust), and quality pots and pans since they do all the cooking." These same items, he notes, are important in the home kitchen as well.

Chef Josef left the Homestead in 2005 to supervise Virginia Tech's planned closing of the Donaldson Brown Hotel and Conference Center and to become the first executive chef at the The Inn at Virginia Tech and Skelton Conference Center. At the new hotel, he managed the full-service kitchen as it supported daily conference meals and breaks, the fine-dining restaurant Preston's, room service, and banquets. His position also required that he plan menus and develop recipes for both daily meals and special events.

He has always taken delight in all aspects of his profession, even going to market. "When I go shopping for fresh ingredients, I am inspired like 'a child in a toy store,'" he says. The most challenging part of the job is "racing against the clock! There always seems to be something that needs to be done within the limited hours in the day."

He now works as a chef in West Virginia, where he continues to focus on "local, fresh, seasonal ingredients, including fish products," which, he notes, is "really important to me." And even after all of these years as a chef, he remains excited by "all the amazing produce that we are going to be getting in with the upcoming spring and summer seasons. Whether it's using one ingredient with several different preparations in one dish to enhance the flavor of that star ingredient or creating an intricate presentation of a dish for a customized menu or guests, I always try to apply a refined, fresh take and style to a dish."

His life's journeys have taught him "that life is really so simple," he says, adding, "In cooking, simple flavors and great combinations of food to serve can be very rewarding."

Photo by Kelsey Kradel

Recipes from the Grove

Definitions

A

al dente: an Italian expression for cooking a food item (generally pasta but also vegetables) until it is firm but not hard

amaretto: an almond-flavored liqueur

ancho: a large, usually dried, aromatic variety of chili pepper; the most commonly used pepper in Mexico

Arborio rice: the traditional rice used in risotto, it is high in starch, round-grained, produced in Italy, and named for the town of Arborio

arrowroot: a large perennial herb used as a thickener for sauces and soups that need to be cooked at low temperatures

arugula: an aromatic salad green

Asiago: a semi-hard, sweet, nutty-flavored cheese produced in the Alpine region of Italy

B

baste: pouring juices over meat during the cooking process to keep the meat moist

béchamel sauce: a medium-thick, classic French white sauce

Belgian endive: a leafy, cylinder-shaped vegetable rich in vitamins and minerals

bibb lettuce: a small, dark green, loose-leaved butterhead lettuce with lots of flavor; also known as limestone lettuce

bisque: a rich, creamy, seasoned soup, usually based on a strained broth from crustaceans, although pureed vegetables can serve as the base

Black Forest ham: a slow-cooked, smoked ham produced in Germany's Black Forest region

blood orange: a variety of orange smaller than an average orange that has crimson-colored flesh

Boursin cheese: a soft, smooth, creamy cheese developed in France and formed into cylindrical shapes

bread boules: round bread

brioche: a rich, light French pastry with a high egg and butter content

brunoise: very small dice cut, traditionally resulting in about ⅛-inch cubes

C

chanterelle: a wild, bright yellow to orange mushroom that has a convex to funnel-shaped cap

chervil: a delicate herb in the parsley family

chèvre: a sharp-tasting cheese made from goat milk; the generic term for goat cheese, the word is French for goat

chiffonade: a way of cutting flat leafy vegetables and herbs, resulting in uniform, curly strips

China cap chinois: a very fine, cone-shaped strainer

chipotle: a type of chili pepper produced in the state of Chihuahua in Mexico

confit: the French word for "preserved"; used to describe meat that has been cooked and preserved in its own fat

coulis: a thick sauce made from puréed fruits and vegetables

crème de cassis: a sweet, red liqueur made from black currants

croquette: a small fried food roll usually containing a mashed vegetable or minced meat as its main ingredient

Cryovac bags: sealed bags with air removed

D

deglaze: to moisten, often with wine, and remove browned food bits that stick to a pan

E

elephant garlic: not a true garlic, this plant forms a bulb of very large, garlic-like cloves that, while resembling the taste of garlic, are milder and sweeter

Emmental (also Emmenthal): a hard, cooked, pressed Swiss cheese with walnut-sized holes

F

fontina cheese: a mild, somewhat nutty-flavored, semi-soft cheese made from cow's milk; it has been made in the Aosta Valley of Italy since the 12th century

framboise: a Belgian beer that has a raspberry flavor

frangelico: a hazelnut liqueur developed in Italy

G

garnish: a decoration added to the top of food dishes

Grand Marnier: an orange-flavored liqueur

Gruyère: a semi-soft, nutty-flavored cheese with a hard brown rind that is named for the Swiss town of Gruyères

H

habañero: an intensely spicy hot chili pepper that most commonly ripens from green to red or orange

hake: a member of the cod family of fish

hummus: a dip or spread made from chickpeas, also known as garbanzo beans, that dates back to ancient Egypt

hydrate: to take up a liquid or to combine with a liquid

I

ice bath: dipping cooked food into a container of ice and water to quickly stop the cooking process

J

jalapeño: a very hot, medium-sized, green chili pepper

jicama: a root vegetable with a slightly sweet apple flavor that has the texture of a potato

julienne, julienned: slice or sliced into thin, matchstick-size strips

K

kecap manis: a dark brown, syrupy-thick, sweet Indonesian soy sauce also known as kekap manis

kirsch: a dry, colorless brandy that is made in the Black Forest of Germany and has been distilled from the fermented juice of black morello cherries

L

lemongrass: an herb-type grass, popular in Thai and Vietnamese cooking, that has a lemony aroma and flavor

lobster medallions: sliced lobster tail

M

mâche: a salad green, also known as corn salad and lamb's lettuce, that has a mild nutty flavor and can be purchased as mâche rosettes

Maggi liquid seasoning: a dark sauce similar to soy sauce

mahi mahi: another name for the common dolphin fish

mandolin slicer: a slicer that allows precise control over the size of cuts

marbling: small streaks of fat in meat

Marsala wine: a dark, sweet dessert wine resembling sherry that is produced in the region around the town of Marsala in Sicily

masa harina: finely ground flour made from corn that has been dried, cooked, ground up, and re-dried; a traditional flour used in Mexican cooking

mascarpone: a soft, white, rich cream cheese made in Italy from cow's milk

mesclun: a salad comprised of a mixture of small, young salad greens

meunière: cooked or served in lightly browned butter with lemon juice and parsley added; usually refers to a way to prepare fish

micro-greens: small, young sprouts of root vegetables

mirepoix: a mixture of chopped carrots, celery, and onions, generally used in soups and sauces to add flavor and aroma

Mornay sauce: a béchamel sauce (see definition under B) to which shredded or grated cheese has been added

morel: an edible wild mushroom with a honeycomb-textured upper portion

N

napa cabbage: a crisp, mildly flavored cabbage originating in China; also known as celery cabbage and Chinese cabbage

O

orange roughy: a deep-sea fish in the slimehead family of fish

P

pancetta: Italian bacon, which is salt-cured and seasoned with spices

panko: Japanese breadcrumbs

par cook: to partially cook vegetables (until they start to soften) so the cooking process can be completed later

pâté: a spreadable paste that includes ground meat, usually poultry, or meat organs

pequin: a hot chili pepper that has a slightly elongated oval shape; the smallest of the chili peppers

phyllo: an unleavened flour dough made into paper-thin sheets

poblano: a mild chili pepper usually shaped like a heart

pommes frites: fried potato strips

prosciutto: a specialty ham that is salted and air-cured

purée: a pasty substance resulting from cooking a food and then finely grinding it

Q

quinoa: a seed considered to be a whole grain that can be prepared like whole grains such as rice

R

ramekins: small, individual-size ceramic or glass bowls

reduction: the process of thickening a liquid mixture by boiling

rémoulade: a sauce, similar to tartar sauce, that was invented in France

render, rendered: melt down by cooking, melted down by cooking

reserve: put aside for later use

ricotta: an Italian dairy product made from milk whey left over in cheese-making; the word is Italian for "re-cooked"

risotto: an Italian dish of rice that is generally cooked in broth until it becomes creamy, like porridge

rosette: a circular arrangement of leaves

roulade: traditionally, a slice of fish rolled around a filling into a tubular shape, from the French word *rouler*, which means "to roll"

roux: a mixture of butter and flour used as a thickener for soups and sauces

S

serrano: a small, green, very hot chili pepper that originated in the mountainous regions of the states of Puebla and Hidalgo in Mexico

Shiraz: an Australian red wine made from Shiraz grapes, the most widely planted grape variety in Australia

simmer: to cook just below or at boiling point

star anise: a star-shaped, licorice-tasting seed pod from an evergreen tree grown in China and Japan

steep: allowing dry ingredients to soak in a liquid until the liquid has absorbed the flavor of the ingredients

Stilton cheese: a type of blue cheese produced in England

streusel: a crumbly topping or filling

strudel: a layered pastry with a filling inside

T

tahini: a paste made from ground sesame seeds

tawny port: a smoother, less sweet wine made from red grapes and aged as much as 20 years in oak barrels

temper: adding ingredients, such as eggs, very slowly to hot liquid so that the added ingredients do not cook into solids

terrine: similar to pâté but consisting of more coarsely chopped ingredients

tomatillo: a small, green, spherical fruit of a plant in the nightshade family; first grown by the Aztecs as much as 1,300 years ago, it has a somewhat lemony taste

truffle oil: an ingredient usually not made from truffles that still has the flavor and aroma of truffles

V

vichyssoise: a thick potato and leek soup traditionally served cold

Z

zest: a scraping, grating, or cutting from the outer, colorful skin of citrus fruits

Selecting Food for Your Meals

By Chef Michael Arrington

When buying ingredients, do not skimp. For example, it serves no purpose to spend money on a nice piece of beef or fish and then use cooking wine for an accent in the sauce served with the beef or fish.

When purchasing beef from a grocer, look at how it is trimmed. Ask the butcher if the beef is select or choice grade, remembering that choice is a higher grade and, thus, a better cut. Check the meat for marbling. Better yet, order grass-fed beef through the mail from a reputable butcher. The flavor profile of grass-fed beef is much better than that of grain-fed beef.

Beef is graded by the United States Department of Agriculture on a marbling scale of 1 to 12 and based on the age of the animal. The top three grades available to most consumers are *prime,* which is the best quality in terms of tenderness, juiciness, and flavor and has a marbling rating of about a 6, meaning that it is moderately abundant in marbling; *choice,* which has a moderate amount of marbling; and *select,* which has slight marbling. Prime grade generally is not available at grocery stores. If you are using a leaner cut of meat and are already spending a great deal of money, go that extra bit for a better cut. Remember that marbling is important since fat is what gives flavor and moistness to the finished product.

When selecting fish, remember that much of the success of your fish dish will depend on how well you choose your product. Color is important. Salmon should be orange, even though the color is feed-created in most instances. Swordfish should have a pink hue. Cod, flounder, Chilean sea bass, orange roughy, and hake should be cream-colored or white. Mahi mahi and tuna should be dark red. If any of these fish are browning or have hints of dull color, they have probably been on the market for a while.

Fresh fish should not have an odor and should look dry. Scales should be firmly in place. If buying whole fish, look for clear eyes and pink gills. Whenever possible, visit a fish mart as opposed to a grocer.

When buying fruits and vegetables, look to local farmers' markets, which are proliferating these days. Find markets that are actually stocked by farms and not by food brokers. If you see large produce boxes lying around, the sellers most likely are stocking their stands from the same vendors used by local grocery stores and restaurants. In such cases, the customer is paying extra money to buy the produce but is not getting the freshness usually found in locally grown fruits and vegetables.

Remember that no matter how well you prepare a recipe, if the ingredients have not been carefully selected for freshness, your dish cannot approach the perfection every cook desires.

Using Salt Blocks for Cooking, Serving, and Curing

By Chef Michael Arrington

Blocks of Himalayan salt have come into use at receptions at The Grove. Removed whole from the Himalayan mountains that were once part of a sea, this pink-streaked salt contains many more nutrients than regular salt. The blocks are wonderful to cook on since salt holds heat well. Their use as serving platters adds color and height to a reception table. And to keep food warm for about an hour, the blocks can be removed from a hot oven and placed under pans of food. They can be used to cold-cure food since the salt allows the removal of moisture, mainly water, both to inhibit bacterial growth and to intensify the flavor of the food being cured.

Salt blocks are available online and come in various sizes.

Cooking on Salt Blocks

Salt is hydrophilic, meaning that it attracts water. So while the salt block sits, it will absorb water from the atmosphere. Heating it at high temperatures without first removing the moisture can lead to cracking.

Salt blocks can be used for cooking either over a gas burner or on a grill. To use a salt block for cooking, ensure that the block is dry and less likely to crack by leaving it in a 200-degree (F) oven for several hours. Note that salt is a natural product and may exhibit minor cracks and seams that will not affect its usage. If it does crack, it can be ground for use as table salt.

Placing food on a salt block over a heating unit will not provide enough heat to cook the food completely, and leaving the food on the block too long will introduce too much salt into the food. One may have to experiment with using salt blocks to learn how much time is too long.

Beef Tenderloin and Ahi Cooked on Salt Blocks

To use the salt-block method of cooking beef tenderloin, roast the meat to rare before finishing it on the salt block. Roast the tenderloin in a 350-degree (F) oven for about one hour or until a thermometer inserted into the thickest part of the meat reads 120 degrees (F). Allow the meat to cool, and slice it about 1-inch thick. Place the slices on a salt block that is placed directly on the grill, and continue cooking until tenderloin has reached desired level of cooking.

Yellowfin tuna, also known as ahi, is generally served rare at The Grove. Thus, the ahi is seared on each side on the salt block, which is placed directly on the grill.

Curing on a Salt Block

Before tuna is served at The Grove, it is first cured on salt blocks. The curing is accomplished by placing one side of a 1 x 1 x 6-inch piece of fish on a salt block and turning it every 45 minutes until all sides of the fish have spent 45 minutes on the block. It is then removed from the block and sliced.

Watermelon can also be cured on a salt block. When it is cured and sliced, watermelon makes a great base for appetizers or salads. To cure watermelon, use a large cut—at The Grove, the watermelon is cut into an elongated cube—and place it on a salt block, turning the chunk of watermelon every 15 minutes until each side has been cured. For saltier watermelon, leave it on the block longer; for a less salty melon, leave it a shorter amount of time.

Mushroom Strudel with Fresh Thyme

Hors d'Oeuvres and Salads

Hors d'Oeuvres

40　Ale-glazed Shallots and Sharp Cheddar Cheese Toasts

41　Belgian Endive Leaves with Roasted Yellow Pepper Hummus and Whipped Boursin

42　Chicken Liver Pâté with Green Peppercorns and Port Wine

43　Cheese Straws

45　Parmesan, Cheddar Cheese, and Onion Toast

46　Cucumber Watercress Sandwiches

46　Deviled Ham Dip

47　Heirloom Tomato Finger Sandwiches with Pancetta and Basil

47　Hummus

49　Crab and Avocado Terrine

50　Grilled Vegetables

51　Fresh Asparagus Wrapped in Prosciutto Ham and Baked Phyllo with Parmesan Cheese

52　Sage Stuffing Rounds with Cranberry Chutney and Roast Turkey Pinwheels with Toasted Chestnut and Cream

53　Mesquite-smoked Chicken Strips

54　Cherry-wood Smoked Duck Breast with Cherry Chipotle Glaze

55　Mushroom Strudel with Fresh Thyme

56　Hot Smoked Wild Salmon with Sauce or Relish

58　Thai Crab Salad in Bread Cups

59　Smoked Salmon Roulades

Salads

60　Mesclun Salad with Grilled Butternut Squash

60　Pecan Sweet Potato Salad

61　Mâche with Charred Tomatoes, Vidalia Onion, and Avocado

62　Jicama Slaw

63　Granny Smith Apple and Fennel Slaw

65　Strawberry and Poblano Salad

66　Seasonal Salad: Grilled Romaine Lettuce with Grilled Vegetables

67　Seasonal Salad: Arugula with Poached Pears, Port Syrup, Spicy Walnuts, and Stilton Cheese Salad

67　Seasonal Salad: Spinach, Sliced Strawberries, and Almond-crusted Goat Cheese Salad

Chef Michael demonstrated the preparation of this canapé recipe, which is his version of a Chef Josef recipe, for the Faculty Women's Club's Friday Forum.

Ale-glazed Shallots and Sharp Cheddar Cheese Toasts

1. In a sauté pan, melt 1 tablespoon butter over low heat. Add shallots; continue cooking over low heat. Cook until shallots turn a dark brown and get sticky, about 20 - 30 minutes.* When browned, add ale; increase heat to medium. Reduce liquid until almost evaporated, about 5 - 10 minutes. Remove from stovetop; let cool.

2. Preheat oven to 250 degrees (F).

3. Melt 2 tablespoons butter in a small pan over low heat. Using a pastry brush, lightly brush bread rounds on one side with melted butter. Place bread on a sheet tray, butter side up; bake in oven until crunchy, about 15 minutes. Remove from oven; cool.

4. Shred cheddar. Once shallots have cooled, place shallots and cheddar in a food processor. Use pulse setting until ingredients are well blended and smooth.

5. Turn oven to broil.

6. Using a spoon, place a dollop of cheese mixture in center of each bread round, and lightly sprinkle with cayenne pepper. Place rounds in oven; heat until cheese is melted and bubbly. Serve immediately.

*Be careful to continuously watch and stir shallots since sugars are drawn from the shallots during the cooking process, and they can burn.

Yield: 50 (serves 25)

3 tablespoons butter, divided
10 shallots, julienned
½ cup flavorful ale
white bread, cut into 50 small rounds
    or other decorative shapes
8 ounces sharp white or yellow
    cheddar cheese
dash of cayenne pepper

Certain vegetables can hold a filling, and Chef Michael developed this canapé using Belgian endive leaves as the "holder." He prepared this recipe at The Grove during a cooking demonstration.

Belgian Endive Leaves with Roasted Yellow Pepper Hummus and Whipped Boursin

1. To make the yellow pepper hummus, combine all ingredients except Boursin, endive leaves, chives for garnish, and yellow peppers for garnish in a food processor. Blend until smooth.

2. In another bowl, whip Boursin with a whisk until smooth.

3. Using a pastry bag, pipe both spreads onto the "spoon" end of endive leaves, keeping spreads separate.

4. Garnish Boursin with snipped chives, and garnish hummus with brunoise-cut yellow peppers.

*Another nut butter can be substituted if tahini is not available.

**Found canned in some specialty food sections.

Yield: 50 canapés

2 ½ cups chickpeas (garbanzo beans), drained and rinsed
1 tablespoon tahini*
1 tablespoon roasted garlic
juice of 1 lemon
salt to taste
1 yellow pepper, roasted**
16 ounces Boursin cheese
50 Belgian endive leaves
chives for garnish, snipped
yellow peppers for garnish, brunoise cut

Chef Michael demonstrates the preparation of special dishes at a meeting of the Friday Forum group of the Virginia Tech Faculty Women's Club.

According to Chef Josef's research, this hors d'oeuvre or a variation of it was served at The Grove in the 1950s, a time when President Newman and his family lived in the residence.

Chicken Liver Pâté with Green Peppercorns and Port Wine

1. Melt 6 teaspoons butter in a skillet. Add onion, garlic, celery, and thyme. Cover; cook over medium-low heat for about 25 minutes or until onion is tender and lightly colored.

2. Meanwhile, add black peppercorns, salt, and bay leaves to water in a saucepan. Bring to a boil over medium-high heat. Reduce heat; simmer for 10 minutes.

3. Add chicken livers to water mixture, and simmer gently for about 10 minutes (livers should still be pink inside). Drain livers, and discard bay leaves and black peppercorns.

4. Place sautéed onion mixture in the bowl of a food processor fitted with a steel blade. Purée until onion mixture is finely textured. Add livers. Little by little, add ⅔ pound butter, port wine, and cognac. Process until smooth. Pour in cream, and process again to blend.

5. Transfer liver mixture to a bowl. Stir in green peppercorns and parsley. Serve with crackers or toast, cut into rounds, triangles, or squares.

Serves: at least 8

6 teaspoons unsalted sweet butter
½ cup yellow onions, finely minced
2 garlic cloves, peeled and chopped
½ cup celery, no leaves
1 teaspoon dried thyme
10 black peppercorns
½ teaspoon salt
2 bay leaves
6 cups water
1 ¼ pounds chicken livers
⅔ pound unsalted sweet butter, softened
½ cup port wine
2 tablespoons cognac
¼ cup heavy cream
4 teaspoons water-packed green peppercorns, drained
1 teaspoon parsley, chopped

These cheese straws developed by Chef Michael serve as a great appetizer or reception treat, or they can be used as an accent to soups or salads.

Cheese Straws

1. Preheat oven to 350 degrees (F).

2. Lightly flour work surface; using a rolling pin, roll puff pastry out to double its area. Sprinkle a quarter of cheese and a quarter of parsley over half the pastry. Fold pastry over so that cheese and parsley are enclosed. Sprinkle with flour and roll out again.

3. Repeat with a quarter of cheese and a quarter of parsley. Continue process until all the cheese and all the parsley have been worked into dough.

4. Cut dough into strips, approximately 3 inches long and 1 inch wide.

5. Starting at one corner of strip, roll up diagonally. Place on a parchment-lined sheet tray; brush with egg wash.

6. Bake in preheated oven until straws are puffed and brown, about 20 minutes. Remove from oven; cool to room temperature.

Yield: about 20 straws

flour
1 sheet puff pastry, thawed
½ cup Parmesan cheese
¼ cup fresh parsley, chopped
egg wash (2 eggs and 2 tablespoons
    water, beaten until well mixed)
parchment paper

Chef Josef shared this recipe with Chef Michael, who continues to use it at as an appetizer at The Grove, sometimes adding ale to the caramelized onion for another taste option.

Parmesan, Cheddar Cheese, and Onion Toast

1. Preheat oven to 250 degrees (F).

2. Lightly oil a baking sheet, and place bread rounds on it. Bake in preheated oven until rounds are toasted and dried, with most of moisture gone, about 20 - 30 minutes. Remove.

3. Turn oven to broil.

4. In a saucepan, melt butter over medium heat. Add onion; cook, stirring occasionally until onion is browned and becoming sticky, about 20 minutes. Be careful not to burn. Remove from heat.

5. In a food processor, add cheeses, onion, and cayenne. Salt to taste. Process until smooth. Top each toasted bread round with a dollop of cheese mixture.

6. Broil until cheese begins to brown, about 5 minutes.

7. Garnish with chives.

Yield: 50 bread rounds

oil
1 loaf white bread, cut into
   ½-inch rounds
1 tablespoon unsalted butter
1 sweet yellow onion, small dice
8 ounces sharp cheddar cheese,
   shredded
2 ounces Parmesan cheese, grated
dash of cayenne pepper
salt to taste
chives, freshly snipped, for garnish

This hors d'oeuvre developed by Chef Michael is a favorite finger food at receptions.

Cucumber Watercress Sandwiches

1. Lay cucumber slices on a rack over a sheet pan. Sprinkle with coarse salt. Let sit until salt pulls a fair amount of liquid from slices. Rinse slices, pat dry, and set aside.

2. In a food processor, add cream cheese, cayenne, and watercress. Process until smooth.

3. Spread cream cheese mixture on one side of half of the bread slices. Top cream cheese mixture with cucumber slices; cover each with second slice of bread to form sandwich.

4. Trim crust; cut sandwich into 4 triangles or squares.

Yield: approximately 64 sandwiches

2 seedless cucumbers, peeled and
    sliced lengthwise
1 tablespoon coarse salt
4 ounces cream cheese
1/8 teaspoon cayenne pepper
1/4 cup watercress, cleaned and
    chopped
Pepperidge Farm very thin sliced
    white bread

Although the timeframe and origin are unknown, this hors d'oeuvre was prepared for receptions and cocktail parties at Virginia Tech, according to information uncovered during Chef Josef's research.

Deviled Ham Dip

1. In a skillet, sauté onion in butter for 2 minutes on medium heat or until onion is soft but not brown; cool.

2. In a mixer, combine onion and remaining ingredients, except chopped parsley, until blended; refrigerate.

3. After garnishing with chopped parsley, serve with celery sticks, on toast points, or as the filling for finger sandwiches.

Yield: 1 pint

1 tablespoon onion, finely chopped
1 teaspoon butter
3 ounces diced pimiento
3 ounces processed cheddar cheese
1/2 cup mayonnaise
8 ounces cooked Virginia ham,
    finely chopped
pinch of cayenne pepper
salt and pepper to taste
1 teaspoon parsley, chopped

With this recipe, Chef Michael has created an Italian spin on the traditional BLT. He prepares the sandwiches for receptions at The Grove.

Heirloom Tomato Finger Sandwiches with Pancetta and Basil

1. Preheat oven to 275 degrees (F).

2. Slice pancetta. Place on a rack in a pan*; bake in preheated oven until crispy.

3. In processor, combine cream cheese, basil, olive oil, and garlic; puree until smooth.

4. Spread mixture on slices of bread. Top with tomato slices and pancetta, followed by another slice of bread. Trim crusts; cut each into 4 sandwiches, either shaped as triangles or squares.

*The pan will catch the rendered fat.

Yield: about 60 finger sandwiches

2 pounds pancetta (Italian bacon)
4 ounces cream cheese
2 ounces basil leaves
2 ounces olive oil, high quality
1 garlic clove, roasted
Pepperidge Farm very thin sliced
    whole wheat bread
8 heirloom tomatoes, thinly sliced

Hummus is a classic Middle Eastern dip or spread that began to appear at parties in the United States in the 1970s, perhaps spurred by the growing vegetarian movement, Chef Josef says. Hummus, which is the Arabic word for "chickpea," dates back to ancient Egypt. The chef's recipe for the centuries-old food follows.

Hummus

1. In blender or food processor, place beans, reserved liquid, lemon juice, sesame seed oil, cumin, garlic, ½ tablespoon parsley, salt, and pepper. Cover. Blend on high speed, stopping occasionally to scrape sides if necessary, until uniform consistency is reached.

2. Spoon dip into serving dish. Sprinkle with remaining parsley and sesame seeds. Serve with pita-bread wedges, crackers, or vegetables.

*Note that garbanzo beans and chickpeas are the same thing.

Serves: 15 - 18

1 15-ounce can chickpeas or garbanzo
    beans,* drained, reserving ⅓ cup
    liquid
3 tablespoons lemon juice
½ teaspoon sesame seed oil
⅛ teaspoon cumin
1 garlic clove, crushed
1 tablespoon fresh parsley, chopped
    and divided
½ teaspoon salt
pinch of ground black pepper
¼ cup sesame seeds

This terrine is Chef Michael's variation on a pâté and is served at receptions at The Grove.

Crab and Avocado Terrine

1. In a saucepan, sprinkle gelatin over cold water. Let sit to hydrate gelatin.

2. In a bowl, combine sour cream, mashed avocados, lime juice, and cilantro.

3. In a food processor, place cream cheese; process until smooth. Gradually add mayonnaise, mustard, Worcestershire, and Tabasco. Move to a second bowl; fold in crab meat and Old Bay seasoning.

4. Heat hydrated gelatin over low heat until liquid. Pour half in avocado mixture and half in crab mixture.

5. Line a terrine mold with plastic wrap. Place half of avocado slices and half of red pepper slices in bottom of mold. Cover with half of avocado mixture. Press remaining avocado slices and red pepper slices on top of avocado mixture. Cover with remaining avocado mixture. Top with crab mixture. Fold edges of plastic wrap over sides of the terrine mold; refrigerate until set.

6. To unmold, dip bottom of terrine mold briefly in warm water. Place serving tray over terrine mold and invert. Shake gently until mold releases contents. Remove plastic wrap.

7. Garnish molded mixture with lime slices. Serve with French bread toasts and crackers.

Serves: 8 - 10

2 packets unflavored gelatin
⅓ cup cold water
8 ounces sour cream
2 ripe avocados, mashed
juice of 1 lime
¼ tablespoon cilantro, chopped
8 ounces cream cheese, softened
¼ cup mayonnaise
1 tablespoon Dijon mustard
dash of Worcestershire sauce
dash of Tabasco sauce
½ pound blue crab claw and backfin
1 teaspoon Old Bay seasoning
1 avocado, sliced
1 red pepper, roasted and sliced
lime slices for garnish

Chef Michael's grilled vegetable recipe, which produces one of the more popular foods he prepares for receptions, is a simple, colorful (depending on the vegetables), and attractive alternative to the traditional vegetable/dip tray.

Grilled Vegetables

1. Place vegetables and vinaigrette in a sealable bag.† Marinate vegetables overnight.

2. Remove from bag; char on a charcoal grill. For small bite-size pieces, use either a small oven rack or an aluminum roasting-pan with holes poked in it.

3. Allow to cool; arrange artistically on a platter. No dip is needed but can be provided if desired.

*Salt eggplant to remove liquid from it. Liquid in eggplant is high in alkali, which has a bitter taste. By salting and then pressing the eggplant, one can remove most of this bitter liquid. Salting and pressing also allow cell membranes to better absorb marinade.

**Per Cryovac bag. When using a sealable bag instead of a Cryovac bag, use enough oil to cover the vegetables, occasionally turning the bag over to keep the vegetables well marinated.

† Chef Michael prefers to use Cryovac bags, which help force the marinade into the vegetables.

Serves: 20 - 25

1 red pepper, cut in quarters
    with seeds and stem removed
1 yellow pepper, cut in quarters
    with seeds and stem removed
1 orange pepper, cut in quarters
    with seeds and stem removed
1 red onion, cut into bite-size pieces
1 bunch asparagus spears, bottom
    trimmed, cut in bite-size pieces
2 zucchinis, halved
2 crookneck squashes, halved
1 eggplant, sliced and salted*
¼ cup** Italian vinaigrette, good
    quality

Optional Vegetables

- cherry or grape tomatoes: Cut in half and toss with sugar, salt, dried oregano, dried basil, and olive oil.
- portabella mushrooms: Remove gills; marinate in garlic, olive oil, salt, sugar, and balsamic vinegar.
- baby carrots with stem: Toss with butter, cinnamon, brown sugar, and apple-cider vinegar. Roast in 250-degree (F) oven for 45 minutes.
- new potatoes: Quarter and toss with truffle oil, salt, and pepper. Roast in 250-degree (F) oven for 30 minutes.
- cauliflower: Remove florets. Parboil in a mixture of sugar, vinegar, and water. If using white cauliflower, add ¼ teaspoon of turmeric.

This tasty hors d'oeuvre was developed by Chef Josef.

Fresh Asparagus Wrapped in Prosciutto Ham and Baked in Phyllo with Parmesan Cheese

1. Blend olive oil with melted butter; set aside.

2. Preheat oven to 400 degrees (F).

3. Add water to a stainless steel saucepan; bring to a boil over medium heat. Add asparagus; blanch until crisp-tender, about ½ - 1 minute depending on size of asparagus. Cool spears under cold water; pat very dry with paper towels or a napkin.

4. Roll 4 spears, salted to taste, in 2 slices prosciutto. Repeat with remaining asparagus and ham.

5. Spread 1 sheet of phyllo on work surface; brush with butter/olive oil mixture. Place ½ of wrapped asparagus on short end of phyllo; roll it up snugly. Brush second sheet of phyllo with butter/olive oil mixture. Place first roll on second sheet; roll up snugly. Repeat process with remaining phyllo, asparagus, and prosciutto.

6. Brush phyllo rolls with butter/olive oil mixture, dust with Parmesan, and set on a baking sheet.

7. Bake on top shelf of preheated oven for 10 -16 minutes or until golden brown and crisp.

8. Remove from oven; let rolls cool slightly before slicing them at an angle into bite-size pieces.

*Note that large asparagus spears will need to be peeled.

Yield: 10 pieces

1 tablespoon olive oil
1 tablespoon unsalted butter, melted
4 cups water
8 asparagus spears*
salt to taste
4 very thin slices prosciutto ham
4 sheets phyllo dough
1 tablespoon Parmesan cheese, freshly grated

In a February 2007 presentation at The Grove for the Virginia Tech Faculty Women's Club, Chef Michael demonstrated the preparation of canapés, including the ones that follow.

Sage Stuffing Rounds with Cranberry Chutney and Roast Turkey Pinwheels with Toasted Chestnut and Cream

Yield: about 25

Sage Stuffing Rounds

1 tablespoon butter or oil
2 tablespoons onions, finely chopped
2 tablespoons celery, finely diced
1 cup chicken stock (recipe on page 81)
2 tablespoons fresh sage, finely minced
2 cups coarse breadcrumbs*
1 egg
salt and pepper to taste
canola oil

1. Melt butter in a sauté pan. Add onions and celery; cook until tender. Add chicken stock, sage, and breadcrumbs. Cook until heated through and all liquid is absorbed. Allow to cool. Add egg; salt and pepper to taste. Refrigerate.

2. When chilled, place stuffing between two sheets of wax paper. Press out, using a rolling pin if desired, to about ½-inch thickness. Using a small, round biscuit cutter, cut into about 25 circles.

3. In a sauté pan, fry rounds (in batches) in oil (enough to reach 1-inch deep in pan) over medium heat. Drain well.

*Japanese breadcrumbs, known as panko, work well.

Cranberry Chutney*

1 cup cranberry juice
juice of 1 lemon
1 cup dried cranberries
1 teaspoon ginger
¼ teaspoon ground cloves
2 tablespoons brown sugar

1. Add all ingredients in a saucepan; cook over medium heat until liquid has evaporated and chutney is sticky.

2. Remove from heat; run through a food processor.

*Make a day ahead and chill to meld flavors.

Roast Turkey Pinwheel Canapés

toasted chestnut and cream filling (recipe below)
¼ pound roasted deli turkey, sliced thin enough to roll but thick enough to hold together

1. Prepare toasted chestnut and cream filling.

2. On a piece of plastic wrap, lay out sliced turkey with slices slightly overlapping. Spread chestnut and cream filling over turkey to about 1 inch from edges. Using plastic wrap, roll turkey over lengthwise. Roll turkey/chestnut and cream mixture into a tube shape, wrap tube in plastic wrap, and freeze at least 1 hour.

3. Remove from freezer, remove plastic wrap, and slice into ¼-inch-thick rounds. Allow pinwheels to reach room temperature.

4. To serve, place a small amount of cranberry chutney (recipe below left) on a sage stuffing round (recipe above left). Top with turkey pinwheel slice. Garnish, if desired, with a small amount of chutney.*

*Chef Michael prefers not to garnish this canapé and recommends that if a garnish is used, it should not completely cover the pinwheel.

Toasted Chestnut and Cream Filling

1 ounce chestnut meats
1 teaspoon walnut oil
2 ounces cream cheese

1. Preheat oven to 250 degrees (F).

2. In a baking pan, toss chestnut meats in walnut oil. Cook in preheated oven until lightly browned, about 10 - 15 minutes. Watch closely since nuts burn quickly.

3. Add nuts and cream cheese to a food processor; purée until ingredients are smooth in texture.

Smoked chicken, such as that prepared from Chef Michael's recipe below, sliced into bite sizes and served chilled with sauce makes a tasty reception dish. At The Grove, homemade white rolls (recipe on page 74) usually accompany the smoked chicken.

Mesquite-smoked Chicken Strips

1. In a bowl, combine all seasonings.

2. Trim fat from chicken thighs. Add trimmed chicken to the bowl of seasonings; toss to coat. Refrigerate for about 2 - 3 hours.

3. Remove; let drain on rack.

4. Turn on grill; leave covered to preheat to high. Turn one side off; place a pie pan full of water under the rack on this side.

5. Soak mesquite wood for at least 10 minutes in water. Place mesquite on side of grill that is on.

6. Place chicken on side of grill that is off. Cook until internal temperature of chicken reaches 165 degrees (F), about 25 - 30 minutes. Rotate chicken pieces so that all are toward the side that is on for an equal amount of time. Remove from grill when done, and allow to cool.

7. Refrigerate until chilled.

8. Remove from refrigerator, slice, and serve with a sauce and slaw.

Serves: 20 - 25 in reception-style platters

¼ cup brown sugar
1 tablespoon kosher salt
1 teaspoon curing salt
1 tablespoon paprika
1 tablespoon chili powder
1 teaspoon garlic powder
1 teaspoon dry oregano
5 pounds boneless chicken thighs
mesquite wood
water

Chef Michael prepares a variety of canapés, all pleasing to the palate. His smoked duck breast falls in this category, and the appetizing recipe follows.

Cherry-wood Smoked Duck Breast with Cherry Chipotle Glaze

1. Pour half of cherry chipotle glaze over duck breast; let marinate for 1 hour. (Note: The longer the duck sits in the glaze, the more water will be pulled from the breast.) Reserve remaining glaze for use during grilling process and to use as a dipping sauce.

2. Heat outdoor grill to high. Place wood chips on a piece of aluminum foil; fold into a cup shape. Place foil directly on coals; wait until wood chips begin to smoke.

3. Place marinated duck breast on grill. Close lid of grill; reduce heat to medium. Close vents almost all the way; keep grill lid closed as much as possible.* Cook about 7 minutes.

4. Open grill, turn duck, and brush it with cherry chipotle glaze. Close grill; cook another 4 - 5 minutes.

5. Remove duck; let rest for at least 10 minutes; refrigerate until completely cooled.

6. Preheat oven to 200 degrees (F).

7. Cut bread slices into 1-inch squares with canapé cutter. Brush lightly with oil; toast in preheated oven for 10 - 15 minutes or until dried out.

8. Cut duck breast into strips; serve with reserved glaze on bread toasts.

*Refrain from lifting the grill lid to check on the duck.

Serves: 25

2 pounds duck breast, skin removed
cherry chipotle glaze (recipe below)
1 cup cherry-wood chips, soaked
  in water
1 loaf thick-sliced white bread
oil

Cherry Chipotle Glaze

1. In a saucepan, combine white wine and raspberry vinegar. Bring to a boil; add cherries. Cook until reduced by half. Add lime juice, chipotle peppers, brown sugar, and jam. Heat until just combined.

2. Remove from heat; add cilantro. Let cool.

3. Move mixture to food processor; purée. Push through a fine strainer.

1 cup white wine
¼ cup raspberry vinegar
1 pint cherries, fresh or frozen
juice of 1 lime
2 ounces chipotle peppers in adobe
  sauce, diced
¼ cup brown sugar
1 8-ounce jar red currant jam
1 tablespoon cilantro, chopped

This recipe from Chef Michael made its debut at The Grove in September 2011.

Mushroom Strudel with Fresh Thyme

1. Preheat oven to 325 degrees (F).

2. Place mushrooms and shallots with regular oil in sauté pan, and cook over medium heat until mushrooms give off juice. Strain; reserve juice for use in sherry sauce.

3. In food processor, add mushrooms and shallots; pulse to chop finely. Move to mixing bowl.

4. Add ricotta to a food processor with eggs, truffle and porcini oils, salt, pepper, and thyme. Purée until curds are smooth. Add to mushrooms. Add enough breadcrumbs to make mixture firm.

5. On a floured surface, roll out 1 puff pastry. Add half of mushroom mixture, stopping about 1 inch from edge. Brush edges of puff pastry with egg wash; roll pastry around mushroom mixture. Fold ends to seal; place on parchment-lined sheet pan. Repeat with remaining sheet of pastry.

6. Cut vent holes in top of pastry; bake in preheated oven for about 1 hour. Remove; let rest 15 minutes.

7. Slice and place over sherry sauce. Garnish with fresh thyme.

*Chef Michael uses dried morels and fresh chanterelles. When using dried mushrooms, use weight when reconstituted.

Fresh Ricotta

1. Place all ingredients in a pot; heat over medium heat, stirring occasionally. Wait for milk to form curds.

2. Strain through a China cap chinois (a very fine, cone-shaped strainer). Place strained curds in strainer lined with coffee filters or cheesecloth.

3. Let sit overnight in refrigerator to strain off liquid*; discard liquid.

 *Place a pan under the strainer to catch the liquid.

Serves: 12

2 pounds mushrooms*
¼ cup shallots
1 tablespoon oil
2 ½ pounds fresh ricotta (recipe below)
2 eggs
1 tablespoon truffle oil
1 tablespoon porcini oil
1 tablespoon salt
1 tablespoon black pepper
3 tablespoons fresh thyme leaves
½ cup breadcrumbs
flour
2 sheets puff pastry
egg wash (2 eggs and 2 tablespoons water, beaten together until well mixed)
sherry sauce (recipe on page 103)
fresh thyme
parchment paper

1 gallon whole milk
¼ cup sherry vinegar
1 tablespoon salt

Depending on the type of wood used to smoke the salmon in this recipe, Chef Michael has developed a variety of sauces and relishes that blend with the wood-smoke taste and are paired with the type of wood used.

Hot Smoked Wild Salmon with Sauce or Relish

Hot Smoked Wild Salmon

1. Before smoking the salmon, cure it for at least 1 day and up to 3 days.† Use a mixture of curing salt†† and brown sugar, and cover salmon completely. When you have cured salmon to your liking, rinse and let it sit long enough to dry. The surface of the salmon should be tacky to help the smoke adhere to it better.

2. Place wood chips over hot charcoals on one side of grill; put salmon on opposite side, away from heat. Place a pan of water under the salmon. Close lid to grill. Let salmon smoke for about 10 minutes per inch of thickness at thickest part or until internal temperature reaches 140 degrees (F). Turn salmon midway through cooking so that both ends spend equal time closest to the heat.

3. After smoking salmon, prepare sauce or relish (recipes on facing page) depending on type of wood used in smoking.

*Bourbon is casked in oak and made of corn.

**Think Pacific Northwest.

†Curing removes water from the salmon, adds flavor, and helps prevent bacterial growth. If curing for longer than 1 day, rinse salmon daily, and reapply cure after each rinse. Follow directions on curing salt package.

††Curing salt contains nitrates that prohibit the growth of botulism. The concentration of nitrates can differ in the curing salt, so follow manufacturer's directions since nitrates in high concentrations can be dangerous for consumption.

Serves: 25

curing salt
brown sugar
1 pound wild salmon (king, sockeye, Coho)
¼ cup wood chips (fruitwood such as peach, oak, mild soft wood such as alder or cedar)
sauce or relish (recipes on facing page)

Wood - sauce combinations:
for peach fruitwood, peach horseradish relish
for oak, charred corn or bourbon mustard sauce*
for soft woods, blueberry juniper relish**

Peach Horseradish Relish

Mix peaches and horseradish. Place peach-wood-smoked salmon on bread slices; spread relish on top of salmon; serve.

*White peaches are sweeter, even before they become soft.

2 firm, white peaches,* diced
1 tablespoon prepared horseradish
    or freshly grated horseradish root
pumpernickel bread, sliced

Charred Corn

1. Preheat oven to 250 degrees (F).

2. Leave ears of corn in husks; place on charcoal grill. Cook until husk is completely charred, turning to char all sides.

3. Place on a sheet pan; roast an additional 25 minutes in preheated oven.

4. Remove and let cool. Remove husks and silk. Slice corn off cob with a sharp knife. Add salt, pepper, sugar, and vinegar. Place on top of oak-smoked salmon; serve.

2 ears sweet yellow corn
salt and pepper to taste
1 tablespoon white sugar
1 tablespoon white vinegar

Bourbon Mustard Sauce

1. Cook bourbon over medium heat until reduced to ¼ cup.

2. Combine Dijon and sugar in medium-size bowl. Add bourbon, mixing well.

3. Spread sauce over salmon; serve.

2 cups bourbon
1 cup Dijon mustard
¼ cup light brown sugar

Blueberry Juniper Relish

Add juniper berries to blueberries. Add salt, pepper, sugar, and lemon juice. Place alder- or cedar-smoked salmon on toast; top with relish; serve.

*Place in a bag; pound with hammer.

1 tablespoon dried juniper berries,
    crushed*
½ cup blueberries, roughly chopped
salt and pepper to taste
1 tablespoon sugar
1 tablespoon lemon juice
sourdough bread, sliced and toasted

According to Chef Michael, some canapés consist of cups filled with a salad, something finely diced or shredded, or something hot served with a sauce. This recipe developed by the chef is an example of a filled-cup canapé and is one he demonstrated at The Grove for the university's Faculty Women's Club.

Thai Crab Salad in Bread Cups

Thai Crab Salad

1. Pick through crabmeat, removing cartilage and shell.

2. Split lemongrass stalk, and remove middle stem for use.** Finely dice (julienne) stalk.

3. In a bowl, combine lemongrass, cilantro, basil, coconut milk, and mayonnaise. Let sit for at least 1 hour. Fold in crabmeat, being careful to keep lumps of crab intact.

4. Place in bread cups; top with red curry sauce (recipe on page 97). Garnish with coconut, lemongrass, or cilantro. Serve chilled.

*Celery can be substituted if necessary.

**Middle stems are less fibrous and more tender.

Bread Cups

1. Preheat oven to 200 degrees (F).

2. Using a biscuit or cookie cutter, cut bread slices into rounds, ensuring that the rounds are larger in diameter than mini-muffin pan holes. Brush top side with butter.

3. Spray mini-muffin pans with non-stick spray. Press bread rounds, butter side up, firmly into muffin holes so that the bread comes up the sides, forming bread cups. Bake in preheated oven until well toasted, about 15 - 20 minutes.

4. Remove bread cups; let sit until they reach room temperature before completing the canapés.

Serves about 18

1 ½ pounds crabmeat, lump or backfin
1 stalk lemongrass*
2 tablespoons chopped cilantro
2 tablespoons chiffonade of fresh basil
1 tablespoon coconut milk
2 tablespoons mayonnaise
50 white bread cups (recipe below)
coconut, toasted, for garnish
lemongrass, julienned, for garnish
cilantro, chopped, for garnish

1 loaf thick-sliced white bread
4 ounces butter, melted
non-stick spray

Salmon is the basic ingredient of this Chef Michael canapé, another favorite of guests at receptions.

Smoked Salmon Roulades

1. On parchment paper, lay sliced smoked salmon, overlapping slices. Freeze for 30 - 60 minutes.

2. Place cream cheese, lemon juice, capers, dill, and pickle in a processor. Purée until smooth.

3. Remove parchment with salmon slices from freezer. Spread cream cheese mixture over slices within ½ inch of border. Roll salmon by folding parchment over salmon, pulling parchment back to keep from rolling it up in the salmon, then folding again; repeat until salmon is in one roll. Wrap with parchment; seal ends. Freeze.

4. To serve, remove from freezer; allow to thaw slightly.* Slice into ⅛-inch thick pieces. Place on pumpernickel toasts; serve.

*The roll will slice best if cream cheese is still frozen in the middle.

Serves: 25

1 pound smoked salmon, sliced
4 ounces cream cheese
1 tablespoon lemon juice
1 tablespoon capers
3 tablespoons snipped fresh dill
½ dill pickle spear
pumpernickel bread, toasted
parchment paper

Chef Michael demonstrates the preparation steps for smoked salmon roulades.

This Chef Michael creation combines traditional fall flavors in a tasty salad. He served it as the opening course to a pan-seared scallop dish for a board of visitors' spouses' lunch in November 2008.

Mesclun Salad with Grilled Butternut Squash*

1. Cut squash into large pieces, each with surface area large enough to show grill marks.

2. In a bowl, add vinegar, sugar, cinnamon, cloves, and sea salt. Place squash in the bowl, and toss to coat. Cover and refrigerate at least 5 hours.

3. Preheat grill or broiler. Preheat oven to 350 degrees (F).

4. Grill pieces of squash until lightly charred.

5. Move to greased sheet pan, and bake in preheated oven until soft, about 15 - 20 minutes. Keep warm.

6. Arrange each salad plate with greens, place squash to the side. Top greens with cranberries and walnuts, and dress with cranberry vinaigrette (recipe on page 89).

*Can be prepared a day ahead.

Serves: 10 - 12

1 small butternut squash, peeled and cut in half lengthwise
1 cup cider vinegar
¼ cup light brown sugar
⅛ teaspoon cinnamon
3 whole cloves
1 teaspoon sea salt
3 cups mixed baby greens
¼ cup dried cranberries
¼ cup walnuts, chopped

Chef Michael calls this salad a new, healthier way to eat sweet potatoes during the holiday season.

Pecan Sweet Potato Salad

1. Place potatoes in a stockpot; cover with water. Bring to a boil, and reduce heat to simmer. Cook until tender (but not mushy), about 20 minutes.

2. Drain potatoes, and run under cold water to stop cooking. Place in the refrigerator, and allow to cool.

3. To serve, toss with dressing (recipe below), and garnish with pecans.

Dressing

In a small bowl, whisk together all ingredients.

Yield: ½ gallon of salad

3 pounds sweet potatoes, peeled and diced into 1-inch cubes
1 cup spicy candied pecans (recipe on page 153)

½ cup yogurt
¼ cup brown sugar
2 tablespoons orange juice
⅛ teaspoon ground cinnamon
dash of ground cloves

For a great start to dinner, try this salad developed by Chef Michael to serve at The Grove.

Mâche with Charred Tomatoes, Vidalia Onion, and Avocado

1. Turn charcoal grill to high, preheating with cover closed. Preheat oven to 350 degrees (F).

2. Brush onion slices with olive oil; sprinkle with sea salt. Place slices on grill, and char for about 3 minutes. Make a quarter turn of onion slices; grill an additional 3 minutes. Turn onions over and repeat grilling process.

3. Remove slices from grill; place on a sheet pan. Roast in preheated oven until soft and very browned, about 10 minutes. Chop onion; reserve.

4. Place tomato slices on rack; sprinkle with sugar. Let sit for 5 minutes, turn over, and sprinkle other side with sugar. Let sit another 5 minutes. Using a blowtorch, char tomatoes. Turn and char other side.

5. To make the salad, place two slices of tomato on each plate. Top with ½-cup mâche, avocado, and chopped onion. Dress with chive vinaigrette.

Serves: 8

1 Vidalia onion, sliced ½-inch thick
1 tablespoon olive oil
1 teaspoon sea salt
4 heirloom tomatoes, sliced ½-inch thick
1 tablespoon white sugar
4 cups mâche rosettes
1 avocado, peeled, pitted, and sliced
2 cups chive vinaigrette (recipe on page 88)

This slaw recipe developed by Chef Michael was inspired by a chef with whom he worked years ago. A version of the slaw was served in a seafood restaurant and opened Chef Michael's eyes to different styles of slaw, not just that made from cabbage. In presenting the recipe, the executive chef of The Grove offers his thanks to Chef Tom.

Jicama Slaw*

1. Place all vegetables in a bowl; toss in sugar and salt; let sit 5 minutes.

2. Place vegetables in a colander over a bowl; allow to drain in the refrigerator for at least 1 hour.

3. Remove and rinse. Place in dry bowl, and toss with dressing (recipe below).

*The vegetables used in this recipe are best when they are cut shoestring size. If lacking the knife skills for the julienne cut, use a mandolin slicer.

Dressing

Mix all ingredients until well blended.

Yield: 2 quarts

1 medium jicama, peeled and julienned
1 red pepper, cored and julienned
1 medium carrot, peeled and julienned
4 ribs celery, peeled and julienned
4 shallots, peeled and julienned
1 jalapeño, seeded and minced
2 tablespoons white sugar
1 tablespoon kosher salt

½ cup mayonnaise
2 tablespoons Dijon mustard
¼ cup ketchup
1 tablespoon chili powder
1 teaspoon ground cumin
1 teaspoon garlic powder
dash of cayenne pepper
juice of 1 lime
1 tablespoon cilantro, chopped
dash of Worcestershire sauce
dash of Tabasco sauce

This creation of Chef Michael is served with barbecue and smoked foods, but it also makes an excellent side dish for crab cakes and fish, particularly halibut.

Granny Smith Apple and Fennel Slaw

1. Toss onion, apples, fennel, and cabbage with salt and sugar. Place in a colander over a bowl; cover mixture with a dinner plate with a heavy weight on it. Allow to drain for at least 1 hour or under refrigeration overnight.

2. Remove colander from refrigerator; pour juice from bowl into a saucepot with cider vinegar and apple cider. Cook over medium heat until reduced to ½ cup. Let juice cool.

3. In a bowl, combine apple-cabbage mixture, juice, mayonnaise, mustard, Worcestershire, and Tabasco; add fennel fronds. Refrigerate. Drain before serving.

Yield: 6 cups

1 Vidalia onion, julienned
6 Granny Smith apples, cored
   and grated
1 fennel bulb, quartered and thinly
   shaved, reserving fronds (leaves)
1 napa cabbage, sliced very thinly
1 tablespoon salt
¼ cup white sugar
¼ cup cider vinegar
1 cup apple cider
1 cup mayonnaise
2 tablespoons Dijon mustard
dash of Worcestershire sauce
dash of Tabasco sauce

This salad creation of Chef Michael was an opening course for a board of visitors dinner that featured Parmesan-crusted sole. The chef was interested in celebrating the new spring with a light salad with berries. He used a bitter green, a peppery green, and a nutty green and added something sweet, which he countered with a mild chili. He then tied the various flavors together with a tart berry dressing.

Strawberry and Poblano Salad

1. Turn oven to broil.

2. Pour oil into a bowl; add salt and peppers. Toss to coat.

3. Place peppers on sheet pan; place under broiler. Cook until skin blackens. Turn peppers. Repeat process until skin is blackened on all sides. Remove from oven, and place back in bowl. Cover; let sit for 10 minutes.

4. Move bowl to sink. With cold water running into bowl, peel off charred skin; remove seeds. Slice peppers into strips.

5. Place strawberries in a bowl; toss with sugar. Let sit until juice begins to release from berries.

6. Put equal amounts of greens on each plate, and top with strawberries and pepper strips. Dress with berry vinaigrette (recipe on page 88) before serving.

Serves: 8

1 tablespoon oil
1 teaspoon salt
4 medium poblano peppers or other mild chili peppers
1 quart strawberries, hulled and sliced
1 tablespoon white sugar
1 cup baby spinach, washed and stems removed
1 cup arugula, torn into bite-size pieces
1 cup mâche rosettes

The ingredients of salads served at The Grove generally depend on the season. In the spring, Chef Michael likes to use young greens, a sweeter-style (like Bibb) lettuce, bitter greens (such as a type of spinach), or nutty mâche. He generally pairs these greens with strawberries or oranges. In the summer, he favors large, mature lettuce (such as crisp head—iceberg lettuce falls in this group) or romaine and prefers to mix them with grilled vegetables (like tomatoes and onions). In fall and winter, he leans toward peppery greens (as the weather gets colder, he likes to serve something that warms the guests) or a spicier style of greens (like arugala or garden cress). In the fall, he roasts pears, apples, or squash to accompany the greens, and in the winter, he uses root vegetables (like beets) and squashes (like butternut). He often uses nuts to enhance his salads, preferring almonds in the spring, macadamias in the summer, and pecans and walnuts in fall and winter. Cheese is another enhancer frequently used by Chef Michael. He considers a nice goat cheese to be a refreshing addition in the spring, a mild mozzarella a great accompaniment in the summer, a salty Parmesan good for fall, and strong bleu or Stilton cheese perfect in the winter.

Following are examples of these salads.

Seasonal Salads
Each serves: 8

Grilled Romaine Lettuce with Grilled Vegetables

1. Heat charcoal grill, making sure that it is very hot. Preheat oven to 350 degrees (F).

2. Brush tomatoes, onion, and peppers with oil; sprinkle with salt. Grill vegetables on all sides until well charred.*

3. Place onion on a sheet pan; continue roasting in preheated oven for another 20 minutes. Cool and chill.

4. Chop vegetables.

5. Cut romaine in half. Brush cut side with oil; season with salt. Place cut side on grill; char. Remove from grill; cut in half width-wise.

6. To serve, place 1 romaine quarter on plate, still warm. Top with charred vegetables; dress with Dijon/herb vinaigrette. Top with macadamia nuts and Asiago cheese.

*Tomatoes should not be charred as long as the onion and peppers, or they will not hold their form.

1 yellow tomato, thickly sliced
1 red tomato, thickly sliced
1 sweet yellow onion, such as Maui or Vidalia, sliced thickly
1 red pepper, seeds removed
1 green pepper, seeds removed
¼ cup olive oil
2 tablespoons sea salt
2 heads romaine lettuce, outer leaves removed
1 cup Dijon/herb vinaigrette (recipe on page 89)
macadamia nuts, finely chopped
Asiago cheese, shaved

Arugula with Poached Pears, Port Syrup, Spicy Walnuts, and Stilton Cheese Salad

1. Place arugula on individual plates. Place pear slices over arugula, drizzle with port syrup, and top with walnuts and Stilton cheese.

2. Dress with red wine vinaigrette.

3 cups arugula
8 poached pear halves (recipe below)
¼ cup port syrup (recipe below)
1 cup spicy walnuts (recipe on page 153)
4 ounces Stilton cheese, crumbled
1 cup red wine vinaigrette (recipe on page 90)

Poached Pears and Port Syrup
Yield: 8 pear halves and about ¼ cup of port syrup

1. In a saucepan, combine all ingredients except pears. Bring to a boil over medium-high heat; reduce heat to a simmer. Add pears; simmer until pears are fork tender. Remove pears from liquid; reserve for use on salad.

2. Strain solids from port mixture, reserving the liquid. Continue to heat liquid over medium heat until thick and syrupy, being careful not to burn the mixture. Cool.

2 cups port wine
1 quart water
1 teaspoon whole cloves
1 cinnamon stick
½ teaspoon juniper berries
4 Bosc pears, peeled, cored, and cut in half

Spinach, Sliced Strawberries, and Almond-crusted Goat Cheese Salad

1. In a food processor, place goat cheese, cream cheese, almond oil, and salt. Process until smooth. Refrigerate to firm.

2. Remove from refrigerator; divide into 16 balls. Roll balls in almonds; refrigerate.

3. To serve, place spinach on plate; top with sliced strawberries. Place two balls of goat cheese mixture on the plate. Dress with strawberry/almond vinaigrette.

8 ounces goat cheese (also known as chèvre cheese)
2 tablespoons cream cheese
1 tablespoon almond oil
1 teaspoon sea salt
1 cup sliced almonds, toasted and chopped
3 cups baby spinach, stems removed and washed
2 pints strawberries, stems removed, washed, and sliced
1 cup strawberry/almond vinaigrette (recipe on page 90)

Wheat Rolls

Breads and Cereals

The dining table in the second-floor foyer at The Grove has been set and awaits overnight guests, who will enjoy a breakfast of various food items, including homemade granola.

Chef Michael developed this version of granola to serve at The Grove, and it has become a breakfast favorite of health-conscious guests.

Homemade Granola

1. Preheat oven to 225 degrees (F).

2. In a large bowl, combine oats, wheat germ or bran, flax, coconut, nuts, and cinnamon.

3. In another bowl, combine honey and water. Pour over dry mixture and mix well. Spread on two ungreased cookie sheets.

4. Bake granola mixture in preheated oven for 1 hour or until golden brown, stirring about every 15 minutes.

5. Remove from oven; allow to cool. Stir in raisins and currants.

6. Place in a covered jar; store in a cool, dry place or refrigerate.

7. Use ½ cup of milk or vanilla soy milk for each serving.

*May substitute dried cranberries, dried blueberries, dried cherries, dates, or other dried fruit, diced small.

Serves: 12 (½-cup servings)

3 cups rolled oats
1 cup wheat germ or bran
1 ½ cups ground flax seed
½ cup shredded coconut (may substitute other dried fruit)
⅓ cup chopped pecans, almonds, or walnuts
1 teaspoon cinnamon
3 tablespoons honey
3 tablespoons water
¾ cup raisins, golden raisins, and currants*

Chef Michael manipulated this Southern concoction, a cross between a biscuit and a roll, to make it his own recipe. It has become a staple at fall receptions preceding football games. Oftentimes, the biscuits are filled with thinly sliced country ham to create a popular finger food.

Angel Biscuits

1. In a small bowl, combine water, yeast, and 1 tablespoon sugar. Whisk to combine; let foam.

2. In the bowl of a mixer set with a paddle attachment, add butter, flour, ⅔ cup sugar, baking powder, and salt. Mix on low until mixture is crumbly and no butter is visible. Continue mixing; add yeast mixture and buttermilk.

3. Lightly flour table; turn out mixture onto lightly floured surface. Form into a ball. Wrap airtight; refrigerate until chilled. Remove from refrigerator.

4. Preheat oven to 350 degrees (F).

5. Unwrap dough ball; place on a lightly floured surface. Flour top of dough ball, and roll out to ½-inch thick sheet. Using a biscuit cutter, cut out biscuits; place on parchment-lined sheet pan. Bake in preheated oven until golden, about 20 minutes.

Yield: 75 mini-biscuits

¼ cup warm water
1 tablespoon active dry yeast
1 tablespoon white sugar
12 ounces chilled butter,
  cut into cubes
5 cups all-purpose flour
⅔ cup white sugar
1 tablespoon baking powder
1 tablespoon salt
1 ¼ cups buttermilk
flour
parchment paper

This breakfast dish known as Johnny cakes was a staple of the early South, where it was originally a flatbread. Chef Michael, who has prepared the dish for an early football-game brunch-type reception, has cut the amount of cornmeal in the recipe and added leavening so that the Johnny cakes are very similar to pancakes. He recommends that they be served with bourbon vanilla syrup.

Johnny Cakes with Bourbon Vanilla Syrup

Johnny Cakes

1. In a saucepan, combine cornmeal and water; bring to a boil over high heat. Reduce heat to medium; cook until cornmeal has absorbed all of the water and has come together and begun to pull away from the sides of the pan, about 10 minutes.

2. Remove from heat; allow to cool slightly. Mix in milk and ⅓ cup oil. Whisk eggs together, and whisk into batter.

3. Combine flour, sugar, salt, and baking soda; mix into batter. Add lime juice and butter.

4. Pour ¼ cup oil into a sauté pan; heat on medium-high. Pour small amount of batter into oil. Turn over when batter begins to bubble on top.

5. Serve topped with fresh berries and bourbon vanilla syrup (recipe below).

Bourbon Vanilla Syrup

Combine all ingredients. Cook over low heat until mixture becomes syrupy, about 20 minutes. Serve warm.

Yield: 8 – 10 small cakes

½ cup white cornmeal
3 cups water
1 cup milk
⅓ cup canola oil
2 eggs
1 ¼ cups white flour
¼ cup sugar
1 teaspoon salt
½ teaspoon baking soda
1 tablespoon key lime juice
1 tablespoon butter, melted
¼ cup canola oil
1 pint fresh berries

Yield: about 1½ cups

2 ½ cups bourbon
1 vanilla bean, halved and scraped
11 ounces cane syrup
1 tablespoon lime juice

Chef Michael makes these white rolls for luncheons and dinners, and they are always popular with guests at the president's home. They can also be filled with various spreads and meats to create sandwich-type finger-foods for receptions.

White Rolls

1. In a bowl, combine warm water, yeast, sugar, and gluten; whisk. Set aside until frothy, about 30 minutes. Add all ingredients except for 1 tablespoon canola oil; work into a dough. Allow flour to become fully hydrated, about 10 minutes.

2. Lightly flour work surface. Turn dough out onto work surface, lightly flour dough, and begin to knead. At this point, you can continue to knead to activate gluten, or you can work the flour into a ball, lightly oil with second (1 tablespoon) canola oil, cover, and refrigerate overnight.* If you prefer to knead to activate the gluten, continue to knead the dough until it becomes elastic, adding more flour as necessary. Dough should be slightly sticky.

3. Place dough in a bowl large enough to accommodate the rising of the dough to double in volume. Cover; store in a warm place until it has risen to double in volume. Punch dough down, and knead briefly.

4. Preheat oven to 350 degrees (F).

5. Flour work surface again, and turn dough out onto surface. Scale dough down into ½-inch balls, and place on parchment-lined sheet pan. Place dough balls (rolls) up against each other so they can push against each other to help them rise. Cover rolls with a damp towel; store in a damp place to rise for about 30 minutes.

6. Remove towel; bake in preheated oven for about 30 - 40 minutes. Rotate pan half way through baking.

7. If dough is refrigerated overnight,** remove from refrigerator; begin punching dough down as with first method; and follow remaining directions (above) from that step.

*Either method will activate the gluten necessary for having the bread hold gases given off by fermenting sugars in the dough. Chef Michael uses the refrigeration method.

**Cold dough is easier to work with.

Yield: 25 - 30 1-ounce rolls

2 cups warm water (100 degrees F)
1 tablespoon active yeast
2 tablespoons white sugar
1 teaspoon wheat gluten
½ cup buttermilk
1 tablespoon sea salt
3 tablespoons canola oil
5 ½ cups all-purpose flour plus
   extra flour for kneading
1 tablespoon canola oil
parchment paper

Chef Michael creates these homemade wheat rolls for meals and uses them with carved meats at receptions. He also uses this recipe to make a loaf of bread for the continental breakfast service arranged for overnight guests at The Grove.

Wheat Rolls

1. In a bowl, combine warm water, yeast, sugar, and gluten. Whisk; set aside until frothy, about 30 minutes. Add bran, flax seed, sea salt, ⅓ cup canola oil, and buttermilk. Let sit to hydrate flax and bran, about 10 minutes. Add flour, and work into dough. Allow flour to become fully hydrated, about 10 minutes.

2. Lightly flour work surface. Turn dough out onto work surface, lightly flour dough, and begin to knead. At this point, you can continue to knead to activate gluten, or you can work the flour into a ball, lightly oil it with 1 tablespoon canola oil, cover, and refrigerate overnight.* If kneading to activate the gluten, continue to knead until dough becomes elastic, adding more flour as necessary. Dough should be slightly sticky.

3. Preheat oven to 350 degrees (F).

4. Place dough in a bowl large enough to accommodate the rising of the dough to double in volume. Cover; store in a warm place until it has risen to double in volume. Punch dough down, and knead briefly.

5. Flour work surface again, and turn dough out onto surface. Scale dough down into ½-inch balls, and place on parchment-lined sheet pan. Place dough balls (rolls) up against each other so they can use each other to help them rise. Cover rolls with a damp towel; store in a damp place to rise for about 30 minutes.

6. Remove towel; bake in preheated oven for about 30 - 40 minutes. Rotate pan half way through baking.

7. If dough is refrigerated overnight,** remove from refrigerator; begin punching dough down as with first method; follow remaining directions (above) from that step.

*Either method will activate the gluten necessary for making the bread retain gases given off by fermenting sugars in the dough. Chef Michael uses the refrigeration method.

**Cold dough is easier to work with.

Yield: 25 - 30 1-ounce rolls

2 cups warm water (100 degrees F)
1 tablespoon active yeast
⅓ cup brown sugar, packed
1 tablespoon wheat gluten
½ cup wheat bran
¼ cup flax seed meal
1 tablespoon sea salt
⅓ cup canola oil
⅓ cup buttermilk
3 ½ cups whole-wheat flour plus extra flour for kneading
1 tablespoon canola oil
parchment paper

Chef Michael developed the recipe for these rolls to provide a cheesy-flavored bread for various occasions.

Parmesan and Chive Rolls

1. In a bowl, combine warm water, yeast, sugar, and gluten. Whisk; set aside until frothy, about 30 minutes.

2. Add remaining ingredients except for 1 tablespoon canola oil. Work into a dough. Allow flour to become fully hydrated, about 10 minutes.

3. Lightly flour work surface. Turn dough out onto work surface, lightly flour dough, and begin to knead. At this point, you can continue to knead to activate gluten, or you can work the flour into a ball, lightly oil with 1 tablespoon canola oil, cover, and refrigerate overnight.* If kneading to activate the gluten, continue to knead until dough becomes elastic, adding more flour as necessary. Dough should be slightly sticky.

4. Preheat oven to 350 degrees (F).

5. Place dough in a bowl large enough to accommodate the rising of the dough to double in volume. Cover; store in a warm place until it has risen to double its volume. Punch dough down, and knead briefly.

6. Flour work surface again, and turn dough out onto surface. Sprinkle Parmesan cheese and chives over dough, and knead into it.

7. Scale dough down into ½-inch balls; place on parchment-lined sheet pan. Place dough balls (rolls) up against each other so they can use each other to help them rise. Cover rolls with a damp towel; store in a damp place to rise for about 30 minutes.

8. Remove towel; bake in preheated oven for about 30 - 40 minutes. Rotate pan half way through baking.

9. If dough is refrigerated overnight,** remove from refrigerator; begin punching dough down as with first method; follow remaining directions (above) from that step.

*Either method will activate the gluten necessary for making the bread hold gases given off by fermenting sugars in the dough. Chef Michael uses the refrigeration method.

**Cold dough is easier to work with.

Yield: 25 - 30 1-ounce rolls

2 cups warm water (100 degrees F)
1 tablespoon active yeast
2 tablespoons white sugar
1 teaspoon wheat gluten
½ cup buttermilk
1 tablespoon sea salt
3 tablespoons canola oil
5 cups all-purpose flour plus extra
    flour for kneading
½ cup Parmesan cheese, finely grated
¼ cup fresh chives, minced
1 tablespoon canola oil
parchment paper

Chef Michael serves his pumpernickel rolls with his wheat rolls and white rolls to provide guests dining at The Grove with a choice of breads. He also uses it for sandwiches at receptions.

Pumpernickel Rolls

1. In a bowl, combine warm water, yeast, sugar, and gluten. Whisk; set aside until frothy, about 30 minutes.

2. Meanwhile, whisk cocoa powder into melted butter; cool to warm temperature, not more than 105 degrees (F).

3. To the yeast mixture, add buttermilk, salt, molasses, and butter/cocoa mixture; combine. Add flours, and combine into a dough. Allow flour to become fully hydrated, about 10 minutes.

4. Lightly flour work surface. Turn dough out onto work surface, lightly flour dough, and begin to knead. At this point, you can continue to knead to activate gluten, or you can work the flour into a ball, lightly oil it with second (1 tablespoon) canola oil, cover, and refrigerate overnight.* If kneading to activate the gluten, continue to knead until dough becomes elastic, adding more flour as necessary. Dough should be slightly sticky.

5. Preheat oven to 350 degrees (F).

6. Place dough in a bowl large enough to accommodate the rising of the dough to double in volume. Cover; store in a warm place until it has risen to double in volume. Punch dough down, and knead briefly.

7. Flour work surface again, and turn dough out onto surface. Scale dough down into ½-inch balls, and place on parchment-lined sheet pan. Place balls up against each other so they can push against each other to rise. Cover with damp towel; store in a damp place to rise for about 30 minutes. Remove towel; bake in preheated oven for about 30 - 40 minutes. Rotate pan half way through baking.

8. If dough is refrigerated overnight,** remove from refrigerator; begin punching dough down as with first method; follow remaining directions (above) from that step.

*Either method will activate the gluten necessary for making the bread retain gases given off by fermenting sugars in the dough. Chef Michael uses the refrigeration method.

**Cold dough is easier to work with.

Yield: about 40 1-ounce rolls

2 cups warm water (100 degrees F)
1 tablespoon active yeast
⅓ cup brown sugar, packed
1 tablespoon wheat gluten
3 tablespoons cocoa powder
2 ounces butter, melted
½ cup buttermilk
1 tablespoon sea salt
¼ cup molasses
3 cups all-purpose flour plus
    extra flour for kneading
2 cups rye flour
1 cup whole-wheat flour
1 tablespoon canola oil
parchment paper

Butternut Squash Bisque with Squash Croquettes

Soups and Sauces

This Chef Josef recipe can be used as a base for soups or sauces that are served with beef.

Brown Beef Stock

1. Preheat oven to 450 degrees (F). Lightly grease a roasting pan.

2. Strew bones in pan. Place in preheated oven. When bones are lightly browned, reduce heat to 350 degrees (F). Watch bones carefully to prevent them from burning or turning dark brown because this produces a bitter-tasting stock. Add next 10 ingredients, continuing to roast for approximately 15 minutes, stirring frequently. Drain off all grease, and deglaze pan with white wine to loosen all brown bits.

3. Transfer bones, vegetables, and seasoning to stockpot; add enough water to cover bones and vegetables. Bring contents to a boil very slowly (this may require as much as 30 minutes) to ensure that stock stays as clear as possible. If it is brought to a boil too quickly, the stock will assume a cloudiness that is very difficult to remove. Once the boil is reached, immediately reduce heat to low or to a level where it will maintain the stock at a simmer. Simmer for 5 - 6 hours or until stock is reduced by half, skimming if necessary.

4. Strain stock into a second stockpot, season lightly with salt and pepper, and bring to a boil for 5 minutes. Finish the brown stock by cooling it in an ice bath. Refrigerated stock will keep for about 1 week; frozen stock, for many months.

Yield: approximately 2 quarts

vegetable oil
10 pounds soup bones, either all veal
   or half veal and half beef
2 large onions, sliced
2 large tomatoes, chopped
1 medium carrot, sliced
1 celery stalk, sliced in 1-inch pieces
2 garlic cloves
2 sprigs fresh parsley
2 bay leaves
2 pinches thyme
6 black peppercorns, crushed
1 cup tomato paste
1 cup dry white wine
water
salt and pepper to taste

Chef Michael developed this recipe to use as the base for soups, an accent for entrées, and an ingredient in other dishes served at The Grove.

Chicken Stock

1. Preheat oven to 350 degrees (F).

2. Toss chicken in kosher salt and coarse ground pepper until coated.

3. Place chicken, celery, carrots, and onions in a large roasting pan. Place in preheated oven, and roast for 45 minutes. Move chicken and vegetables to a large stockpot.

4. Place roasting pan on stove, and add white wine to drippings left in pan. Stir wine, scraping to loosen any brown bits from pan. De-fat drippings.*

5. Add drippings to large stockpot containing chicken and vegetables. Add bay leaves, garlic, peppercorns, and water. Turn heat to medium, and bring to just a simmer; simmer about 45 - 60 minutes. Reduce heat to low. Cook until liquid is reduced by half. Strain off vegetables and chicken. Return liquid to stockpot. Continue cooking until liquid is reduced to 2 ½ quarts.

*Remove rendered chicken fat from the drippings. Chef Michael suggests moving the drippings to a tall, clear container and skimming separated fat from the drippings or refrigerating the drippings and waiting for the fat to harden before removing it.

Yield: 2 ½ quarts

2 pounds chicken legs
1 tablespoon kosher salt
1 teaspoon coarse ground pepper
½ head celery, roughly chopped
½ pound carrots, roughly chopped
2 medium yellow onions, roughly
  chopped
1 cup white wine
4 bay leaves
10 garlic cloves
1 tablespoon peppercorns
3 ½ gallons water

A soup recipe similar to this one, which was developed by Chef Josef, probably would have been served at The Grove in the 1960s or early 1970s.

Split Pea Soup with Virginia Ham Hocks

1. In a large saucepot, add oil, onion, celery, and carrots; sauté over medium-high heat for 1 minute. Add split peas, shredded potatoes, and ham hock; cover with chicken stock. Bring to a boil; simmer for about 1 ½ hours, stirring frequently to keep from burning, until soup is thick and peas have almost disintegrated.

2. Remove ham hock; let cool until meat can be pulled from ham bone and shredded. Add shredded ham back to soup, season to taste, and keep soup warm until ready to serve.

3. Garnish with toasted bread (croutons) and parsley before serving.

Serves: 4 - 6

¼ cup olive oil
1 large yellow onion, finely diced
2 celery stalks, finely diced
2 carrots, finely diced
1 pound split peas, rinsed
1 Idaho potato, peeled and finely shredded
1 ½ pounds ham hock
2 quarts chicken stock (recipe on page 81)
salt and pepper to taste
2 slices white bread, diced and toasted
1 teaspoon fresh parsley, chopped

Research by Chef Josef revealed that beef stew was served at Virginia Tech—and probably at The Grove—in the early 1920s. The original directions for preparing the stew have been modified by Chef Michael.

Virginia Beef Stew

1. Preheat oven to 350 degrees (F).

2. Melt Crisco in large Dutch oven over medium heat. Add a batch of meat to Dutch oven, taking care not to overcrowd pan. Brown meat thoroughly, turning to brown all sides. Remove meat. Continue browning batches of meat until all of it is browned.

3. Return all meat to Dutch oven; add tomatoes and enough water to cover meat. Bring to a boil. Add carrot and onions. Cover and move to oven. Bake in preheated oven for 3 hours or until meat is tender.

4. Add potatoes; continue cooking for another 30 minutes.

5. Season with salt and pepper to taste.

*2 ½ pounds from the hind shank of beef, which is largely lean meat and bone, may also be used and costs less than chuck.

Serves: 12

4 tablespoons Crisco vegetable shortening
2 ½ pounds chuck beef roast,* cut into small pieces
2 tomatoes, cleaned and chopped
water
1 carrot, peeled and sliced
3 onions, peeled and sliced
6 potatoes, pared, rinsed, parboiled, and drained
salt and pepper to taste

For elegant dinners at The Grove, Chef Michael prepares this lobster bisque, serving it before the main course.

Lobster Bisque

1. In a stockpot, bring water to boil. Add lobster; cook about 8 - 10 minutes. Remove lobster; cool. Retain water in stockpot; add onion, red pepper, celery, and carrots. Turn heat down; simmer until stock is reduced to about 2 ½ quarts.

2. Remove tail and claw meat from lobster; reserve.

3. Crush lobster shell with knife. Place crushed shell, cognac, and sherry in a pan; cook over low heat for 10 minutes, pressing shells into pan. Strain cognac/sherry/shell mixture into stockpot.

4. In a small pot over low heat, melt butter; add flour to form a roux. Whisk in paprika and cayenne; continue cooking over low heat for about 10 minutes. Remove from heat. Stir into stockpot a little at a time until desired thickness is reached.** Whisk in cream and tomato paste. Remove from heat; add lobster meat. Salt and pepper to taste.

*Chef Michael generally uses live lobsters, but frozen lobster tails can be substituted.

**Since people have individual preferences for the thickness of soup, some roux may be left over. Any remaining roux can be stored at room temperature and used to thicken other soups and sauces.

Yield: 2 quarts (about 10 servings)

3 ½ gallons water
1 whole lobster*
1 yellow onion, diced
1 red pepper, seeded and diced
4 celery ribs, diced
2 medium carrots, peeled and diced
¼ cup cognac
1 cup sherry
1 pound butter
2 cups all-purpose flour
2 tablespoons paprika
dash of cayenne
2 cups heavy cream
1 tablespoon tomato paste
sea salt to taste
pepper to taste

The trick to creating Chef Josef's elegant classic soup is to begin with beef stock made with roasted beef bones, vegetables, and herbs. Another important element is to properly caramelize the onions by cooking the onion slices at least 20 minutes over medium-high heat.

French Onion Soup with Cheese Croutons

1. In a large saucepan over medium heat, sauté onions in butter until well browned, but not burned, about 18 - 20 minutes. Add garlic; sauté for 1 minute. Add vermouth, beef stock, bay leaf, and thyme, stirring well. Bring to a boil. Reduce heat; simmer until flavors are well blended, about 35 minutes. Season to taste with salt and pepper.

2. Remove from heat; discard bay leaf.

3. Preheat oven to 250 degrees (F).

4. To make the croutons, arrange bread slices on baking sheet; place in middle level of preheated oven. Bake until golden brown.

5. Just before serving soup, preheat oven broiler.

6. Ladle soup into individual ovenproof crocks or bowls, float croutons on top of each and sprinkle cheeses over croutons.

7. Cook under broiler until cheese is melted and bubbly. Serve at once.

Serves: 4 - 5

6 large yellow onions, peeled and sliced
4 tablespoons unsalted butter
2 garlic cloves, minced
½ cup dry vermouth or dry white wine
8 cups beef stock (recipe on
   page 80)
1 bay leaf
¼ teaspoon dried thyme
salt and pepper to taste
8 slices French bread
1 ½ cups Swiss Gruyère and grated
   Parmesan cheese, mixed together

Vichyssoise was created in New York City in the 1920s by the Ritz Carlton's French-born chef, Louis Diat. Chef Joseph has given the recipe his own personal flair, and it has been one of his classics over the past 35 years. With the added touch of tasty caramelized shallot and Yukon gold croquettes, this soup is hard to beat.

Vichyssoise - Cold Potato and Leek Soup

1. Prepare the vegetables. Leeks must be thoroughly washed to remove all clinging dirt by separating the long stalks and cleaning them under running water.

2. In a soup pot, melt butter; add leeks, onion, and celery. Sauté for a few minutes; add diced potatoes and broth; season with salt, pepper, and Maggi. Bring to a boil, reduce heat to a simmer, and cover pot with a lid. Cook for approximately 30 minutes or until potatoes are soft.

3. Purée soup in a blender, food mill, or food processor. Refrigerate 2 - 3 hours, stirring occasionally.

4. When soup is well chilled, whisk in half-and-half and chives, reserving enough chives for garnishing. Extra half-and-half may be added if soup is too thick.

5. Serve in chilled cups. Place caramelized shallot and Yukon gold croquettes (recipe on page 148) on top in center; garnish with chives. Soup can also be served hot; see the variation below.

Variation

Served hot, vichyssoise is commonly known as potato and leek soup or potage Parisienne. Begin with preparation steps above. After puréeing the soup, bring it to a simmer for a couple of minutes while adding the half-and-half and chives, reserving enough chives for garnishing. Pour into individual serving cups; garnish with chives.

Yield: about 6 cups (serves 6 - 8)

1 tablespoon unsalted butter
4 medium leeks, white and inner green
 parts only, cleaned and diced
1 medium onion, diced
½ celery stalk, diced
2 pounds Idaho potatoes, peeled
 and diced
4 cups white chicken broth
salt and ground white pepper to taste
¼ teaspoon Maggi liquid seasoning
1 cup half-and-half (milk/cream)
2 tablespoons fresh chives, chopped

Chef Michael uses chicken stock in most of the soups he makes since it serves as a good generic base. However, vegetable stock can be substituted to keep this particular soup vegetarian.

Butternut Squash Bisque with Squash Croquettes

1. Preheat oven to 250 degrees (F).

2. Rub squash halves with oil; place on sheet pan. Roast in preheated oven until soft, 60 - 90 minutes. Allow to cool. Scrape out, removing seeds. Reserve seeds.

3. Scrape squash pulp into processor with brown sugar, cinnamon, and cayenne. Add ¼ cup cream; process until smooth.

4. In a saucepot, add stock; bring to a boil. Add carrots, celery, onion, and vinegar. Reduce heat to low; simmer 15 - 20 minutes or until vegetables are soft. Add squash purée; whisk in remaining cream.

5. In a separate pan, combine melted butter and flour to form roux. Heat until mixture becomes tan in color. Add roux to vegetable mixture a little at a time until desired thickness is reached. ** Simmer 15 - 20 minutes, stirring occasionally.

6. To serve, pour into bread boules (round bread) or warm soup bowls. For an even better presentation, pour into roasted squash halves. For an elegant appearance, top each bowl of bisque with a squash croquette (recipe on facing page), and add 2 - 3 seeds as a garnish.

*Toast seeds removed from the butternut squash, or purchase pumpkin seeds from a grocery store to use as garnish.

**Since people have individual preferences for the thickness of soup, some roux may be left over. Any remaining roux can be stored at room temperature and used to thicken other soups and sauces.

Serves: 10 (makes 2 quarts)

1 butternut squash, halved
oil
½ cup brown sugar
1 teaspoon cinnamon
½ teaspoon cayenne pepper
2 cups heavy cream, divided
1 quart chicken or vegetable stock
    (chicken stock recipe on page 81)
2 medium carrots, peeled and diced
3 celery ribs, diced
1 yellow onion, diced
¼ cup apple-cider vinegar
1 pound butter, melted
2 cups all-purpose flour
20 - 30 pumpkin seeds or squash
    seeds, toasted* for garnish

Squash Croquettes

1. Preheat oven to 350 degrees (F).

2. Whip egg yolk into squash purée. Add first breadcrumbs until mixture reaches a solid consistency.* Form into 1-inch diameter spheres; freeze.

3. Place egg wash, flour, and 2 cups breadcrumbs in 3 separate pie pans, one ingredient in each pan. Remove croquettes from freezer; dredge in egg wash, then in flour, then in egg wash again, and finally in breadcrumbs.

4. Heat oil (enough to cover croquettes) in 2-quart stockpot until candy or fry thermometer reaches 350 degrees (F). Add croquettes to oil, and deep fry until golden in color.

5. Move to sheet pan, and heat in preheated oven about 10 minutes or until internal temperature reaches 145 degrees (F).

6. Use as a garnish with butternut squash bisque.

*Add too many breadcrumbs, and croquettes will be dry; add too little, and croquettes cannot be formed.

1 egg yolk
1 cup puréed squash (see facing page)
breadcrumbs
egg wash (2 eggs and 2 tablespoons water, beaten until well mixed)
2 cups all-purpose flour
2 cups breadcrumbs
oil

This dressing was developed by Chef Michael to serve with his strawberry and poblano salad (recipe on page 65), but it could be used with any number of salads.

Berry Vinaigrette

1. In a saucepan, add all ingredients except strawberries and oil. Simmer over medium heat. Cook until reduced to ½ cup.

2. Remove from heat; allow to cool. Add to food processor; purée. Add strawberries; process until smooth.

3. Strain through a fine sieve to remove strawberry seeds. Pour strained liquid back into processor. With blades running, slowly drizzle in oil.

Yield: about 2 cups

1 cup dry white wine
½ cup raspberry vinegar
1 shallot, sliced
3 garlic cloves, crushed
3 whole black peppercorns
¼ cup white sugar
1 teaspoon salt
5 large strawberries
2 cups canola oil

Developed by Chef Michael to enhance the flavor of his mâche with charred tomatoes, Vidalia onion, and avocado salad (recipe on page 61), this vinaigrette is a good one to offer guests to dress a variety of salad greens.

Chive Vinaigrette

1. In a saucepan, combine wine, vinegar, garlic, shallot, sugar, and peppercorns. Simmer over medium heat until contents are reduced to ½ cup.

2. Remove from stovetop, pour into processor, and purée until smooth. Add lime juice, lime zest, mustard, salt, and chives. Purée until smooth. With processor blades turning, add olive oil in a steady stream.

Yield: about 2 cups

1 cup white wine
½ cup white wine vinegar
3 garlic cloves, crushed
1 shallot, sliced
1 tablespoon white sugar
3 whole peppercorns
1 tablespoon lime juice
1 teaspoon lime zest
1 tablespoon Dijon mustard
1 tablespoon sea salt
1 bunch chives, freshly snipped
2 cups extra virgin olive oil

This Chef Michael creation was developed specifically to dress his mesclun salad with grilled butternut squash (recipe on page 60), but like his other vinaigrettes, it should not be limited to a single type of salad. It is especially good in the fall, when fresh cranberries are available.

Cranberry Vinaigrette

1. In a saucepan, add cranberries, Shiraz, cranberry juice, shallot, garlic, pink peppercorns, zest, sugar, salt, and vinegar. Turn heat to high; cook until liquid is reduced to ½ cup, about 45 minutes. Remove from heat, and allow to cool.

2. Place in a processor; purée until smooth. With blades of processor still running, add oils in a slow stream until ingredients are combined. Pour through fine strainer.

Yield: about 2 ½ cups

1 cup fresh cranberries
1 cup dry Shiraz wine
1 cup Ocean Spray cranberry juice
1 shallot, sliced
3 garlic cloves, crushed
3 whole pink peppercorns
1 tablespoon orange zest
¼ cup white sugar
1 teaspoon sea salt
¼ cup red wine vinegar
1 ½ cups canola oil
½ cup walnut oil

Chef Michael likes to pair this dressing with his summer salads, when an abundance of fresh herbs are available in the garden at The Grove.

Dijon/Herb Vinaigrette

1. In a saucepan, combine wine, lemon juice, zest, sugar, peppercorns, salt, shallot, garlic, and vinegar. Simmer over medium heat until liquid is reduced to a quarter of the original amount. Remove from stove top; cool.

2. Move mixture to a blender. Add herbs and mustard; purée on high speed. Reduce speed to medium; pour oil into mixture in a steady stream.

Yield: 2 cups

1 cup white wine
1 tablespoon lemon juice
zest of 1 lemon
1 tablespoon white sugar
1 teaspoon peppercorns
1 teaspoon sea salt
1 shallot, chopped
3 garlic cloves, smashed
¼ cup champagne vinegar
3 large fresh basil leaves
¼ cup fresh parsley
2 tablespoons fresh thyme
1 tablespoon fresh oregano
¼ cup Dijon mustard
1 cup olive oil

This dressing created by Chef Michael can be used on any variety of salads, but the chef particularly likes to use it to enhance the flavor of his fall and winter salads.

Red Wine Vinaigrette

1. In a saucepan, combine all ingredients except olive oil. Simmer over medium heat until reduced to a quarter of the original amount of liquid. Remove from heat; allow to cool.

2. Move liquid to a blender; purée on high speed. Reduce speed to medium; slowly add oil in a steady stream.

Yield: 1½ cups

1 cup red wine
¼ cup red wine vinegar
1 shallot, chopped
1 garlic clove, smashed
1 teaspoon peppercorns
1 tablespoon Dijon mustard
1 teaspoon sea salt
1 tablespoon sugar
1 cup olive oil

Chef Michael developed this dressisng to serve with salads he prepares in the spring, when fresh strawberries are at their peak.

Strawberry/Almond Vinaigrette

1. In a saucepan, combine wine, vinegar, shallot, garlic, peppercorns, and salt. Simmer over medium heat until reduced to a quarter of the original amount of liquid. Remove from heat; allow to cool at room temperature.

2. Place in a blender; add strawberries and sugar. Purée on high. Reduce speed to medium, and pour in oils in a slow, steady stream. Strain through a fine strainer to remove strawberry seeds.

Yield: 2 cups

1 cup white wine
¼ cup raspberry vinegar
1 shallot, roughly chopped
1 garlic clove, smashed
1 teaspoon peppercorns
½ teaspoon sea salt
2 large strawberries
2 tablespoons white sugar
¼ cup almond oil
¾ cup canola oil

An excellent accompaniment to seafood dishes, this Chef Michael creation goes particularly well with the chef's baked halibut stuffed with blue crab (recipe on page 112).

Lemon Butter Sauce

1. In a saucepan, heat wine, lemon juice, lemon zest, and shallots. Cook over medium heat until reduced to ¼ cup.

2. Place mixture in a food processor; process until smooth.

3. Move back to saucepan; turn heat to low. Add butter cubes, stirring until all butter is melted, about 5 minutes. Remove immediately from heat; keep in a warm place (if sauce gets too hot or too cold, it will separate) until served.

Yield: about 2 - 3 cups

1 cup dry white wine
¼ cup lemon juice
1 teaspoon lemon zest
3 shallots, sliced
1 pound butter, cut into cubes

Chef Michael particularly likes to use this recipe to embellish the flavors of his marbled rye bread pudding with Black Forest ham (recipe on page 125). However, it can add a special touch to a variety of dishes.

Mornay Sauce

1. In a saucepan, melt butter over medium heat. Add flour; stir. Continue cooking until slightly browned. Add heavy cream, milk, water, salt, and pepper. Heat until mixture is thickened. Turn heat to low. Start adding cheeses to mixture, a little at a time, stirring after each addition. Continue until all cheeses are incorporated.

2. Serve warm.

Yield: about 3 cups

4 tablespoons butter
⅓ cup all-purpose flour
1 cup heavy cream
2 cups milk
1 cup water
1 teaspoon salt
pinch of white pepper
4 ounces Gruyère cheese
8 ounces Emmental cheese

The sauce made from this Chef Josef recipe enhances the flavor of a variety of meat dishes.

Ancho Citrus Sauce

1. Combine arrowroot and water in a small bowl; set aside.

2. Sauté butter and garlic in a large pan over medium heat. Add white wine, and cook until liquid is reduced to half. Add concentrates, cumin, honey, and kecap manis. Bring to a boil, and simmer for 3 minutes. Add lemon juice. Add arrowroot mixture, and stir until sauce is thickened to a loose consistently.

3. Keep warm; serve with sautéed chicken breast, beef medallions, or pork tenderloin.

Yield: about 4 - 5 cups

¼ cup arrowroot
⅓ cup cold water
1 teaspoon unsalted butter
2 teaspoons garlic, chopped
⅓ bottle white wine
2 tablespoons blood-orange concentrate
½ quart orange concentrate
½ teaspoon cumin
¼ cup honey
¼ cup kecap manis
¼ quart fresh lemon juice

Chef Michael's version of the classic Newburg seafood sauce is served with cooked seafood to make a stew-like entrée.

Newburg Sauce

1. Add stock, sherry, shallots, and mushrooms to a stock pan. Bring to a boil; reduce to a simmer.

2. In a separate pot, melt butter; whisk in cayenne and paprika; and add flour, mixing well. Cook over medium heat until roux (the flour mixture) has nutty aroma, about 10 minutes.

3. Whisk roux into stock mixture (sauce) a little at a time until sauce reaches desired consistency. Whisk in cream; season to taste with salt.

4. To serve, fold cooked seafood such as shrimp, scallops, and crabs into sauce; spoon over white rice.

Yield: 1 ½ quarts

1 quart seafood stock, such as lobster or crab
1 cup sherry
¼ cup shallots, minced
3 pounds button mushrooms, quartered
8 tablespoons butter
⅛ teaspoon cayenne
¼ cup paprika
½ cup all-purpose flour
2 cups cream
salt to taste

According to Chef Michael, when using pepper, chefs abide by the classic rule to use the same color pepper as what they are cooking, i.e., black pepper in brown sauces, white pepper in white sauces, and cayenne in red sauces. For a different level of flavor, he suggests using pink and green peppercorns, which can add pepper flavor without as much heat. Four varieties of peppercorn berries are available (cayenne is from a completely different family and is actually a ground chili). Black peppercorns are the ripe berries, green peppercorns are immature berries, and pink peppercorns are the step between green and black. White peppercorns are actually black peppercorns with the outside removed. There are also many varieties of long-tail peppers (looking like food pellets rather than pods) that have subtle flavor differences. Experiment with each to learn about their respective subtle flavors.

Compound Lobster Butter

1. Crack uncooked lobster tail; remove meat from shell. Reserve meat.

2. Crush shell, and place in a saucepan with canola oil. Heat over medium heat, stirring until shell turns a bright red. Add brandy; reduce heat to low; cook about 10 minutes. Remove and discard shell. Add peppercorns; heat over low heat for another 10 minutes. Add lobster meat and all other ingredients except butter. Turn heat to medium; cook until liquid has almost evaporated. Turn off heat; allow mixture to cool to room temperature.

3. Place mixture in a food processor; process until smooth. Add butter, a few cubes at a time; process until butter is incorporated into mixture.

4. Pour mixture onto a sheet of parchment paper, and roll into a cylinder. Refrigerate until ready to use.

5. Use to top seafood dishes, to finish sauces, and as a topping for soups.

*Cold-water lobsters usually come from Maine or Canada. Lobsters from the Gulf of Mexico are not cold-water lobsters.

**For milder flavor, use pink or green peppercorns.

Yield: 1 ¼ pounds

1 4-ounce lobster tail, preferably
   from a cold-water lobster*
1 tablespoon canola oil
½ cup brandy
2 - 3 whole peppercorns**
2 shallots, roughly chopped
3 - 4 fresh tarragon sprigs, leaves
   removed from stems
zest of 1 lemon
1 tablespoon Dijon mustard
1 pound butter, chilled and cut
   into small cubes
parchment paper

Sauces enhance the flavor of many dishes, and this peppercorn sauce developed by Chef Michael to serve with lobster medallions is no exception. The chef also uses the sauce for chilled seafood platters, which are served at receptions.

Cognac Peppercorn Sauce

1. In a saucepan, combine cognac, sugar, and peppercorns. Simmer over low heat until reduced by a quarter.

2. Remove to a mixing bowl, add mayonnaise and mustard, and stir until well blended. Chill.

Yield: about 1 ½ cups

1 cup cognac or brandy, good quality
1 teaspoon white sugar
3 tablespoons green peppercorns
1 cup mayonnaise
1 tablespoon Dijon mustard

Especially good when accompanying a number of seafood dishes, this rémoulade is Chef Michael's variation of the sauce that was first developed in France.

Rémoulade

1. In a bowl, combine onion, green pepper, and celery. Let sit for 5 minutes. Add remaining ingredients. Chill in refrigerator.

2. Serve with fried seafood or lump crabmeat.

Yield: about 1 ¾ cups

1 tablespoon onion, minced
1 tablespoon green pepper, minced
1 tablespoon celery, minced
1 cup mayonnaise
¼ cup ketchup, good quality
¼ cup Dijon mustard
1 tablespoon lemon juice
1 tablespoon capers
1 teaspoon sea salt
1 tablespoon paprika
1 teaspoon granulated garlic
1 teaspoon dry thyme
1 teaspoon coarse ground black pepper
½ teaspoon ground white pepper
⅛ teaspoon cayenne pepper

This chutney, along with strawberry habañero relish (recipe below), accompanies Chef Michael's grilled swordfish steak (recipe on page 112) when he serves the popular dish at receptions.

Strawberry and Habañero Chutney

1. In a saucepan, cook canola oil over medium heat. Add garlic, and sauté until translucent, about 3 - 4 minutes. Add strawberries, lime juice, ginger, tequila, habañero, water, and cinnamon stick. Bring to a simmer; reduce heat to low. Cook until strawberries are reconstituted, about 20 minutes.

2. Stir in preserves; heat until liquid, another 10 minutes. Remove cinnamon stick; reserve for another purpose if desired.

3. Transfer mixture to food processor; add cilantro. Pulse processor until strawberries are coarsely chopped.

Yield: about 2 cups

1 teaspoon canola oil
1 tablespoon garlic, minced
4 ounces dried strawberries
2 tablespoons key lime juice
1 teaspoon fresh ginger, grated
¼ cup tequila
½ habañero pepper, seeded and minced
1 cup water
1 cinnamon stick
¼ cup seedless strawberry preserves
1 tablespoon fresh cilantro, chopped

Strawberry and Habañero Relish

1. In a bowl, combine all ingredients. Refrigerate for at least 10 minutes and no longer than 1 hour before serving.

Yield: about 2 cups

1 pint strawberries, hulled and diced
½ habañero pepper, seeded and minced
1 tablespoon fresh cilantro, chopped
1 tablespoon white sugar
pinch of salt

According to Chef Josef, compound butters can provide a delightful finishing touch to grilled fish, poultry, and beef cooked in various ways. These butters also can be used for finishing simple sauces and whenever one wants an extra flair for vegetables and starchy foods. Chef Josef's classic compound butter recipe has been used at The Grove with grilled meats.

Maître d'Hôtel Butter (Compound Butter)

1. Add all ingredients except butter, parsley, and chives to a saucepot; bring to a boil over high heat. Turn heat to medium; cook until almost all of the liquid has evaporated. Remove from heat; allow to cool.

2. Place mixture in a food processor; process. Add butter, a few cubes at a time, and process until all of butter has been incorporated. Add parsley and chives.

3. Use 1 ounce of maître d'hôtel butter on each piece of grilled meat as it is served. If not used immediately, compound butter can be placed on parchment paper, shaped into a log roll, and stored in the refrigerator or freezer. It can then be sliced — as one would slice a log of cookie dough — when needed.

Yield: 1 ½ pounds

3 shallots, finely chopped
6 garlic cloves, finely chopped
¼ teaspoon green peppercorns
¼ cup lemon juice
1 cup white wine
zest of 1 lemon
½ teaspoon dried chervil
1 teaspoon fresh thyme
dash of Worcestershire sauce
salt and pepper to taste
1 pound butter, cut into cubes
    and softened to room temperature
1 bunch fresh parsley, minced
1 tablespoon chives, finely cut

This zesty sauce was created by Chef Michael to serve with his Thai crab salad in bread cups (recipe on page 58) but can used to enhance the flavor of other seafood dishes as well.

Red Curry Sauce*

1. In a saucepan, cook oil over medium heat.

2. Add shallots and garlic; cook until tender. Add curry paste; stir. Heat thoroughly. Except for peanut butter, add remaining ingredients, cooking over medium heat; whisk until smooth. Whisk in peanut butter.

3. Remove from heat; chill.

*Best if made a day before it is served.

Yield: about 1 ½ cups

1 tablespoon vegetable oil
1 tablespoon shallots, minced
½ tablespoon fresh garlic, minced
1 tablespoon red curry paste
1 can coconut milk, less 1 tablespoon
½ tablespoon fresh ginger, grated
1 tablespoon sugar
2 tablespoons peanut butter

This sauce developed by Chef Michael is a perfect accompaniment to his Parmesan-crusted fillets of sole (recipe on page 116), but it is excellent for pairing with other seafood and chicken dishes.

Caper Sauce

1. In a saucepan, heat wine, shallots, garlic, and peppercorns.

2. Cut lemons in half; squeeze to soften pulp; add lemon halves to wine mixture. Continue cooking until almost all of the liquid has evaporated.

3. Remove from heat; allow to cool. Add butter; place back on heat, stirring constantly until butter is melted. Remove immediately from heat.

4. Strain off solids. Stir capers into sauce.

5. Store sauce in a warm place until time to spoon it over fish fillets or other dishes.

Yield: about 2 cups

1 cup dry white wine
2 shallots
1 garlic clove
1 teaspoon black peppercorns
2 lemons
1 pound butter, cut into small cubes
1 3-ounce bottle capers, drained

This sauce developed by Chef Josef can be used to perk up the flavor of a variety of entrées, vegetables, and pasta dishes.

Red Pepper Butter Sauce

1. Combine arrowroot and water in a small bowl; set aside.

2. In a large skillet, sauté peppers in olive oil over medium heat for 3 - 4 minutes. Reduce heat, and add garlic and shallots; cook for ½ minute. Add red wine, vinegar, and lemon juice; continue cooking until peppers are partially cooked. Remove from heat; let cool.

3. Add pepper mixture to a food processor; blend until smooth. Return mixture to skillet; simmer over medium heat for 1 minute. Add arrowroot mixture to firm up the sauce.

4. Remove from heat, and gradually whisk in softened butter until sauce is smooth. Season with salt and pepper to taste.

5. Keep sauce warm until served. If sauce must be re-heated to serve, make sure that it is never boiled, or it will separate.

Yield: 4 - 6 servings

2 teaspoons arrowroot powder
2 tablespoons cold water
4 - 5 medium red bell peppers, cleaned, cut in half, seeds and pulp removed, coarsely chopped
1 tablespoon olive oil
½ garlic clove, finely chopped
1 tablespoon shallots, finely chopped
½ cup red wine
½ cup red wine vinegar
l tablespoon fresh lemon juice
1 cup butter, softened at room temperature
salt and ground black pepper to taste

This barbecue sauce is a version of the vinegar mustard sauce used in eastern North Carolina. Developed by Chef Michael, it boosts the taste of smoked pulled pork, a favorite dish for receptions at The Grove.

North Carolina Barbecue Sauce

1. In a small saucepan, heat oil over medium heat. Add mustard seeds; cook until toasted, about 3 minutes. Add red and black pepper; cook another minute. Add vinegar, mustard, 2 cups water, and brown sugar. Reduce heat to low; simmer for 30 minutes.

2. In a small bowl, combine cornstarch or arrowroot and 1 tablespoon of water. Add to sauce to thicken it.

3. For better flavor, add 1 cup reserved drippings from smoked pork that has been defatted. The sauce is an excellent accompaniment when served warm with applewood-smoked pork tenderloin (recipe on page 129).

Yield: approximately 3 - 3 ½ cups

1 teaspoon vegetable oil
1 tablespoon mustard seeds
1 teaspoon flaked red pepper
1 teaspoon coarse ground black pepper
1 cup cider vinegar
2 tablespoons Dijon mustard
2 cups water
¼ cup light brown sugar
1 tablespoon cornstarch or arrowroot
1 tablespoon water

*Chef Michael uses the following savory sauce in any dish
that requires tomato sauce.*

Roasted Tomato Sauce

1. Preheat oven to 250 degrees (F).

2. Cut tomatoes in half, and coat with olive oil. Place cut side down on a sheet pan. Place pan in preheated oven; roast for 60 - 90 minutes. Remove and chill.

3. Peel skin from tomatoes. Dice and place in casserole dish.

4. Mix together vegetable juice, wine, tomato paste, onion, green pepper, garlic, bay leaves, salt, red pepper, and sugar.

5. In a blender, combine vinegar, basil, oregano, sage, and rosemary; purée. Blend with vegetable juice mixture; pour over tomatoes.

6. Place casserole dish in preheated oven; bake for 3 - 4 hours or until sauce is thickened.

*Chef Michael uses V8 juice.

Yield: about 8 cups

12 Roma tomatoes
¼ cup olive oil
2 6-ounce cans of vegetable juice*
1 cup red wine
4 ounces tomato paste
1 yellow onion, sliced
1 green pepper, diced
1 head elephant garlic, cloves
    roasted and chopped
3 bay leaves
salt to taste
1 tablespoon flaked red pepper
3 tablespoons white sugar
½ cup red wine vinegar
4 ounces fresh basil
2 ounces fresh oregano
½ ounce fresh sage
¼ ounce fresh rosemary

*Chef Michael developed this version of a classic sauce
to enhance the taste of roasted beef.*

Horseradish Cream

Combine all ingredients; mix well.

Yield: approximately ½ quart

1 cup mayonnaise
1 cup sour cream
½ cup prepared horseradish
1 teaspoon sea salt
1 tablespoon coarse ground black
    pepper
dash of Worcestershire sauce
dash of hot sauce
1 tablespoon lemon juice

This sauce created by Chef Michael is excellent with Mexican dishes and particularly with the chef's Latin spiced pork tenderloin (recipe on page 127).

Mole Sauce

1. Add oil to saucepan; cook over medium heat. Add seeds; toast lightly before adding garlic, onion, celery, jalapeño, and carrots. Sauté until translucent. Add chicken stock, lime juice, lime zest, and tomatoes. Bring to a boil; reduce heat to low. Simmer for 45 minutes. Allow to cool.

2. Purée in blender; strain through a sieve.

3. Put back on stove; bring to a boil over high heat. Reduce heat to medium; add chocolate. Whisk until chocolate is melted. Whisk in peanut butter.

4. Remove from heat; serve immediately.

Yield: about 2 ½ - 3 ½ cups

1 tablespoon vegetable oil
1 tablespoon coriander seeds
2 teaspoons cumin seeds
¼ cup garlic cloves, minced
1 yellow onion, diced
4 celery ribs, diced
1 jalapeño pepper, diced
2 medium carrots, peeled and diced
2 cups chicken stock (recipe on page 81)
juice of 2 limes plus zest
4 Roma tomatoes, diced
2 ounces dark chocolate (60 percent cocoa or greater)
1 tablespoon peanut butter

Chef Michael developed this quick version of the holiday classic cranberry sauce and demonstrated its preparation for the university's Faculty Women's Club.

Cranberry Sauce

1. In a small bowl, mix arrowroot and water. Set aside.

2. Place all ingredients except arrowroot mixture in a saucepot. Cook over medium heat until cranberries burst and mixture thickens, about 20 minutes. Stir in arrowroot; heat until thickened, another 5 - 10 minutes.

3. Refrigerate. Serve chilled as an accompaniment to roast turkey.

Variation

For an extravagant boost, whisk in ¼ cup Grand Marnier just before removing the sauce from the heat.

Yield: about 1 quart

¼ cup arrowroot
¼ cup water
1 bag fresh cranberries
½ cup dry white wine
1 cup orange juice
½ cup white sugar

This Chef Michael concoction goes particularly well with the roasted venison tenderloin (recipe on page 123) that he prepares for receptions at The Grove, but it also makes an excellent addition to most game dishes.

Blackberry Port Chutney

1. In a sauce pot, place port, 1 pint blackberries, vinegar, shallots, garlic, ginger, juniper, and peppercorns. Bring to a boil; boil until mixture is reduced to half.

2. Remove from heat; place in a blender; liquefy.

3. Strain through a fine strainer. Place strained liquid back into pot, bring to a simmer, and whisk in jam.

3. Remove from heat; stir in ½ pint blackberries.

4. Chill in refrigerator until served.

Yield: about 1 ½ cups

2 cups ruby port wine
1 ½ pints fresh blackberries, divided
¼ cup raspberry vinegar
2 shallots, chopped
1 elephant garlic clove, chopped
2 tablespoons fresh ginger, grated
1 teaspoon juniper berries, crushed
1 teaspoon black peppercorns
1 tablespoon black currant jam

Chef Michael developed this cocktail sauce to accompany shrimp and other seafood.

Cocktail Sauce

Combine all ingredients; blend well.

Yield: 4 - 5 cups

4 cups ketchup, good quality
1 cup prepared horseradish
2 tablespoons Worcestershire sauce
¼ cup lemon juice
dash of hot sauce
dash of cayenne pepper

Chef Michael amended Chef Joseph's recipe for this sauce by adding bacon. The sauce is served at The Grove with sliced beef tenderloin and roasted pork loin.

Sauce Chasseur*

In a saucepan, fry bacon over medium heat until browned; crumble bacon. Add oil to saucepan. When heated, add butter, shallots, and garlic; simmer for 1 minute or until soft and lightly brown. Add mushrooms; sauté for 3 minutes. Add wine; cook until liquid is reduced to half. Add brown stock; simmer until a third of liquid evaporates. Add tomatoes; simmer for 5 minutes. Finish with parsley; salt and pepper to taste.

* Also known as Hunter Sauce or Rustic Mushroom and Tomato Sauce

Yield: about 1 ½ - 2 cups

¼ pound bacon
1 teaspoon olive oil
1 tablespoon unsalted butter
1 teaspoon shallots, finely chopped
½ teaspoon garlic cloves, finely chopped
8 ounces fresh mushrooms, sliced
1 cup dry red wine, good quality
1 cup brown stock (recipe on page 80)
2 Roma tomatoes, peeled and
    coarsely diced
½ teaspoon fresh parsley, chopped
salt and pepper to taste

This spicy apple butter was developed by Chef Michael to accompany pork and poultry.

Chipotle Apple Butter

1. Cut apples into quarters; add to a large crock-pot. Add remaining ingredients; heat on high. Bring to boil; turn heat to low. Cover; cook for 24 hours.

2. Uncover; continue cooking until liquid is reduced to a thick and syrupy consistency.

3. Remove apple mixture to a strainer over a large bowl, and push solids through the strainer. Cool to room temperature; refrigerate.

4. Serve chilled.

Yield: ½ gallon

2 Granny Smith apples, peeled
    and cored
2 red delicious apples, peeled and cored
2 gala apples, peeled and cored
2 golden delicious apples, peeled
    and cored
1 quart apple cider
1 cinnamon stick
1 teaspoon whole cloves
1 tablespoon whole allspice
1 whole nutmeg
½ cup apple-cider vinegar
1 cup brown sugar
¼ cup molasses
2 ounces chipotle peppers, puréed

Chef Michael uses brown sauce prepared from the following recipe as a base for soups and for sauces served with beef.

Demi Glace (Brown Sauce Base)

1. Preheat oven to 350 degrees (F).

2. In a roasting pan, place bones and beef trimmings; roast in preheated oven until browned. Deglaze pan with wine, scraping up brown bits.

3. Add pan juices to a large pot. Add all other ingredients; heat over medium-high heat. When stock starts to simmer, reduce heat to low. Continue simmering until stock is reduced by half, then strain into a smaller pot.

4. Return to heat; simmer until stock is reduced to about 1 quart.

5. Cool and refrigerate for up to 2 weeks.

6. Remove from refrigerator. Reserve hardened fat for basting beef when roasting or grilling for a less healthy but more flavorful option. Cut gelatinized brown sauce into cubes; freeze up to 6 months for use in recipes.

*Beef bones can be purchased at grocery stores.

Yield: 1 quart

2 pounds beef bones*
1 ½ pounds beef trimmings from roast
1 quart dry red wine
12 - 15 garlic cloves
2 tomatoes, chopped
2 Bermuda onions with skin, chopped
1 whole head of celery, chopped
½ pound carrots, chopped
2 bay leaves
1 tablespoon peppercorns
½ cup tomato paste
4 gallons cold water

This sauce was developed by Chef Michael to serve with the hors d'oeuvre mushroom strudel (recipe on page 55), but, as with the other sauces, it will go with a variety of dishes.

Sherry Sauce

1. In saucepan over medium heat, melt 4 ounces butter; add flour. Cook, stirring until mixture is a tan color.

2. In a separate saucepan, add sherry and reserved juice. Cook over medium heat for about 10 minutes. Add flour mixture a little at a time until thickened. Whisk in cream; heat until hot.

3. Remove from heat; whisk in 2 tablespoons butter. Serve warm.

*Use the reserved juice from cooking mushrooms and shallots in preparing mushroom strudel.

Yield: about 2 - 3 cups

4 ounces butter
⅓ cup all-purpose flour
2 cups sherry
reserved mushroom juice*
½ cup cream
2 tablespoons butter, cut into small cubes

Chef Michael uses this stirred custard as a creamy addition to many desserts.

Crème Anglaise

1. Cut bean in half, and scrape out seeds; add seeds and pod to heavy saucepan. Add cream and sugar. Heat over medium heat until mixture simmers, about 10 minutes. Remove from heat; allow to cool. Remove vanilla bean pod; reserve for another use.

2. When cool, gradually whisk cream mixture into egg yolks in a metal bowl. Place bowl over pot of simmering water, and stir constantly until mixture is thickened or reaches 175 degrees (F), about 20 - 25 minutes.

3. Serve chilled with dessert of choice.

Yield: about 1 ½ cups

1 vanilla bean
1 cup heavy cream
½ cup white sugar
4 egg yolks

This dessert sauce was developed by Chef Michael, particularly to serve with his white chocolate bread pudding (recipe on page 173).

Amaretto Sauce

1. Mix all ingredients in a small saucepan. Heat over low heat until slightly thickened or temperature reaches 175 degrees (F).

2. Use as an accompaniment to desserts, especially bread puddings.

Yield: about 1 ½ - 1 ¾ cups

1 cup heavy cream
1 tablespoon corn starch
½ cup white sugar
¼ teaspoon almond extract
½ cup amaretto liqueur

This recipe, developed by Chef Michael, delivers a great sauce to serve with a variety of desserts.

Caramel Sauce

1. Combine cornstarch and water; set aside.

2. In a saucepot, combine cream and sugar. Bring to a boil over medium heat; add cornstarch mixture. Cook until thickened.

3. Serve warm with dessert.

Yield: about 2 cups

1 tablespoon cornstarch
¼ cup cold water
½ cup heavy cream
2 cups brown sugar

When a dessert calls for a fruity accompaniment, try this recipe, part of Chef Michael's repertoire of sauces.

Raspberry Coulis

1. Place all ingredients in a pot; bring to a boil over medium heat.

2. Remove from heat; place in a blender. Purée on high speed.

3. Strain to remove raspberry seeds.

4. Chill before serving with desserts.

Yield: about 2 - 3 cups

2 pints fresh raspberries
2 tablespoons raspberry vinegar
½ cup white sugar
½ cup water
2 tablespoons Chambord or other
    berry-flavored liqueur

This Chef Michael sauce is a standard one he often uses with desserts served at The Grove.

Chocolate Sauce

1. In a saucepot, combine chocolate and cream. Heat on medium setting, stirring often, until chocolate is melted. Add sugar; whisk in nut butter.

2. Serve warm with dessert.

Yield: about 1 ¼ cups

4 ounces bittersweet chocolate, chopped
1 cup cream
¼ cup white sugar
1 tablespoon nut butter such as peanut butter

Chef Michael developed this dessert sauce to complement his Black Forest bread pudding (recipe on page 170), both part of a cooking demonstration he gave at the executive residence.

Kirsch Sauce

1. Drain juice from cherries; put juice into a saucepan; add cherries and juice from 1 can, reserving cherries from other can. Add wine, sugar, and vinegar; cook over medium heat until mixture is reduced by half.

2. Pour mixture into a blender; purée until smooth.

3. Return mixture to saucepan; add kirsch. Cook over medium heat until mixture is syrupy. Remove from heat; add reserved cherries. Serve warm.

*Additional sugar may be used if a sweeter sauce is desired.

Yield: about 2 cups

2 8-ounce cans pitted dark cherries
½ cup dry red wine
1 tablespoon white sugar*
1 teaspoon balsamic vinegar
¼ cup kirsch liqueur

This Chef Joseph creation makes any number of desserts luscious, not only in presentation but also on the palate.

Vanilla Bourbon Sauce

1. Add bourbon to a saucepan. Cook over medium heat until bourbon starts to bubble; then reduce heat to low.

2. Cut vanilla bean in half, and scrape out seeds with a knife. Add seeds and pod to bourbon. Cook over low heat until bourbon is reduced by half. Add heavy cream and sugar; continue to cook until sugar is dissolved, about 10 minutes. Add arrowroot mixture; heat until thickened, about 10 more minutes.

3. Serve either warm or chilled with a variety of desserts.

*Some bourbon bottles include tasting notes on the labels.

Yield: 1 ½ cups

½ cup bourbon, good quality,
   preferably with vanilla accents*
1 vanilla bean
1 cup heavy cream
¼ cup white sugar
2 tablespoons arrowroot combined
   with 2 tablespoons cold water
   to form paste

Chef Michael has demonstrated the preparation of several recipes in this book for the Friday Forum of the Virginia Tech Faculty Women's Club. Members of the club then sampled the results of those demonstrations, as shown above.

The Grove's Crab Cakes

Main Dishes

Are you looking for a color combination in your food that will reflect Virginia Tech's official colors of orange and maroon? If so, try this recipe developed by Chef Michael, who prepares the dish for various winter events at The Grove.

Pan-seared Black Cod with Puréed Ginger Carrots and Beet Salad

1. Heat oil in a large pan.

2. Mix flour, salt, and pepper in a bowl. Dredge fillets in flour mixture; place fillets in the hot oil. Cook until browned, about 5 minutes. Turn the fillets over; cook another 3 - 4 minutes. Remove from pan, and place on paper towels to absorb oil.

3. To serve, place a small amount of puréed ginger carrots (recipe below) on a plate. Top the carrots with fish, and garnish with beet salad (recipe below).

Serves: 4

¼ cup canola oil
1 cup all-purpose flour
1 tablespoon salt
1 tablespoon pepper
4 6-ounce portions black cod

Puréed Ginger Carrots

1. Bring ginger ale to boil in a pot. Add carrots, and cook until soft.

2. Place carrots in food processor with 1 tablespoon cooked ginger ale liquid (reserve remaining liquid to cook beets in recipe below) and remaining ingredients. Purée in processor. Keep hot.

1 quart ginger ale
2 pounds carrots
¼ cup milk
1 ounce butter
2 tablespoons ginger, grated
½ teaspoon salt
dash of cayenne pepper

Beet Salad*

1. Return carrot cooking-liquid (from recipe above) to heat. Add beet strips; par cook until al dente (soft but still firm). Drain; rinse well with cold water.

2. In a bowl, mix remaining ingredients. Add cooled beet strips; toss.

*Make salad a day ahead so that the acid has time to "cook" the beets.

1 large (about 10 ounces) beet, peeled and julienned (sliced into thin strips)
1 tablespoon sesame oil
1 tablespoon orange juice
dash of salt
1 tablespoon rice vinegar
1 teaspoon ginger, grated
1 teaspoon white sugar

The fried softshell crabs made from this Chef Josef recipe are pure pleasure for the palate, and the fried parsley garnish adds an elegant touch. The chef recommends that the crabs be served with slaw on the side.

Breaded Fried Softshell Crabs with Fried Parsley

Breaded Fried Softshell Crabs

1. In a shallow bowl, combine salt, pepper, and milk. Place flour in a second shallow bowl. In a third shallow bowl, combine eggs and water. Place breadcrumbs in a fourth shallow bowl.

2. Dip crabs in milk mixture first, then in flour to coat. Next, dip them in egg mixture, followed by breadcrumbs, lightly patting the crumbs onto the crabs.

3. To cook softshell crabs in a skillet or deep-fat fryer, heat oil in pan to about 360 - 375 degrees (F). Add crabs slowly, 1 by 1, into the hot oil. If using a skillet, do not crowd the crabs. Cook until golden brown, about 4 - 5 minutes, depending upon size of crabs. Reserve hot oil for fried parsley (recipe below).

4. Place crabs on platter, and garnish with fried parsley.

*To make at home, cut crust from white bread; chop bread in a chopper until fine.

** Count on 2 - 3 crabs per serving, depending on size.

Serves: 4 - 6

salt to taste
white pepper, freshly ground, to taste
½ cup milk
1 cup all-purpose flour
2 eggs
1 tablespoon water
2 cups fine white breadcrumbs*
12 fresh softshell crabs,** cleaned
vegetable oil

Fried Parsley

1. In a mixing bowl, combine milk, egg yolk, flour, salt, and pepper; blend well.

2. In a separate bowl, whip egg white until stiff; blend into batter with rubber spatula.

3. Dip parsley sprigs, 1 by 1, into batter, letting excess batter drip off gently.

4. Drop each sprig into hot oil; fry until golden brown, turning with a skimmer to brown evenly, approximately 1 minute.

⅓ cup milk
1 egg, separated
⅓ cup all-purpose flour
pinch of salt and white pepper
1 bunch parsley
oil (reserved from frying crabs)

Guests at a pre-football game reception held at The Grove in the fall of 2011 enjoyed the dish prepared using this recipe created by Chef Michael, who carved a whole roasted swordfish and served it with chutney and relish.

Grilled Swordfish Steak

1. Brush steaks with oil; season with sea salt.

2. Grill on one side for 8 minutes, turning a quarter turn half way through. Turn steaks over; grill another 6 minutes, again turning a quarter half way through.

3. Remove steaks to platter; tent for 15 minutes. To serve, place strawberry and habañero chutney (recipe on page 95) on plate; place swordfish over it. Top with strawberry and habañero relish (recipe on page 95).

Serves: 6

6 6 - 8-ounce swordfish steaks
¼ cup olive oil
1 tablespoon sea salt

This recipe is Chef Michael's version of a dish prepared at a restaurant where he had worked.

Baked Halibut Stuffed with Blue Crab

1. Preheat oven to 350 degrees (F).

2. In a bowl, combine mayonnaise, mustard, hot sauce, Worcestershire, and egg yolks. Fold in lump crab, taking care not to break up lumps.

3. Lay fillets on cutting board. Starting to the left of center, slice fillets on the bias back to the right about ¾ of the way through. Open slit in halibut; stuff with crab mixture to overflowing. Place in a shallow baking dish; top with wine and lemon slices.

4. Bake in preheated oven until cooked through, about 10 minutes per inch of thickness. Top with lemon butter sauce (recipe on page 91).

*The freshness of the halibut is key to this dish. Choose thicker fillets.

Serves: 6

¼ cup mayonnaise
1 tablespoon Dijon mustard
dash of hot sauce
1 tablespoon Worcestershire sauce
2 egg yolks
1 pound jumbo lump blue crab
6 5 - 6-ounce halibut fillets*
1 cup dry white wine
6 lemon slices (1 per halibut fillet) for garnish

Chef Michael developed this recipe from ideas garnered while working at hotel and seafood restaurants. He has prepared it for both luncheons and dinners at The Grove—and at Preston's, the restaurant at The Inn at Virginia Tech.

The Grove's Crab Cakes

1. Prepare dressing. Fold in crabmeat.* Fold in bread cubes. Refrigerate for at least 1 hour to allow bread to absorb dressing and bind cakes.

2. Remove from refrigerator; form into 3-ounce cakes.

3. Preheat oven to 350 degrees (F).

4. Heat oil in a skillet on medium-high heat. Add crab cakes; pan-sear both sides. Remove cakes to a sheet pan lined with paper towels. When all cakes have been seared, move to another sheet pan. Heat through in preheated oven, about 15 minutes.

5. Serve warm. Chef Michael likes to serve the crab cakes with jicama slaw (recipe on page 62) or apple fennel slaw (recipe on page 63).

*The secret of good crab cakes is not to break any or as few as possible of the lumps of crab.

Dressing

Mix ingredients in a bowl.

Yield: 6 3-ounce crab cakes

dressing (recipe below)
1 pound jumbo lump or lump crabmeat
4 slices soft white bread, cut into very small cubes after removing crust
2 tablespoons canola oil

⅓ cup mayonnaise
2 tablespoons Dijon mustard
½ tablespoon Old Bay seasoning
1 egg yolk
dash of Worcestershire sauce
dash of Tabasco sauce

The crunchy panko and wasabi crust used in this recipe from Chef Josef adds an exciting twist to the flavor and texture of an otherwise mild and tender fish.

Panko and Wasabi-crusted Baked Salmon

1. Preheat oven to 350 degrees (F).

2. Combine water and wasabi powder in a small bowl until well blended; reserve for later use.

3. In a food processor, add panko, lime zest, ginger, and garlic; pulse twice. After the second pulse, add olive oil, salt, and pepper; pulse until mixture becomes coarsely ground and evenly sized.

4. Add oil to a large, heavy sauté pan, and heat to medium-high. Salt and pepper salmon fillets to taste; move fillets to sauté pan, leaving space between fillets. Sear over medium-high heat, about 1 ½ minutes on each side. Remove salmon from sauté pan onto a lightly oiled sheet pan.

5. Rub wasabi mixture onto salmon; roll in panko mixture. Place pan in preheated oven; cook for about 10 - 12 minutes.

6. Remove from oven, and place on individual plates; serve with lime wedges and lemon butter sauce (recipe on page 91).

Serves: 4

1 ½ teaspoons cold water
1 teaspoon wasabi powder
½ cup panko
2 teaspoons lime zest
2 teaspoons fresh ginger, minced
¼ teaspoon fresh garlic, minced
1 teaspoon olive oil
salt and pepper to taste
1 teaspoon vegetable oil
4 6 - 7-ounce thick-cut skinless
   salmon fillets
1 soft lime, cut into 4 wedges

This recipe, Chef Michael's variation of a sole dish, is a popular entrée at The Grove.

Parmesan-crusted Fillets of Sole

1. Place flour in a pie dish. Place egg wash in another pie dish. In a third pie dish, add cheese and panko, mixed together.

2. Rinse fillets in cold running water.

3. Dredge fillets in flour, then in egg wash, and finally in panko/cheese mixture. Place aside while preparing caper sauce.

4. Add oil to pan, and heat to medium high. Add fillets to pan; sauté in hot oil, about 3 - 5 minutes or until browned.* Flip fillets; sauté about 3 – 4 minutes.

5. Remove fillets to serving plate; spoon caper sauce over them.

*Keep adding oil as needed between frying batches of sole fillets, keeping the pan coated with oil.

Serves: 4

1 cup all-purpose flour
egg wash (2 eggs and 2 tablespoons water, beaten together until well mixed)
¼ cup Parmesan cheese, grated
1 cup panko
2 pounds 2 - 3-ounce sole fillets
¼ cup canola oil
caper sauce (recipe on page 97)

This upscale dish from 1941 may well have been prepared at The Grove during the mid-1900s, according to Chef Josef's research, but the recipes for Mornay sauce and compound lobster butter included in the list of ingredients are modern-day additions from Chef Michael.

Fillets of Sole with Shrimp and Oysters

1. Sauté mushrooms* in pan over medium heat; season with salt and pepper to taste. Reserve liquid.

2. Poach fillets in liquid from mushrooms. Remove fillets from liquid, keeping liquid warm. Move fillets to heat-proof serving dish; garnish with oysters, shrimp, and sautéed mushrooms.

3. Mix Mornay sauce with lobster butter.

4. In a saucepan, cook mushroom liquid over medium heat until reduced to 1/3 original amount; add to Mornay sauce/lobster butter mixture. Add whipped cream; pour over fillets. Sprinkle with cheese; brown under a broiler.

*Mushrooms give off a lot of liquid when cooked.

Serves: 4

4 mushrooms
salt and pepper to taste
4 6 - 8-ounce fillets of sole
12 oysters, cooked
12 medium-size shrimp, cleaned and cooked
1 tablespoon Mornay sauce (recipe on page 91)
2 tablespoons compound lobster butter (recipe on page 93)
1 tablespoon whipped cream
1 tablespoon Parmesan cheese, grated

This recipe from Chef Josef is a simple yet delicious way to prepare and protect the flavor of any delicate fish. The chef recommends that only fresh trout be used and suggests that fishing for and catching one's own trout is the best way to ensure the freshest fish.

Rainbow Trout Meunière*

1. Rinse trout inside and out with cold running water; cut fillets from fish, leaving skin on. De-bone fillets. Soak trout fillets in half-and-half for 10 minutes.

2. On waxed paper, combine flour, salt, and pepper.

3. Remove trout from cream; dredge through flour mixture, coating sides evenly and shaking off excess flour.

4. Preheat a 12-inch skillet over medium heat; add 2 tablespoons oil to skillet. Add trout fillets; sauté 2 ½ minutes on each side or until light brown. Transfer fillets to platter; keep warm. Repeat process with remaining oil and remaining fish.

5. Pour off any fat remaining in skillet, and wipe it out or start with a new skillet. Return skillet to medium heat. Add butter; cook until lightly foamy, about 2 minutes. Stir in parsley, lemon juice, salt, and pepper.

6. Pour butter mixture over rainbow trout fillets. Add 1 lemon wedge for each fillet, garnish with parsley sprigs, pecans, and grapes.

*For Trout Amandine, add ¼ cup toasted sliced almonds; garnish with fresh seedless grapes.

Serves: 6

6 fresh rainbow trout
½ cup half-and-half
1 cup all-purpose flour, sifted
salt and pepper to taste
½ cup vegetable oil, divided
6 tablespoons unsalted butter
1 tablespoon fresh parsley, chopped
3 teaspoons fresh lemon juice
6 lemon wedges
sprigs of fresh parsley for garnish
pecans, halved, for garnish
seedless grapes for garnish

Chef Michael prepared this entrée in September 2005 for his first event at The Grove; the meal was part of his obviously successful job application process.

Grilled Fillet Mignon with Cabernet Reduction

Grilled Fillet Mignon

1. Place oil in a pan, roll steaks in oil, and rub steaks with salt and pepper. Place on a charcoal grill. Cook for about 5 minutes. Turn steaks one-quarter turn; cook another 3 - 4 minutes. Turn steaks over; cook 2 - 3 minutes. Turn steaks a quarter; cook another 4 minutes for medium rare or until a thermometer inserted into middle of steaks registers 140 degrees (F).

2. Remove steaks from grill; place on platter. Tent with aluminum foil, allowing to sit a minimum of 15 minutes and up to 30 minutes.*

3. To serve, spoon cabernet reduction sauce (recipe below) over and around steaks.

*Resting the steaks allows juices to be reabsorbed so that these juices do not leak out on a plate when served.

Serves: 4

1 tablespoon vegetable oil (per steak)
4 6 - 8-ounce center-cut beef tenderloin
   steaks, 2 - 2 ½-inches thick
salt and pepper to taste

Cabernet Reduction

1. In a saucepan on high heat, bring wine, vinegar, grapes, shallots, garlic, and peppercorns to a boil. Reduce heat to medium; simmer, stirring occasionally until wine is reduced to half.

2. Strain, pressing solids through strainer, into a pot. Add brown beef stock; bring back to simmer. Cook until thickened.

3. Remove from heat; whisk in butter.

1 bottle dry cabernet wine
¼ cup red wine vinegar
½ cup red grapes, roughly chopped
2 shallots, roughly chopped
2 garlic cloves, roughly chopped
1 tablespoon black peppercorns
½ cup brown beef stock (recipe
   on page 80)
¼ cup butter, cut into cubes

A standard dish for tailgates, Chef Michael's chili is just as popular at receptions held at The Grove before football games.

Texas-style Chili with Black Beans

Chili Sauce

1. Combine all ingredients in a saucepan. Bring to a boil over high heat. Reduce heat to medium; cook until liquid is reduced by half. Turn off heat; allow to cool.

2. Place mixture, in batches, in a blender; purée. Strain through a fine strainer. Use as ingredient in Texas-style chili with black beans (recipe below).

3. Some, if not all, of this sauce can be kept on hand in the freezer. Freeze it in ice-cube trays to add spice to sauces.

* Chef Michael likes to use larger-size chilis, like anchos, which have more flavor and less heat. However, he suggests that cooks should feel free to add some smaller chili peppers, such as pequins, for a spicier dish.

Yield: 1 ½ gallons

2 ounces dried red chilis*
8 cups water
1 cup prunes
2 tablespoons cumin seed
1 cinnamon stick
1 teaspoon dried oregano
12 garlic cloves

Chili with Black Beans

In a large stockpot,* heat canola oil over medium-high heat. Add meat and cumin; cook until meat is browned. Add onion and green pepper; continue to cook until vegetables are translucent, about 5 minutes. Add chili powder; cook for 5 more minutes. Add remaining ingredients. Bring to a boil. Reduce heat to low; simmer for 3 - 4 hours or until meat begins to shred.

*The chili can also be prepared in a crockpot.

¼ cup canola oil
3 - 4 pounds chuck roast, cut into
    1-inch cubes
1 tablespoon cumin seed
1 yellow onion, diced
1 green pepper, diced
¼ cup chili powder
4 cups beef stock (recipe on page 80)
6 cups water
2 bay leaves
2 14 ½-ounce cans diced tomatoes
1 26 ½-ounce can black beans
1 tablespoon key lime juice
2 tablespoons kosher salt
chili sauce (recipe above)

This version of a traditional entrée was developed by Chef Josef.

Old Fashioned Meat Loaf

1. Melt butter in a sauté pan, add onions and garlic, and sauté over medium heat until just golden but not too brown. Let cool.

2. In a small bowl, soak diced bread in milk.

3. In a large bowl, mix ground beef with sautéed onions/garlic and soaked bread. Add eggs, salt, pepper, mustard, parsley, thyme, and marjoram. Mix until completely combined.

4. Pat into a loaf shape; place in lightly oiled baking pan, leaving at least 1 inch of space around edges to allow fat to run off. Brush top of meat with tomato purée, sprinkle with plain breadcrumbs, and sprinkle some vegetable oil over the breadcrumbs to keep them from burning. Refrigerate for 1 - 2 hours to allow flavors to penetrate and firm up the loaf.

5. Preheat oven to 350 degrees (F).

6. Bake meat loaf on lower rack of preheated oven for 1 hour or until meat is cooked through.** Pour off accumulated fat several times while baking and after meat is fully cooked.

7. Let stand on wire rack for 5 minutes before slicing and serving.

*Should be at least 80 percent lean.

**Inner temperature of the loaf should be 165 degrees (F) or higher.

Serves: 6

2 teaspoons unsalted butter
1 cup onions, finely chopped
2 garlic cloves, minced
2 slices white bread, finely diced
⅓ cup whole milk
2 pounds lean ground beef*
2 eggs, lightly beaten
1 teaspoon salt
ground black pepper to taste
¼ teaspoon yellow mustard
1 teaspoon fresh parsley, finely chopped
½ teaspoon thyme
½ teaspoon marjoram
2 tablespoons tomato purée
2 - 3 tablespoons plain breadcrumbs
½ teaspoon vegetable oil

Chef Michael's smoked duck breast (recipe on page 54) can be paired with vegetables for tasty main courses.

Duck with Lentils and Duck with Pommes Frites

Duck Confit

1. Preheat oven to 350 degrees (F).

2. Break duck into pieces (breast, legs, and thighs). Roast pieces in preheated oven for 1 hour and 30 minutes.

3. Remove from oven, and allow to cool. Pour drippings into clear container. Skim off fat when it separates. Reserve fat and drippings separately.

4. Place roasting pan over heat, and add port. Heat, scraping any brown bits from the bottom. Reserve.

5. Meanwhile, remove meat from bones; mince. Add 1 tablespoon skimmed fat to minced duck; refrigerate.

1 whole duck
2 cups tawny port wine
1 tablespoon skimmed fat (from roasting duck)

Duck Stock

1. Rough chop all vegetables.

2. Combine vegetables and remaining ingredients in a large stockpot. Bring to a simmer over high heat. Reduce heat to low; simmer about 3 hours.

3. Strain and discard solids. Return liquid to pot; continue to cook until reduced to 1 gallon.

2 yellow onions
¾ head celery
1 pound carrots
12 garlic cloves
½ pint raspberries
¼ cup juniper berries
1 tablespoon black peppercorns
2 bay leaves
2 gallons water
reserved drippings (not fat) from duck confit
reserved port from pan in duck confit
bones from roasted duck

Duck with Lentils

1. In a saucepot, combine lentils and stock. Add cumin, and bring to a boil. Reduce heat to low; simmer until most of liquid is absorbed, about 1 hour. Stir in confit and cherries; continue to heat until heated through.

2. Serve duck breast over lentils.

Serves: 4

1 cup lentils
2 cups duck stock (recipe on facing page)
1 teaspoon ground cumin
reserved duck confit (recipe on facing page)
2 ounces dried cherries
1 duck breast (recipe on page 54)

Duck with Pommes Frites

1. In a large stockpot, add potatoes and duck stock; bring to a boil. Turn heat to low; simmer until potatoes are tender when pierced with a fork. Strain off stock; reserve for another use. Let potatoes cool.

2. In a large sauté pan, add duck fat; heat on medium-high heat. Add potatoes and cook, turning often until well browned, about 10 - 15 minutes.

3. Remove to a pan lined with paper towels; let drain.

4. Move to a bowl; add salt. Toss to coat, and serve as a side dish with duck breast.

Serves: 4

1½ pounds baby potatoes, peeled
1 gallon duck stock (recipe on facing page)
⅔ cup duck fat (reserved from duck confit recipe on facing page)
1 teaspoon salt
1 duck breast (recipe on page 54)

Although Chef Michael serves this dish only for receptions, it could be used as a dinner entrée for guests who enjoy the taste of wild game.

Roasted Venison Tenderloin

1. Bring tenderloin to room temperature. Rub with juniper, pepper, and salt.* Sear tenderloin in a very hot pan.

2. Remove from pan; move to roasting pan. Allow to return to room temperature, about 15 minutes.

3. Preheat oven to 250 degrees (F).

4. Place in preheated oven, and cook until internal temperature reaches 140 degrees (F) for medium rare, about 60 minutes.

5. Remove from oven; tent with foil. Allow to sit for 15 minutes.

6. Slice tenderloin to desired thickness; serve with blackberry port chutney (recipe on page 101) on the side.

*This process is known as "crusting."

Serves: 4

1 venison tenderloin, cleaned and silver skin removed
¼ cup juniper berries, crushed
¼ cup cracked black pepper
1 tablespoon kosher salt

This entrée developed by Chef Michael was first served at The Grove in September 2011, making it one of the newer recipes in the book.

Seared Beef Tenderloin with Currant and Pink Peppercorn Sauce

Seared Beef Tenderloin

1. Preheat oven to 400 degrees (F).

2. Rub tenderloin with kosher salt and pepper to taste. Allow tenderloin to reach room temperature, about 15 minutes. Place in preheated oven; cook for 10 - 20 minutes or until outside of roast begins to brown. Remove tenderloin from oven.

3. Lower oven temperature to 250 degrees (F).

4. Let tenderloin return to room temperature before placing it back into preheated oven. Cook until tenderloin reaches an internal temperature of 140 degrees (F) for medium to medium rare.

5. Remove; tent with foil. Let stand at least 15 minutes and as much as 30 minutes.

6. To serve, spoon currant and peppercorn sauce onto plate. Place dollop of parsnip purée in center. Slice tenderloin; place over purée. Top with micro-parsnip greens (small, young sprouts available at farmers' markets) or sprouts of other root vegetables.

*Although choice-grade tenderloin can be used, Chef Michael recommends using prime beef, which must be ordered, for better results. If using a highly marbled beef, which will be more expensive, cook it only to medium rare or rare. The chef says that cooking the beef more renders all of the marbling, for which one pays extra, out of the beef. The more marbling the beef has, the more moist and flavorful it will be.

**Chef Michael reserves trimmings to make brown sauce as a basis for his other sauces.

Serves: 6 - 10

1 whole beef tenderloin,* trimmed, silver removed, head (shoulder tender) removed (reserve and freeze for up to 6 months for later use in stew or for kabobs or steaks), chain (opposite side of head; includes fat, gristle, and silver skin) removed**
kosher salt and black pepper to taste
currant and pink peppercorn sauce (recipe on facing page)
parsnip purée (recipe on page 149)
micro-parsnip greens or sprouts of other root vegetables as garnish

Currant and Pink Peppercorn Sauce

1. In a saucepan, combine red currants, wine, shallots, and garlic. Bring to a boil, mashing currants, for about 20 minutes.

2. Move to a blender; liquefy.

3. Strain through a China cap chinois (a very fine, cone-shaped strainer) back into a pot. Add brown sauce and peppercorns. Cook over medioum heat until reduced by one quarter. Add cream and jelly. Reduce heat to low, cooking until mixture coats back of spoon.

4. Remove from heat; whisk in butter.

½ pound fresh red currants
1 cup dry red wine, preferably the same that will be served with dinner
2 shallots, roughly chopped
2 garlic cloves, roughly chopped
2 cups brown sauce (recipe on page 103)
2 tablespoons pink peppercorns
¼ cup heavy cream
3 tablespoons red currant jelly
¼ cup butter, cubed

Savory bread puddings, rather than sweet bread puddings, are nice alternatives to potatoes, rice, or dressing. This Chef Michael recipe was prepared at The Grove for the Faculty Women's Club in February 2006.

Marbled Rye Bread Pudding with Black Forest Ham

1. Preheat oven to 350 degrees (F).

2. In a bowl, place rye and ham; toss.

3. In a saucepan, scald milk, cream, and butter over medium heat.

4. In a separate bowl, beat egg yolks, mustard, salt, and pepper together. Temper ½ cup milk mixture into egg mixture, whisking constantly. Pour egg mixture into remaining milk mixture, again whisking constantly. Cool.

5. Pour milk and egg mixture over bread and ham. Allow bread to soak up liquid. Let sit in refrigerator until all liquid is absorbed, about 30 minutes.

6. Pour into greased 12 x 6-inch baking pan or individual ramekins; bake in preheated oven until set, 35 - 40 minutes, less for individual portion cups. Serve with warm Mornay sauce (recipe on page 91).

Serves: 12

12 cups stale marbled rye, cubed
2 pounds Black Forest ham
1 cup milk
3 cups heavy cream
2 tablespoons butter
10 egg yolks
¼ cup Dijon mustard
1 tablespoon salt
dash of white pepper

In addition to its use in sweet confections, chocolate can enliven mixes and sauces that are served with meat entrées. The dish made from this recipe, which was developed by Chef Michael, lists cocoa powder as one of the ingredients in the spice mix, and the mole sauce that is served with the entrée includes chocolate.

Latin Spiced Pork Tenderloin

1. Rub spice mix into tenderloin; refrigerate for 4 hours or overnight.

2. Preheat oven to 300 degrees (F).

3. Remove tenderloin from refrigerator. Place on a rack in a roasting pan; roast in preheated oven until meat thermometer inserted into center of tenderloin reads 145 degrees (F).

4. Serve with mole sauce.

Spice Mix

Combine ingredients, stirring until well mixed.

Serves: 4

spice mix (recipe below)
1 pork tenderloin
mole sauce (recipe on page 100)

Yield: about 1 cup

1 ½ tablespoons cocoa powder
2 teaspoons cumin
2 tablespoons chili powder
1 tablespoon ground coriander
1 tablespoon salt
1 tablespoon ground pepper
½ teaspoon ground cinnamon
3 tablespoons brown sugar
1 teaspoon garlic powder
1 tablespoon used coffee grounds

Side dishes that complement this wild-game entrée, courtesy of Chef Josef, include whipped potatoes, sautéed wild mushrooms, Brussels sprouts, and roasted chestnuts with wild rice. Chef Josef recommends obtaining the venison saddle from a butcher shop and asking the butcher to remove the bone from the saddle. Take those bones home to use in the sauce.

Venison Scaloppini Sautéed with Juniper Cream Sauce

Venison Scaloppini

1. Trim bone (reserve for sauce), excess fat, and silver skin from venison saddle (loin cut with bone in). Cut into small slices (2 - 3 ounces), flatten with a meat cleaver, and spread in bottom of a roasting pan. Cover with marinade, adding extra oil, if needed, to completely cover meat (scaloppini). Cover pan tightly, and refrigerate for at least 3 hours (or as long as 3 days if venison comes from a very mature animal, turning the venison over after the second day).

2. Prepare juniper cream sauce.

3. When sauce is ready, remove scaloppini of venison from marinade, season with salt and pepper, and dust with flour.

4. Set sauté pan over high heat until very hot. Skim 3 - 4 tablespoons oil from top of marinade; add to heated pan. Add half of venison slices; sauté, cooking meat until browned, about 1 ½ - 2 minutes on each side (do not cook meat well done). Follow same process for other half of venison.

5. Place scaloppini in serving dish, add juniper cream sauce, and let rest for 1 - 2 minutes before serving.

Serves: 6 - 7

2 ½ pounds boneless venison saddle
marinade (recipe below)
oil, if needed
juniper cream sauce (recipe on
    facing page)
salt and ground black pepper to taste
flour
3 - 4 tablespoons oil from marinade

Marinade

1. Grind pepper; crush juniper berries; chop rosemary.

2. Place ingredients in a large bowl. Add lemon juice and oil mixture, stirring until blended.

2 teaspoons fresh black pepper
6 juniper berries
1 sprig of fresh rosemary
1 teaspoon lemon juice
1 ½ cups olive oil and vegetable oil
    mixture (half olive oil, half vegetable oil)

Juniper Cream Sauce

1. Preheat oven to 375 degrees (F).

2. If not cut by butcher, cut bones into small pieces with a cleaver. Place bones in roasting pan; bake in preheated oven with a little oil for 12 - 18 minutes or until light brown. Remove from oven.

3. Remove fat from pan; add to saucepan. Add onions and wine; sauté for 1 minute on medium heat or until wine has been reduced by half. Add juniper berries and brown beef stock; simmer for 10 minutes. Add cream. Bring sauce back to simmer, and cook 30 - 40 minutes; season with salt and pepper to taste.

4. Strain sauce through a China cap chinois (a very fine, cone-shaped strainer). Put strained sauce back into saucepan over medium heat; boil until sauce has reached the thickness of cream. Remove from heat; pour over venison scaloppini.

bones from venison saddle
oil
2 tablespoons onions, chopped
½ cup dry red wine
4 juniper berries
½ cup brown beef stock (recipe on page 80)
2 cups whipping cream
salt and pepper to taste

Chef Michael developed this dish to use as the main ingredient for scrumptious, reception-style sandwiches, but it can be used as an entrée as well.

Applewood-smoked Pork Tenderloin with Chipotle Apple Butter

1. Combine apple butter and salt.

2. Place pork on piece of plastic wrap. Cover generously with apple butter mixture. Wrap; refrigerate overnight.

3. Remove pork from refrigerator; unwrap. Place in a colander; rinse. Allow to dry at room temperature.

4. Heat one side of a charcoal grill. Place pork on unheated side of grill with a pan filled with water below it.* On hot side of grill, place wood chips in a piece of aluminum foil. Cover grill; allow to smoke until thermometer inserted into pork reads 150 degrees (F), about 20 - 30 minutes. Turn pork half way so that each end spends an equal amount of time closer to heat.

5. Remove and tent. Allow to rest 20 - 30 minutes.

6. Slice; serve with chipotle apple butter. This dish would make a great sandwich, with Granny Smith apple and fennel slaw (recipe on page 63) or dark beer and caraway cabbage (recipe on page 150) on the side.

*The pan of water beneath the pork will help keep the pork from drying out.

Serves: 4

1 cup apple butter
curing salt (follow manufacturer's directions on amounts)
2 pork tenderloins, silver skin removed
apple-wood chips soaked in water
1 cup chipotle apple butter (recipe on page 102)

Chili is one of the popular dishes at receptions held at the president's home preceding fall home football games.

Denver-style Chili

In a large stockpot, heat oil over medium-high heat. Add pork and cumin; brown meat. Add garlic, onion, and green pepper; cook until vegetables are translucent, about 5 minutes. Add stock, water, bay leaves, lime juice, oregano, chilis, tomatoes, and tomatillos. Bring to a boil, and reduce heat to low. Simmer for 3 hours or until pork begins to shred. Add pineapple and apple butter; cook another 10 minutes. Add cilantro and salt. Sprinkle cornmeal over chili, and stir to blend. Cook another 10 minutes until slightly thickened.

*Usually milder green chilis; add jalapeño or Serrano chilis for a spicier dish.

Yield: 1 ¼ gallons

¼ cup canola oil
3 - 4 pounds pork butt, cut into
  1-inch cubes
2 tablespoons cumin seed
6 garlic cloves, minced
1 yellow onion, diced
1 green pepper, diced
4 cups chicken stock (recipe on page 81)
6 cups water
2 bay leaves
¼ cup key lime juice
1 tablespoon dried oregano
2 7-ounce cans diced green chilis*
2 pounds green tomatoes, diced
1 pound tomatillos, diced
4 ounces crushed pineapple
½ cup chipotle apple butter (recipe
  on page 102)
⅓ cup cilantro, chopped
1 tablespooon kosher salt
½ cup white cornmeal or masa harina

Guests attending a pre-football game reception at The Grove feast on a variety of foods, among them Chef Michael's Denver-style chili (recipe above).

This tasty dinner entrée from Chef Josef, made special by the addition of poached plums in a red wine sauce, can be served with a variety of vegetables, but the chef recommends sides of grilled vegetables and sweet potatoes.

Slow-roasted Pork Loin with Poached Plums and Plum Sauce

Slow-roasted Pork Loin

1. Preheat oven to 400 degrees (F).

2. Season pork with salt, garlic, and thyme; brush with olive oil. Place in roasting pan, and cook in preheated oven for 10 minutes. Reduce heat to 230 degrees (F); roast an additional 2 ¼ hours or until meat temperature inserted in center of pork reaches 150 degrees (F).

3. Remove pork from oven; let pork "rest" for 10 minutes. Before serving, heat plums and plum sauce (recipe below) to serve beside the pork. Garnish with chives.

Serves: 6 - 7

2 ½ pounds center-cut pork loin, fat trimmed
salt to taste
2 garlic cloves, minced
thyme to taste
2 tablespoons olive oil
1 teaspoon fresh chives

Poached Plums and Plum Sauce

1. Combine first 5 ingredients in a large saucepan; bring to a boil, stirring until sugar dissolves. Reduce heat; simmer about 20 minutes or until plums are tender.

2. Using a skimmer, transfer plums to a platter; cool. Reserve plums for serving time.

3. Strain wine mixture; reserve.

4. In a saucepan over medium heat, sautée shallots in olive oil; add broth, thyme sprigs, and wine mixture. Bring to a boil; simmer until mixture is reduced to 1 cup, about 25 minutes.

5. Strain sauce; add thyme. Season with salt, pepper, and sugar to taste.

*Available in specialty food stores and Asian markets.

6 - 7 sweet red or dark blue plums, quartered and pitted
2 ½ cups dry red wine
2 pieces whole star anise*
1 medium-size cinnamon stick
¼ cup white sugar
2 tablespoons shallots, finely chopped
1 teaspoon olive oil
2 cups chicken broth
5 fresh thyme sprigs
3 teaspoons fresh thyme, chopped
salt and pepper to taste
sugar to taste

Throughout the fall, smoked pork is a staple at receptions held at the president's home. It has become so popular that Chef Michael made 60 pounds of it in fall 2011, which he hoped would be enough to last throughout the football season. However, he ran out of the popular dish for the last game, and guests at the reception noticed. The Grove has a smoker that uses chips, and for smoking in the grill, the chef uses indirect heat and chunks of wood that are readily available online. Chef Michael uses a mix of hickory, maple, and pecan chunks but recommends experimentation with different combinations of wood for new flavors. The pork can also be used as an entrée.

Smoked Pork

1. In a bowl, mix sugar, salts, and blackened seasoning. Toss pork in the mixture, set it on a rack in a pan, and place it in the refrigerator to drain overnight.

2. Prepare grill. Turn both sides on, and close the lid to preheat.

3. Soak wood for at least 10 minutes.

4. Turn off one side of grill. Fill a pie pan with water; place pan under the rack on side that has been turned off. Place wood on side that is on. Turn heat to low

5. Place pork, fatty side up,** on side of grill that is off, over pie pan. Cook until internal temperature of pork reaches 220 degrees (F), usually 6 - 10 hours at very low heat. If trouble is experienced in keeping the heat that low, smoke pork for 2 hours, and move to a 225-degree (F) oven to finish, rotating pork every hour or so to ensure that one side is not closest to the heat for the whole cooking process.

6. If wood chips are used, add more about every 30 minutes. Wood chunks will last longer but may need to be replaced half way through the cooking process.

7. Remove pork, and allow to cool. Using hands, pull pork apart. An excellent accompaniment is North Carolina barbecue sauce (recipe on page 98).

*Shoulder can be used, but butts shred better.

**Placing the fatty side of the pork up while cooking keeps the pork from drying out.

Yield: 12 - 14 pounds

2 pounds brown sugar
½ cup kosher salt
1 tablespoon curing salt
1 cup blackened seasoning
20 pounds pork butt*
1 - 2 wood chunks (see above left for blend used by Chef Michael)

Through research, Chef Josef learned that this entrée was served at The Grove in years past. He recommends an accompaniment of rice pilaf, fresh asparagus, and baby carrots.

Breast of Chicken in the Style of Kiev

1. Combine butter, parsley, tarragon, lemon juice, kosher salt, and ¼ teaspoon black pepper in bowl of a standard mixer. Place mixture on plastic wrap or waxed paper; roll into a small log; place in freezer.

2. Moisten each chicken breast with water; place each piece, 1 at a time, between 2 pieces of plastic wrap. Moisten top piece of wrap with water. Pound chicken breast to no less than ⅛-inch thick. Be careful not to tear the chicken breasts, each of which needs to be one sheet of meat. Season each breast with salt and pepper to taste.

3. Place each chicken breast on a new piece of plastic wrap. Add ¼ of the frozen butter compound and 1 tablespoon breadcrumbs in center of each breast. Using plastic wrap to assist, fold in ends of breast; roll breast very tightly into a log, completely enclosing butter and breadcrumbs. Place chicken in refrigerator from 2 hours to overnight.

4. Add enough vegetable oil to cover ½ inch of 12-inch sauté pan. Cook over medium to high heat until oil reaches 375 degrees (F).

5. Place egg and water mixture in a pie pan; place 2 cups breadcrumbs in a different pie pan.

6. Dip each breast in egg mixture; then roll in breadcrumbs. Gently place each breast, sealed side down, in oil, and cook until golden brown, approximately 4 - 5 minutes on each side, and internal temperature reaches 165 degrees (F).

7. Remove breasts to a cooling rack set in a sheet pan; drain. Place on plate; serve immediately with lemon slices.

Serves: 4

8 tablespoons unsalted sweet butter, room temperature
1 teaspoon fresh parsley, chopped
1 teaspoon fresh tarragon, chopped
1 teaspoon fresh lemon juice
1 teaspoon kosher salt plus extra for seasoning chicken breast
¼ teaspoon ground black pepper plus extra for seasoning chicken breast
4 boneless, skinless chicken breast halves
water
2 ¼ cups panko or homemade fine white breadcrumbs, divided
vegetable oil
2 large eggs, beaten with 1 teaspoon water
4 lemon slices

Chef Michael, who developed this recipe, serves the dish for lunch at The Grove and has used it for a Virginia Tech Board of Visitors luncheon. It would also make an excellent dinner entrée.

Buttermilk Fried Chicken Breast with Peach Salsa

1. Remove skin and trim fat from chicken breasts. Lay breasts in a deep pan, one layer thick.

2. In a bowl, add buttermilk, honey, and Tabasco; whisk to combine. Pour mixture over chicken breasts. Cover; move to bottom shelf of refrigerator; chill overnight.

3. Preheat oven to 350 degrees (F).

4. Remove chicken from buttermilk mixture, and place in colander to drain.

5. Add oil to large sauté pan; bring to high heat on stovetop.

6. In a bowl, add flour, cornmeal, salt, and pepper. Dredge chicken in flour mixture, and place in hot oil; sauté until golden, about 5 minutes; turn over and cook additional 3 - 4 minutes. Remove pan from heat.

7. Move chicken to baking dish, and place in preheated oven. Bake until done, about 5 - 7 minutes, depending on thickness of breasts. Remove to serving plate; top with peach salsa (recipe below).

Serves: 4

4 chicken breasts
½ gallon buttermilk
¼ cup honey
1 teaspoon Tabasco sauce
¼ cup vegetable oil
1 cup all-purpose flour
2 cups white cornmeal
1 tablespoon salt
1 tablespoon ground black pepper

Peach Salsa

Combine peaches, shallot, chili, and red pepper; toss in sugar until coated. Let sit for 30 minutes. Add lime juice and cilantro.

2 peaches, diced
1 shallot, minced
¼ Serrano chili pepper, seeded and brunoise cut (very small dice)
¼ sweet red pepper, seeded and diced
1 tablespoon white sugar
1 tablespoon key lime juice
2 tablespoons cilantro, chopped

One of the newer recipes in the book, this entrée was developed by Chef Michael and served at a luncheon at The Grove during the winter holidays of 2011. The chef says that veal can be used instead of chicken.

Chicken Marsala with Fontina Cheese

1. Combine cornstarch and water; set aside.

2. In a shallow bowl, mix flour, oregano, garlic powder, salt, and pepper.

3. Lay chicken out on board; cover with plastic wrap. Pound lightly with meat mallet or back of a pan. Dredge breasts in flour mixture; set aside.

4. Preheat oven to 350 degrees (F).

5. Add canola oil to a large sauté pan, and heat over medium heat. Add chicken breasts in batches; cook until brown on each side, about 5 minutes per side. Remove chicken from pan to a sheet tray lined with paper towels.

6. When all chicken has been browned and placed on paper towels, remove sauté pan from heat, and add Marsala. Move pan back to heat; stir, scraping up any brown bits sticking to the pan. Cook until liquid is reduced by half.

7. Add chicken stock. Add shallots, garlic, and mushrooms. Cook again until reduced by half. Add heavy cream, once more cooking until reduced by half. Add cornstarch mixture; stir until thickened. Whisk in butter, and keep warm until sauce is used.

8. Move chicken to sheet pan; top with fontina cheese. Bake in preheated oven about 5 - 7 minutes or until thermometer inserted into thickest part of chicken breasts reads 165 degrees (F).

9. Remove chicken from oven, top with warm Marsala sauce, and serve immediately.

Serves: 12

1 tablespoon cornstarch
1 tablespoon water
2 cups all-purpose flour
1 cup fresh oregano leaves, finely chopped
2 tablespoons garlic powder
1 tablespoon salt
1 tablespoon coarse ground black pepper
12 4-ounce chicken breasts
¼ cup canola oil
1 bottle good dry Marsala wine
2 cups chicken stock (recipe on page 81)
¼ cup shallots, minced
2 tablespoons garlic, minced
1 cup mushrooms (shitake, button, or portabella), sliced
1 cup heavy cream
1 tablespoon butter
1 cup fontina cheese, grated

Winter holidays at The Grove feature special decorations, such as a Christmas tree beside the main staircase, and special dishes, such as chicken marsala with fontina cheese, made from the recipe above.

Chef Josef likes to serve rice dishes as sides to fried chicken made from the following recipe that he developed, along with other vegetable dishes that complement the taste of the entrée.

Fried Chicken Breasts with Roasted Tomatillo and Onion Sauce

Fried Chicken Breasts

1. Salt and pepper chicken breasts to taste.

2. Add vegetable oil to skillet; preheat skillet to medium-low heat. Add seasoned chicken; sauté for approximately 8 minutes on each side or until breasts are completely cooked.

3. Serve each chicken breast with 1 tablespoon of roasted tomatillo and onion sauce (recipe below).

Serves: 4

salt and pepper to taste
4 5-ounce boneless chicken breasts
1 ½ teaspoons vegetable oil

Roasted Tomatillo and Onion Sauce

1. Preheat oven to 375 degrees (F).

2. In a large pan, mix together olive oil, tomatillos, onions, and garlic; place pan in preheated oven for about 20 - 25 minutes, turning vegetables during that time to let them brown on all sides. Remove from oven; let cool to warm.

3. Place contents of pan into a blender or mixer, and purée until mixture is smooth. Add cilantro, lime juice, salt, cayenne pepper, honey, and cumin; purée again until smooth.

4. Move mixture to a saucepan; place over medium heat until sauce reaches a slow simmer.

1 teaspoon olive oil
½ pound tomatillos
⅔ cup onions, cut in 1½-inch squares
1 garlic clove
¼ cup cilantro leaves, chopped
1 tablespoon lime juice
¼ teaspoon salt
pinch of cayenne pepper
¼ teaspoon honey
¼ teaspoon ground cumin

Chef Josef found this recipe for turkey with gravy, which was used at Virginia Agricultural and Mechanical College and Polytechnic Institute (today's Virginia Tech) for the annual Thanksgiving Day dinner in the 1920s and specifically on November 30, 1924. This entrée most likely was served in the dining hall—or mess hall, as the corps of cadets called it — and possibly was also served at The Grove for the special fall holiday.

Roasted Turkey with Giblet Gravy

Roasted Turkey

1. Preheat oven to 325 degrees (F).

2. Wash turkey inside and out; remove giblets and set aside. Lightly salt and pepper turkey inside and out. If desired, cut 1 - 2 tablespoons butter into small pieces and slide under turkey skin; use fingers or wooden spoon handle to gently loosen skin at same time. Rub a little oil or bacon grease on skin.

3. Place carrot and celery chunks in a roasting pan to form a rack; place turkey on chunks.** Fold wings under turkey; tie drumsticks together with twine if not already secured.

4. Place a buttered piece of foil, buttered-side down, over breast of turkey. Place in preheated oven, and roast for 1 hour (change time for larger or smaller turkey accordingly). Remove foil. Continue roasting turkey until inner thigh reaches 165 degrees (F). Occasionally cover turkey with pan drippings during last 20 minutes, if desired. If turkey begins to get too brown, tent again with foil. Total cooking time should be 3 - 3 ½ hours. Add about 45 minutes to cooking time if turkey is stuffed.

5. When turkey is done, turn off oven, cover turkey with foil, and let rest in oven for 20 minutes longer.

6. Remove turkey from oven, leaving juices (drippings from turkey) in roasting pan to use for giblet gravy preparation (recipe facing page). Carve turkey; serve with gravy.

*The original recipe called for Virginia-raised turkey, which was also used in the title of the recipe.

**Instead of carrots and celery, a lightly oiled roasting rack may be used.

Serves: 6 - 8

1 10 - 14-pound turkey*
salt and pepper to taste
1 - 2 tablespoons butter
oil or bacon grease
carrots, cut into chunks
celery, cut into chunks

Giblet Gravy

1. While turkey is roasting, melt butter in saucepan over medium heat, add giblets, and salt and pepper to taste. Sauté seasoned giblets 8 - 10 minutes. Cover with broth or water or a combination of the two. Bring to boil; skim fat from surface. Reduce heat to low, cover pan, and simmer 1 ½ hours.

2. Remove giblets from water and broth. Strain liquid; add additional chicken broth to make 2 - 3 cups. Reserve.

3. Remove meat from neck; chop neck meat, liver, and heart, cutting away and discarding any tough parts and gristles.

4. After removing turkey from roasting pan (recipe on facing page), place pan with roasting juices over medium heat. Stir in flour (1 tablespoon for each cup of broth). Heat, stirring constantly until flour is dissolved in turkey juices. Gradually add chicken broth, stirring and cooking until thickened; simmer 8 - 10 minutes. Add chopped giblets to gravy; add additional broth if taste is too strong.

3 tablespoons butter
turkey giblets (neck, heart, and liver)
salt and pepper to taste
2 - 3 cups water and/or chicken broth
roasting juices from cooking turkey
   (facing page)
2 - 3 tablespoons flour

Members of the corps of cadets feasted on roasted turkey and gravy (see recipes above and on facing page) in the Mess Hall on Thanksgiving Days in the 1920s, while guests at the President's Home (today called The Grove) enjoyed similar fare. Photos courtesy of Special Collections, University Libraries, Virginia Tech

Chef Michael first used this lasagna recipe as a vegetarian dish at a dinner-style reception. After receiving high praise for the entrée, he prepared it as a luncheon dish for the board of visitors in 2010.

Eggplant Lasagna

Fried Eggplant

Serves: 10 - 12

1. Place eggplant slices on rack, lightly salt, and let sit 5 minutes. Turn over, salt other side, and let sit 5 more minutes.

2. Layer slices in a colander. Top slices with a plate; place something heavy on the plate. Allow eggplant to drain for 1 hour or overnight in refrigerator. Remove eggplant, rinse, and pat dry.

3. In a small bowl, combine egg whites and water; beat to make an egg wash. Dip eggplant slices in egg wash; dredge in cornstarch.

4. In a sauté pan, heat oil over medium-high heat. Place eggplant slices in pan; cook until brown and crisp, about 5 minutes. Turn and brown other side, about 3 more minutes. Move slices to a sheet pan lined with paper towels; let drain. Reserve.

3 medium to large eggplants, peeled and sliced into ½-inch thick rounds
2 tablespoons kosher salt
2 egg whites
1 tablespoon water
2 cups cornstarch
¼ cup vegetable oil

Roasted Tomato Sauce*

1. Preheat oven to 200 degrees (F).

2. Toss tomatoes in olive oil, and slice in half lengthwise. Place on an oven rack in a sheet pan. Put pan in preheated oven; roast for 4 hours. Remove from oven, and let cool. Peel skins off tomatoes; dice.**

3. Place tomatoes in a shallow baking pan. Add remaining ingredients; return to oven. Roast another 4 hours, stirring every half hour.

*Can be prepared a day ahead and kept refrigerated. Sauce flavor will be better if cooled and refrigerated overnight and even better if frozen. Can make a big batch to use with spaghetti or other pasta and then freeze in small batches.

**The recipe can be made in a crockpot after roasting tomatoes. Cook sauce on high until hot, about 20 minutes. Turn to low, and cook another 3 ½ hours.

8 Roma tomatoes
¼ cup olive oil
½ garlic clove, minced
1 medium onion, diced
1 small green pepper, diced
½ cup dry red wine
2 tablespoons balsamic vinegar
1 12-ounce can tomato paste
3 bay leaves
1 cup fresh basil
¼ cup fresh oregano
½ teaspoon flaked red pepper
2 tablespoons sugar
1 tablespoon kosher salt

Eggplant Lasagna

1. Preheat oven to 350 degrees (F).

2. In a processor, combine curds, Romano, ¼ cup Parmesan, feta, and eggs; process until smooth.

3. In a 12 x 6-inch oven-safe casserole dish, spread ½ cup tomato sauce. Layer ½ of eggplant slices over sauce. Top with ½ cup tomato sauce. Cover with cheese curd mixture. Top with ½ cup tomato sauce. Layer remaining eggplant over sauce. Top with remaining ½ cup tomato sauce. Top with mozzarella and ½ cup Parmesan. Cover and bake in preheated oven for 30 minutes. Uncover; bake another 15 minutes.

4. Remove from oven; let sit for 15 minutes before slicing and serving.

2 cups fresh cheese curds or ricotta (recipe below)
¼ cup Romano cheese, grated
¼ cup Parmesan cheese, grated
½ cup feta cheese crumbles
2 eggs
2 cups roasted tomato sauce (recipe on facing page)
fried eggplant (recipe on facing page)
8 ounces fresh mozzarella cheese, grated
½ cup Parmesan cheese, grated

Fresh Cheese Curds

1. Combine all ingredients in saucepan. Cook over medium heat until curds begin to separate. Cook for 5 more minutes.

2. Strain curds through a fine sieve. Line colander with coffee filter or cheese cloth. Place over bowl, and let curds drain for at least 1 hour. Or the curds can be prepared a day ahead and drained overnight.

1 gallon whole milk
2 cups heavy cream
¼ cup white balsamic vinegar
2 tablespoons salt

*Cider-glazed Brussels Sprouts
with Golden Delicious
Apples*

Vegetables and Side Dishes

Sweet potatoes have long been a staple with turkey at the Thanksgiving meal, and the holiday feast at The Grove over the years has been no exception. This sweet potato casserole recipe by Chef Joseph adds a special touch to the traditional fare.

Sweet Potato Casserole with Pecan Streusel Topping

1. Preheat oven to 350 degrees (F). Grease a 9 x 13-inch baking dish.

2. In a large bowl, whip eggs lightly; add white sugar, cinnamon, vanilla, maple syrup, orange juice, and melted butter; mix together. Fold in sweet potatoes. Spread sweet potato mixture in prepared baking dish.

3. In a small bowl, mix together brown sugar and flour. Cut softened butter, a little at a time, into flour/sugar mixture. Mix until crumbly, then stir in pecans. Sprinkle pecan mixture over the sweet potatoes.

4. Bake in preheated oven for 25 - 28 minutes or until golden brown.

Serves: 8 - 10

2 eggs
¾ cup white sugar
½ teaspoon cinnamon
½ teaspoon vanilla extract
¼ cup maple syrup
½ cup orange juice
½ cup sweet unsalted butter, melted
4 ½ cups sweet potatoes, cooked and mashed
1 cup light brown sugar
½ cup all-purpose flour
⅓ cup unsalted butter, softened to room temperature
1 cup pecans, chopped

Chef Michael initially developed this recipe for risotto to use in a cooking demonstration. While hearty enough to be an entrée, risottos are usually served as a side dish at The Grove.

Winter Squash Risotto*

1. In a saucepan, heat oil over medium-high heat. Add Arborio, and lightly toast, about 5 minutes. Add cinnamon stick, cloves, and mace; continue to cook another 2 minutes. Start adding chicken stock ½ cup at a time. Do not add next ½ cup of stock until previous addition is absorbed. With last addition, add squash, Gruyère, brown sugar, and cayenne pepper; salt and pepper to taste. Stir until slightly thickened. From first addition of chicken stock to last addition will be about 30 minutes.

2. Remove from heat; let stand 10 minutes before serving.

*Acorn, butternut, or pumpkin squash can be used for this recipe —or use a combination of two of them or all three.

**If pumpkin oil can be found, substitute it for a nice flavor.

Serves 10 - 12 (as a side dish)

2 tablespoons canola oil**
1 cup Arborio rice
1 cinnamon stick
1 teaspoon whole cloves
½ teaspoon mace
5 cups chicken stock (recipe on page 81) or vegetable stock
½ cup orange squash, puréed
4 ounces Gruyère cheese, grated
1 tablespoon brown sugar
dash of cayenne pepper
salt and pepper to taste

This recipe developed by Chef Michael uses quinoa—grain-like, edible seeds that are gluten free—rather than the traditional rice that one usually finds in a pilaf.

Quinoa Pilaf

1. In a pot, heat oil over medium heat.

2. Add onion, celery, carrot, and garlic. Cook about 10 minutes or until vegetables soften. Add quinoa; stir until toasted, about 5 minutes. Add stock and cover.

3. Cook until most of liquid is absorbed and grain opens.

Serves: 8 (as a side dish)

2 tablespoons vegetable oil
1 small yellow onion, diced
2 celery ribs, diced
1 small carrot, diced
1 garlic clove, minced
1 cup quinoa
2 ½ cups vegetable stock

Chef Michael, who developed this recipe for the classic risotto, prefers to prepare the dish during cooler months. He says that the addition of beef, chicken, or shellfish transforms what is usually a side dish into a hearty meal.

Classic Risotto alla Milanese*

1. In a saucepan, heat olive oil over medium-high heat. Add Arborio; cook 5 minutes, stirring constantly. Add onion and garlic; cook another 5 minutes. Add saffron, mushrooms, and red wine; cook until all liquid is absorbed. Add ½ cup of beef stock; cook, stirring continuously until liquid is absorbed. Keep adding stock in ½-cup increments, stirring constantly. Do not add next ½ cup of stock until previous addition is absorbed. When adding last addition, stir in Parmesan. Salt and pepper to taste. Cook until slightly thickened. From first addition to last addition will take approximately 30 minutes.

2. Remove from heat; let stand 10 minutes before serving.

*Chef Michael says that for an extra-rich flavor, add a beef bone that has been roasted and cut to expose the marrow.

Serves: 10 - 12 (as a side dish)

2 tablespoons olive oil
1 cup Arborio rice
1 yellow onion, diced
6 garlic cloves, minced
½ teaspoon saffron threads
    (or ½ teaspoon turmeric)
½ cup mushrooms, sliced
½ cup red wine
4 ½ cups beef stock (recipe on page 80)
8 ounces Parmesan cheese, grated
salt and pepper to taste

A variation of this Chef Josef recipe, a classic Southern comfort food popular with old and young alike, most likely would have been served at The Grove in the 1950s and 1960s.

Corn Pudding

1. Preheat oven to 300 degrees (F).

2. In a large saucepan, heat milk to boiling point over medium heat. With a whisk, stir in cornmeal, sugar, and salt; simmer on low heat, stirring constantly for 5 minutes or until cornmeal thickens.

3. Remove from heat. Add corn kernels and creamed corn; whisk.

4. In a mixing bowl, beat eggs and vanilla until blended; add to corn mixture and mix well. Blend in baking powder and butter.

5. After all ingredients are blended, pour mixture into baking dish; bake in preheated oven for about 20 minutes or until top of pudding is nicely browned.

Serves: 10

3 ½ cups milk
1 cup yellow cornmeal
3 ½ tablespoons white sugar
⅔ teaspoon salt
1 4-ounce can whole corn kernels, including liquid
1 4-ounce can creamed corn, including liquid
3 large eggs
¼ teaspoon vanilla extract
1 teaspoon baking powder
4 tablespoons unsalted butter, room temperature

Although Chef Josef's research indicated that this side dish was served at VPI in the 1920s for the annual Thanksgiving dinner, probably in the dining hall, Chef Michael uses a similar recipe at The Grove today.

Creamed Potatoes

1. Place potatoes in saucepan; cover with water. Bring to a boil. Reduce heat; cook covered for about 10 minutes, making sure that potatoes are not completely cooked. Drain and set aside.

2. In another saucepan, melt butter or margarine. Stir in flour, salt, and pepper; blend until smooth. Slowly add milk; keep stirring. Bring to a boil, stirring all the time. Cook and stir for about 2 minutes or until thickened. Reduce heat, and simmer for 10 minutes without scorching. This mixture is the cream sauce base, which is like a béchamel sauce.

3. Preheat oven to 325 degrees (F).

4. Mix cream sauce and potatoes; blend carefully, and do not break up potatoes. Pour into buttered casserole dish; bake in preheated oven for about 20 minutes.

5. Sprinkle with paprika and parsley before serving.

Serves: 6

6 medium potatoes, peeled and cut into 1-inch cubes
water
3 tablespoons butter or margarine
¼ cup all-purpose flour
1 teaspoon salt
¼ teaspoon black pepper
2 cups milk
paprika for garnish
fresh parsley for garnish

Chef Josef provided this recipe, which he calls a "traditional Virginia tomato dish," that has probably been served at The Grove in times past.

Stewed Tomatoes*

1. Spray an 8-inch deep baking dish with non-stick spray; set baking dish aside.

2. In a small mixing bowl, combine cornstarch and water; set aside.

3. In a large saucepan, combine tomatoes, including juice, with sugar, salt, and pepper. Bring to a boil over medium heat. Simmer for 1 minute; remove from heat, but leave stove-top eye on. Slowly pour cornstarch mixture into tomatoes, stirring constantly with a wooden spoon. When well blended, return mixture to still-heated stove-top eye; bring tomatoes back to a simmer. Turn heat to low; cook gently for 8 - 10 minutes, stirring occasionally.

4. While tomatoes are simmering, place bread cubes on a baking sheet; place under broiler until lightly browned, about 5 - 8 minutes. Remove from oven, arrange toasted bread cubes over the top of the tomatoes, and then drizzle with melted butter.

5. Preheat oven to 350 degrees (F).

6. Bake, uncovered, in preheated oven for 15 minutes or until temperature reaches 155 degrees (F). Remove from oven; serve hot.

*The tomatoes may be prepared several hours ahead, but they should be topped with the bread cubes and butter just before baking.

Serves: 4

1 tablespoon cornstarch
¼ cup cold water
1 28-ounce can whole tomatoes
½ cup white sugar
salt and ground black pepper to taste
2 cups white bread, cut into
   ½-inch-square cubes
⅓ cup unsalted butter, melted

These croquettes developed by Chef Michael can enhance
a number of soups, particularly potato and leek soup.

Caramelized Shallot and Yukon Gold Croquettes

1. Add potatoes to a pot; cover them with water. Boil potatoes until soft, about 30 minutes. Remove and strain. Mash potatoes or whip with mixer. Whisk in milk, butter, and egg yolks. Season to taste with salt and pepper.

2. In a separate small pan, add shallots in enough water to cover them. Warm over low heat until water evaporates and shallots turn a caramel color and are sticky looking. Blend shallots into potato mixture. Spread on a sheet pan; refrigerate until firm.

3. Remove potato mixture from refrigerator. Form into 1-inch-diameter spheres. Roll in panko; freeze.

4. Preheat oven to 350 degrees (f).

5. Place oil in ovenproof pot. On stovetop, preheat over medium-high heat until temperature reaches at least 350 degrees (F).

6. Remove potato spheres from freezer. Deep fry in preheated oil until light brown. Drain on paper towels. Move to preheated oven; bake for about 10 minutes or until croquettes are hot in the center.

7. Serve with soups.

2 pounds Yukon gold potatoes, peeled and diced
water, divided
½ cup milk
2 tablespoons butter
2 egg yolks
salt and pepper to taste
¼ cup shallots, minced
panko, enough to cover potato spheres
at least 1 quart of oil

Research by Chef Josef revealed that this salad-type dish was served at Virginia Tech in the 1940s, 1950s, and 1960s and, because of its popularity at the time, most likely would have been served at The Grove. The chef recommends that it be used as a side dish with sandwiches.

Southern Chow Chow with Roasted Corn

Cabbage Mixture

In a large bowl, mix ingredients. Pour dressing (recipe below) over cabbage mixture; let stand in refrigerator overnight. Can be kept in refrigerator for up to 1 week.

Serves: 20 - 25

6 cups white cabbage, finely diced
2 cups red onions, finely diced
2 cups red peppers, finely diced
2 cups green peppers, finely diced
6 cups frozen corn, roasted lightly
    in oven with some vegetable oil

Dressing

Combine ingredients; pour into a pot; cook over medium-high heat. Bring to a boil, reduce heat, and simmer for 2 minutes. Cool to room temperature. Remove cloves.

2 cups cider vinegar
4 cloves
1 cup white sugar
½ teaspoon turmeric
2 tablespoons coarse mustard
salt and pepper to taste

Chef Michael suggests that this recipe, which he developed, be prepared and used as a side dish in late fall or winter.

Parsnip Purée

1. Fill large stockpot ¾ full of water; add a generous amount of salt. Bring to a boil; add parsnips and potato. Boil until tender.

2. Meanwhile, in a separate saucepan, heat milk and butter until butter melts; reserve.

3. Remove parsnips and potato from heat; drain. Add to food processor with milk mixture and remaining ingredients. Purée until smooth.

Serves: 8 - 10

generously salted water
1 pound parsnips, peeled and diced
1 large russet potato, peeled and cubed
1 cup milk
2 ounces butter
1 tablespoon salt
1 teaspoon white pepper

Variations

1. For an alternative taste, add ¼ cup roasted shallots or garlic.

2. For a thicker, creamier product, add ¼ cup shredded cheese of your choice.

3. For an earthy flavor to go with beef or mushroom dishes, replace ½ ounce butter with 1 tablespoon truffle oil.

This recipe by Chef Josef is a variation of the black-eyed pea dish traditionally served on New Year's Day, supposedly to bring good luck or to ensure prosperity. Since black-eyed peas have been a staple in the Southern diet for well over a century, a simple variation of this modern recipe was likely served at The Grove.

Black-eyed Peas and Rice (Hoppin' John)

1. Soak peas overnight in about 4 - 5 cups of water. Next day, remove any peas that float; drain remaining peas; discard water.

2. In a stockpot, add 3 to 5 cups clean water; heat over medium heat. Add soaked peas and all remaining ingredients except for ham hock, cayenne, rice, and butter. Cover; bring to a boil; simmer for 1¼ hours or until peas are tender and only a small amount of liquid is left.

3. Pick meat from ham hock; discard ham bone. Add pulled meat to peas in stockpot. Season peas to taste with cayenne.

4. Using an amount of rice that will give each person a small serving, cook according to package directions. Finish cooking, and add butter.

5. Mix rice lightly with peas. Cook peas and rice on low heat for 2 - 3 minutes for flavors to blend. Keep warm until served.

*Hog jowl or a hunk of ham can be substituted.

Serves: 10 - 12

1½ cups dried black-eyed peas, washed
7 - 10 cups water, divided
1 teaspoon salt
1½ cups onions, diced
1 medium-size bay leaf
1 garlic clove, minced
1 ham hock*
pinch of cayenne pepper
packaged rice
1 tablespoon unsalted butter

Chef Michael developed this hearty dish, which makes a great side for pork entrées.

Dark Beer and Caraway Cabbage

1. Salt cabbage; place in a colander over a bowl. Cover with a plate, and place something heavy on top of it. Allow to drain for at least 1 hour; reserve liquid. Move cabbage from colander to a bowl.

2. In a large skillet, heat oil over high heat. Add caraway seeds, reduce heat to medium, and cook for about 5 minutes. Add dark beer, mustard, and drained liquid from cabbage. Bring to a boil; cook until reduced by half. Stir in cabbage; cook for another 10 minutes.

3. Remove and chill before serving.

Serves: 6 - 8

2 tablespoons sea salt
1 head napa cabbage, shredded
1 tablespoon canola oil
1 tablespoon caraway seeds
1 bottle good dark beer, preferably German
¼ cup Dijon mustard

This Chef Michael recipe provides a new twist to an otherwise traditional dish and makes an excellent side to beef dishes.

Whipped Yukon Gold Potatoes with Caramelized Shallots

1. In a small, heavy stockpot, add shallots and half the water. Bring to a boil over high heat. Reduce heat to low; cook until almost all of the water has evaporated. Add more water; cook to reduce again. Continue until all of the water is used. When the last of the water has evaporated, stir shallots vigorously while continuing to cook until shallots are brown and becoming sticky. Remove from heat.

2. In a large stockpot, add potatoes and enough cold water to reach about 2 inches over the potatoes. Bring to a boil over medium-high heat; reduce to a simmer. Cook until very tender, about 20 minutes. Remove pot from heat, and drain potatoes.

3. In a separate pan, add milk and butter. Heat over medium heat until butter is melted. Place milk mixture in a blender. Add shallots; purée on high speed.

4. Put milk mixture and potatoes in a mixing bowl, salt and pepper to taste, and begin to mix on low speed. When all milk is incorporated, turn mixer to high; whip until smooth, about 5 minutes, being careful not to over whip, which will make potatoes become gummy.

Serves: 12 -15

2 cups shallots, peeled and sliced
½ cup water
5 pounds Yukon gold potatoes, peeled and small diced
cold water
1 cup whole milk
2 tablespoons butter
salt and white pepper to taste

Chef Joseph's spin on baked potatoes makes them an especially good side dish for beef, pork, chicken, and fish entrées.

Twice-baked Potatoes

1. Preheat oven to 350 degrees (F).

2. Bake potatoes in preheated oven for 45 - 50 minutes or until a fork inserted into them meets no resistance.

3. While potatoes are baking, fry bacon over medium heat until crisp, strain off grease, dice bacon small, and reserve.

4. When potatoes are done, remove from oven, and let cool somewhat (should still be very warm) until they can be handled. Cutting near the top of each horizontal potato, cut a section off lengthwise; discard tops. Scoop out center into medium bowl, leaving ⅛-inch-thick shell. Using a mixer, beat potatoes for 1 minute. Add 4 tablespoons butter, milk, sour cream, bacon, nutmeg, salt, and pepper; beat until fluffy, but not too loose.

5. Stuff potato skins with mixture**; arrange in a baking dish.

6. Combine cracker meal, paprika, and Parmesan in a small bowl, and sprinkle over overstuffed potatoes. Drizzle melted butter over the topping.

7. Bake in preheated oven for 10 minutes or until very hot. Potatoes should be served immediately after removing them from the oven and garnishing them with chives.

*A fine panko can be substituted.

**Potatoes may be stuffed a day before serving. If preparing a day ahead, keep stuffed potatoes covered and refrigerated until the final baking.

Serves: 4

4 baking potatoes (about 2 ½ pounds), cleaned and dried
4 strips bacon
4 tablespoons unsalted butter, room temperature
½ cup milk
4 tablespoons sour cream
pinch of nutmeg
salt and ground pepper to taste
2 teaspoons cracker meal*
⅛ teaspoon paprika powder
1 teaspoon Parmesan cheese, grated
1 teaspoon unsalted butter, melted
2 tablespoons chives, finely sliced

Chef Michael uses spicy walnuts to perk up his fall and winter salads, but they can also be enjoyed as a stand-alone tasty treat.

Spicy Walnuts

1. Preheat oven to 250 degrees (F).

2. In a saucepan, combine water and 1 cup sugar; bring to a boil over high heat. Add walnuts; continue to boil for 10 minutes. Strain walnuts from liquid; allow walnuts to cool.

3. In a medium bowl, combine 2 tablespoons sugar, salt, and cayenne. Toss cooled walnuts in sugar mixture; pour onto well-oiled sheet pan.

4. Bake in preheated oven until nuts begin to brown, about 20 minutes, stirring every 5 minutes or so.

5. Remove; cool, being sure to scrape walnuts from sheet pan before fully cooled.

Yield: 1 cup

2 cups water
1 cup plus 2 tablespoons white sugar, divided
1 cup walnut meats
1 teaspoon sea salt
1/8 teaspoon cayenne pepper
oil

This Chef Michael recipe adds a sweet but spicy touch to foods that are usually served at receptions. It can be added to salads or salsa, or it can be used as a topping for cakes and other desserts.

Spicy Candied Pecans

1. Preheat oven to 300 degrees (F).

2. In a pot, bring water and 1 cup sugar to a boil. Add nuts; reduce to simmer. Cook for 10 minutes. Pour through strainer, reserving pecans.

3. In a bowl, combine 1/4 cup sugar, cayenne, and salt. Toss nuts in sugar mixture. Bake in oven on oiled baking sheet until nuts are toasted, about 15 - 20 minutes. Remove; allow nuts to cool before serving.

*Any nuts can be used, but time in the oven should be adjusted for the oil content of the nuts to avoid burning.

Yield: 1 cup

2 cups water
1 1/4 cups sugar, divided
1 cup whole pecans*
1/8 teaspoon cayenne pepper
1/4 teaspoon salt
oil

Chef Michael finds this concoction to be a great use of leftover mashed potatoes.

Truffle Potato Dumplings with Brown Butter

1. Combine all ingredients except salted water and sage; refrigerate until firm.

2. Lightly flour work surface. Divide mashed potatoes into 2 parts. Roll each part of potato mixture into a cylinder of about ¼ - ½ inch in diameter.* Slice at ¼-inch intervals. Press thumb into center, which allows the mixture to cook more evenly.

3. If using immediately, drop into pot of simmering salted water. Dumplings are ready when they float to the top.

4. If cooking later, toss with additional flour, place on sheet pan, and refrigerate. When ready to use, remove from refrigerator, and follow above procedure for cooking.

5. Toss cooked dumplings with brown butter (recipe below); serve garnished with sage.

*Dumplings cook better when they are small. If they are too large, they will have to cook in the salted water too long, which will cause them to begin to dissolve.

Yield: 100 ½-ounce dumplings (6 - 8 per person)

½ cup all-purpose flour
2 cups mashed potatoes (russet or other high-starch potatoes), chilled, preferably overnight
2 tablespoons black truffle oil
1 egg plus 1 egg yolk, beaten
fresh sage, minced
salted water, based on ratio of ¼ cup salt to 1 gallon water
sage for garnish

Brown Butter

Melt butter over medium heat. Continue cooking until butter starts to foam and milk fat on bottom turns dark brown.

1 pound butter

From the 1900s into the 1950s, pickles were common fare at the beginning of meals served at VPI (today's Virginia Tech) and probably at The Grove. The pickles were most commonly joined on the menu with bleached celery. Chef Josef uncovered the following old pickle recipe, which he tested and adjusted for modern times.

Sweet Mixed Pickles

1. In a large bowl, combine vegetables, sprinkle with kosher salt, cover with cold water, and let stand overnight. Drain, rinse in freshwater, and drain again.

2. Combine vinegar, honey, and turmeric in a large pot. Tie remaining spices in a small piece of cheesecloth; add them to vinegar mixture. Bring mixture to a boil over medium heat; reduce heat, and simmer for 10 - 12 minutes. Add well-drained vegetables, bring to a boil over medium-high heat, and cook for 1 minute.

3. Pack into hot, sterilized canning jars, leaving ½ inch of space at the top of each jar. Place lids on jars; place jars in boiling water bath for 10 - 12 minutes. Remove jars from boiling water; tighten lids; cool. Jars are sealed when lids pop.

* Mustard seeds, bay leaves, allspice, dill seeds, whole cloves, peppercorns, coriander seeds, juniper berries, and some crushed hot pepper generally comprise pickling spices.

Yield: about 8 quarts

8 cups small cucumbers, diced in
   large cubes
8 cups small pearl onions, peeled
1 large cauliflower, cut into florets
2 large sweet red peppers, seeded
   and cut into small strips
4 cups carrots, peeled and cut
   into wafer shapes
¾ cup fine kosher salt
cold water
8 cups apple-cider vinegar
1 ½ cups honey
½ teaspoon turmeric
2 teaspoons pickling spices*
8 whole cloves
2 teaspoons mustard seeds

When Chef Michael chooses side dishes to serve with dinners at The Grove, he generally prefers to season and then roast, steam, or grill vegetables. According to the chef, roasting and grilling bring the natural sugars out in vegetables, and steaming in a bamboo steamer maintains their flavor and texture.

In the recipe that follows, Chef Michael has taken Brussels sprouts and developed a popular dish to serve at dinners at The Grove. He suggests that cooks think of Brussels sprouts as small heads of cabbage and use them accordingly.

Cider-glazed Brussels Sprouts with Golden Delicious Apples

1. Trim outer leaves of sprouts, cut off stems, and halve. Partially cook in a bamboo steamer or colander placed over a pot of boiling water. Remove from steamer; chill under cold water.

2. In a large skillet over medium heat, fry bacon until browned. Add onion; sauté until beginning to brown. Add flour; stir until well combined and toasted, about 5 minutes. Add remaining ingredients except sprouts and apple. Cook over medium heat until sauce thickens. Stir in sprouts and apple, and heat through, about 5 minutes.

3. Remove from heat; serve immediately.

Serves: 8

1 pound Brussels sprouts
4 ounces apple-wood smoked bacon, diced
1 yellow onion, julienned
2 tablespoons all-purpose flour
1 cup apple cider
1 tablespoon apple-cider vinegar
1 tablespoon brown sugar
1 tablespoon black pepper, coarsely ground
1 golden delicious apple, diced

Asparagus is another vegetable Chef Michael roasts and serves as a side dish for dinners, usually in the winter. He developed this particular recipe to use white asparagus, which is regular asparagus grown in the dark so that it has no chlorophyll and has the earthy profile of mushrooms. The white asparagus can be sautéed and combined with mushrooms, such as shitakes, but in the recipe that follows, Chef Michael uses truffle oil in place of mushrooms.

Roasted White Asparagus with Truffle Oil and Fresh Thyme

1. Preheat oven to 350 degrees (F)

2. In a bowl, toss asparagus with other ingredients; place on a sheet pan. Roast in preheated oven until asparagus begins to brown, about 10 - 15 minutes.

3. Remove from oven; serve immediately.

Serves: 8

1 pound white asparagus spears, bottom third removed
2 tablespoons truffle oil
2 tablespoons sea salt
1 teaspoon coarse ground pepper
2 tablespoons fresh thyme

Oyster dressing is a Southern-type addition to a meal featuring turkey and generally is served during the Thanksgiving season. This recipe, uncovered—and updated—by Chef Josef, was probably served at The Grove in times past.

Oyster Dressing

1. Preheat oven to 375 degrees (F).

2. Drain oysters, reserving liquid. Set aside.

3. In a skillet, heat oil over medium-high heat. Add onions, celery, bell peppers, salt, and cayenne; sauté for approximately 5 minutes or until vegetables are soft. Add garlic and parsley; cook for 30 seconds. Add water; cook 2 - 4 minutes, stirring constantly. Add green onions; fold in oyster liquid. Stir to mix well; remove from heat.

4. In a large mixing bowl, combine bread cubes and vegetable mixture; fold in cheese and oysters. Butter baking pan; pour mixture into pan; bake for 1 hour or until bubbly and golden brown.

5. Sprinkle parsley over baked oyster dressing (stuffing) before serving.

Serves: 4 - 6

1 pint shucked oysters with liquid
2 tablespoons vegetable oil
2 cups onions, chopped
1 cup celery, diced
1 cup green bell peppers, diced
1 ½ teaspoons salt
½ teaspoon cayenne pepper
1 tablespoon garlic, minced
1 teaspoon parsley, chopped
1 cup water
¼ cup green onions, finely sliced
4 cups French bread or homemade white bread, cut into 1-inch cubes
⅓ cup fresh Parmesan cheese, grated
2 teaspoons sweet unsalted butter
parsley for garnish

Chef Michael demonstrated how to cook this savory bread pudding recipe for the Virginia Tech Faculty Women's Club in 2006. He suggests using it as an alternative to dressing and serving it with turkey,* or it can be used as an appetizer (see variations below).

Herbed Bread Pudding with Sage and Toasted Walnuts**

1. Preheat oven to 300 degrees (F).

2. In a bowl, combine bread and walnuts; hold in reserve.

3. In a sauté pan, melt 2 tablespoons butter; add all vegetables. Cook over medium-high heat until vegetables are soft. Add to bread and walnuts.

4. In a saucepan, scald milk, cream, and remaining butter over medium heat. Turn off the heat. Add sage; steep for 5 minutes.

5. In a separate bowl, beat egg yolks, salt, and pepper. Add ½ cup of milk mixture very slowly into egg mixture to avoid cooking the eggs into solids, beating constantly. Pour egg mixture into remaining milk mixture, beating constantly. Cool. Pour over bread and walnuts.

6. Pour mixture into greased pan or individual baking cups. Bake in preheated oven for 35 - 40 minutes, less for individual portions, or until set.

Variations

1. For a different approach, pour gravy over the bread pudding. To make the gravy, bring 4 cups of your favorite stock to a boil, and thicken with a mixture of 8 tablespoons butter and ¾ cup flour that has been combined over medium heat to form a roux (a mixture of fat and flour that is cooked to varying degrees for extra flavor and to thicken sauces, soups, and gravies).

2. To use as a holiday hors d'oeuvre, cook bread pudding, and allow to cool. Cut out small rounds of bread; top each with a turkey slice and cranberry mayonnaise (equal parts mayonnaise and cranberry sauce mixed together).

*When using with turkey, pour pan drippings from turkey over the pudding, then reheat in a covered pan in a 275-degree (F) preheated oven for 20 minutes.

**Recipe can be prepared a day ahead of use.

†Toast the nuts for about 10 minutes in an oven preheated to 350 degrees (F).

Serves: 12

12 cups stale herbed bread, cubed
2 cups walnuts, toasted† and then
   roughly chopped
4 tablespoons butter, divided
1 small yellow onion, diced
2 small carrots, peeled and diced
4 celery ribs, small diced
1 ½ cups milk
3 cups heavy cream
1 cup fresh sage, finely chopped
10 egg yolks
1 tablespoon salt
1 tablespoon black pepper

Crème Brûlée

Desserts and Fruit Concoctions

Chef Michael has developed this version of a risotto that can be served as a dessert. Risotto, an Italian rice dish, generally involves cooking rice in a broth until it becomes creamy, like porridge. The classic risotto alla Milanese includes mushrooms and saffron in the dish, but the chef has put a new spin on the classic dish.

Mocha Risotto with Almonds

1. Heat oil in a large saucepan over medium heat. Add rice; sauté until translucent, about 5 - 10 minutes. Add cocoa and espresso; cook until combined, about 1 - 2 minutes. Start adding cream 1 cup at a time. Cook after each cup is added until all liquid is absorbed, about 5 minutes, before adding next cup. Keep adding until all cream is added and absorbed. Add sugar with last cream addition.

2. Turn heat to low; add almond butter, cheese, amaretto, and extract. Cook for about 5 - 10 minutes or until well combined. Risotto should have a creamy oatmeal-like consistency. Turn off heat, and stir in chocolate chips.

3. Garnish with almonds, and serve immediately.

*If almond oil cannot be found at the store, it can be produced by pressing almonds or by altering the way the almonds are toasted in the recipe. When the almonds are toasted, put them in a sauté pan with ¼ cup vegetable oil. After the nuts are toasted, strain off the oil, and use that oil, which will have acquired an almond flavor.

**To make vanilla cream, steep 5 cups of cream with 1 vanilla bean, cut and scraped, over low heat for 20 minutes. The low heat will help infuse the vanilla flavor into the cream without cooking it. Cool and chill. Strain off cream for use in recipe.

Serves: 6

2 tablespoons almond oil*
1 cup Arborio rice
¼ cup cocoa powder
2 tablespoons espresso powder
5 cups vanilla cream**
1 cup white sugar
¼ cup almond butter
8 ounces mascarpone cheese
½ cup amaretto
¼ teaspoon almond extract
1 cup semi-sweet chocolate chips
1 cup sliced almonds, toasted

Another popular dessert at The Grove is this delectable Chef Michael concoction.

Chocolate Soufflé Cake

1. Preheat oven to 325 degrees (F). Butter and line the bottom of 16 6-ounce ramekins with parchment paper.

2. In a bowl over simmering water, melt butter and chocolate. Add egg yolks one at a time; stir into chocolate mixture.

3. Remove from heat; add vanilla and 3 tablespoons sugar. Put aside.

4. In a mixing bowl, beat egg whites with salt until soft peaks form. Gradually add remaining sugar. Continue to beat until stiff peaks form.

5. Whisk ¼ of whipped egg whites into chocolate mixture to lighten its density. Gradually fold in remaining whipped egg whites. Pour batter into ramekins, filling each about ¾ full. Bake in preheated oven about 40 minutes. Allow to cool (cake will fall).

6. To serve, turn out onto plate; top with caramel, chocolate, or raspberry coulis sauce (recipes on pages 105, 106, and 105, respectively).

Serves: 16

2 sticks (1 cup) butter
8 ounces chocolate (between 60 and 70 percent cocoa)
5 eggs, separated
1 tablespoon vanilla extract
6 tablespoons white sugar, run through a processor, divided
1 teaspoon salt
parchment paper

Chef Michael's gingerbread is a special treat for guests visiting The Grove during the winter holidays. The chef's special version is served with caramelized pears and roasted grapes and topped with rum cream.

Gingerbread with Caramelized Pears, Roasted Grapes, and Rum Cream

Soft Gingerbread

1. Preheat oven to 350 degrees (F). Grease a 12 x 6-inch baking pan; set aside.

2. Place butter, sugar, and molasses in a mixing bowl; cream, using a mixer set on medium speed. Turn off mixer; scrape down sides of bowl. Add 1 egg, and turn speed to slow. When egg is incorporated, add the other egg, and mix until incorporated. Add buttermilk; mix on slow speed to combine.

3. In a separate bowl, mix together flours, baking powder, baking soda, and salt. Add cloves, mace, cinnamon, ginger, and cayenne. With mixer on slow, add flour mixture in several additions to sugar/egg mixture, combining each addition before the next one is added.

4. Pour batter into prepared baking dish. Bake in preheated oven for 25 - 30 minutes or until toothpick inserted into batter comes out clean.

5. Cut into squares.

6. Prepare caramelized pears (recipe below), roasted grapes (recipe on facing page), and rum cream (recipe on facing page).

7. To assemble, place gingerbread on plate. Lean pear against gingerbread; pour caramel sauce (see step 7 of recipe below) over pear. Sprinkle with roasted grapes, and top with rum cream.

Serves: 10

4 ounces butter, cut into cubes
½ cup packed light brown sugar
¼ cup molasses
2 eggs
½ cup buttermilk
1 cup all-purpose flour
1 cup wheat flour
1 teaspoon baking powder
½ teaspoon baking soda
1 teaspoon sea salt
¼ teaspoon cloves
½ teaspoon mace
1 tablespoon cinnamon plus cinnamon for garnish
¼ cup fresh ginger, grated
dash of cayenne pepper

Caramelized Pears

1. Preheat oven to 250 degrees (F).

2. Cut pears in half. Place on sheet pan; roast in preheated oven until soft, about 30 - 60 minutes. Remove from oven; allow to cool. Remove core and stems.

4. In a saucepan, bring apple cider, brown sugar, and vinegar to a boil over medium-high heat. Reduce heat to low. Add cinnamon, allspice, and cloves.

5 Bosc pears
1 cup apple cider
1 cup packed brown sugar
2 tablespoons pear-infused vinegar
2 cinnamon sticks
½ teaspoon ground allspice
⅛ teaspoon ground cloves
1 vanilla bean
2 tablespoons butter

(continued on page 165)

5. Cut vanilla bean in half, and scrape out seeds. Add bean and seeds to cider mixture. Add pears; cook over low heat, occasionally spooning sauce over pears. Cook for 30 minutes or until sauce becomes syrupy. Remove vanilla bean.

6. Remove pears; reserve.

7. Whisk butter into syrupy mixture to make caramel sauce.

Roasted Grapes*

1. Preheat oven to 200 degrees (F).

2. Remove grapes from stem. Place on a parchment-lined sheet pan. Roast in preheated oven until grapes begin to shrivel, about 5 hours.

3. Remove; let cool.

4. Place grapes in a container; pour brandy over them.

*Can be prepared a day ahead of use.

1 bunch seedless grapes
½ cup pear brandy
parchment paper

Rum Cream

In a small bowl, combine all ingredients; mix well.

1 cup mascarpone cheese
½ cup powdered sugar
1 teaspoon vanilla extract
½ teaspoon rum flavoring

Chef Michael developed this heavenly treat, which he demonstrated at The Grove for the Virginia Tech Faculty Women's Club in February 2009.

Chocolate Truffles

1. In a saucepan, bring cream and butter to boil over high heat. Reduce heat to medium. Add chocolate; whisk until smooth.

2. Remove from heat; whip in sour cream. Allow to cool at room temperature for about 1 hour.

3. Form into 1-tablespoon-size balls; refrigerate. After balls become cold, remove from refrigerator; roll in cocoa powder.

Variations

1. Add flavorings such as vanilla extract, orange, mint, almond extract, or maple sugar.

2. Add liqueurs such as framboise, amaretto, Grand Marnier, or frangelico.

3. Dip in melted white chocolate or bittersweet chocolate.

4. Roll in coconut, finely chopped nuts, or crushed Oreos.

Yield: about 24

½ cup plus 1 tablespoon whipping cream
6 tablespoons unsalted butter
1 ⅛ pounds bittersweet chocolate
6 tablespoons sour cream
cocoa powder

A version of this dessert has been served at The Grove for years, and it remains a favorite with guests, whatever the occasion.

Apple Cream Cheese Torte

1. Preheat oven to 350 degrees (F).

2. For crust, whip butter, sugar, and vanilla until smooth. Stir in flour to form dough. Press dough into bottom of 10-inch pie pan.

3. Bake in preheated oven until crust begins to brown. Remove and let cool. Place in freezer for 1 hour.

4. For filling, combine cream cheese, sugar, eggs, and vanilla; whip until smooth. Pour over crust.

5. For topping, toss apples with sugar and cinnamon until coated. Let sit for 10 minutes. Layer over cream cheese mixture.

6. Bake in preheated oven until set, about 20 minutes. Allow to cool.

7. Slice into 8 pieces.

Serves: 8

Crust
⅓ cup unsalted butter
⅓ cup white sugar
1 teaspoon vanilla
1 ¼ cups all-purpose flour, sifted

Filling
10 ounces cream cheese
¼ cup white sugar
2 eggs
1 teaspoon vanilla extract

Topping
4 apples, peeled and thinly sliced
2 tablespoons white sugar
1 teaspoon cinnamon

Chef Michael slices apples for his apple cream cheese torte. After preparing the apples, he arranges them on top of the torte.

The fruit prepared using this recipe developed by Chef Michael is a fall favorite at The Grove.

Roasted Fall Fruit

1. Preheat oven to 350 degrees (F).

2. Cut pears, apples, and nectarines in half; place cut side down in a shallow baking dish. Cover with cider; add cinnamon sticks. Cook in preheated oven until fruit softens.*

3. Remove apples first; then nectarines; and, lastly, pears. Allow fruit to cool.

4. Pour apple cider and cinnamon sticks from baking dish into a pot. Add cloves and allspice; bring to a boil. Add arrowroot/water; cook until slightly thickened.

5. Strain, reserving cinnamon sticks for garnish.

6. To serve, spoon out cores of apples and pears; cut fruit into bite-size pieces. Place pieces in a bowl, garnish with blackberries and cinnamon sticks, and pour cider sauce over the concoction.

*Different types of fruit cook at different speeds. Apples cook in about 5 - 10 minutes, nectarines about 15 - 20 minutes, and pears about 30 - 40 minutes.

Serves: 6 - 8

2 Bosc pears
2 pink lady apples
2 nectarines, pits removed
2 cups apple cider
6 - 8 cinnamon sticks
1 teaspoon whole cloves
1 teaspoon whole allspice
2 tablespoons arrowroot combined
   with 2 tablespoons water
1 pint fresh blackberries for garnish

Chef Michael uses this sweet concoction as a dessert at fall receptions and dinners.

White Chocolate Pumpkin Bars

1. Preheat oven to 350 degrees (F). Butter a 12 x 6-inch baking dish; line with parchment paper.

2. In a mixing bowl, cream sugar and butter together. Add vanilla, pumpkin purée, and egg; mix to combine. Add chips.

3. In a separate bowl, combine flour, baking powder, salt, and spices. Stir into pumpkin mixture.

4. Pour batter into baking dish; cover with pecans. Bake in preheated oven for 25 - 30 minutes or until a toothpick inserted into mixture comes out clean.

5. Let cool at least 10 minutes before cutting into 2 x 1-inch squares.

*To purée, cut fresh pumpkin in half, remove pulp and seeds, cover halves with aluminum foil, and bake in 325-degree (F) oven for 1 hour or until tender. Scrape meat from skin into a food processor or blender, and purée.

Yield: approximately 30 bars

¾ cup packed light brown sugar
4 ounces unsalted butter, softened
1 tablespoon vanilla extract
½ cup pumpkin purée*
1 large egg
1 cup white chocolate chips
1 ¼ cups all-purpose flour
½ teaspoon baking powder
¼ teaspoon salt
1 teaspoon cinnamon
½ teaspoon allspice
½ teaspoon mace
¼ teaspoon cloves
1 cup spicy candied pecans (recipe on page 153)
parchment paper

A few extra ingredients can turn a cup of hot chocolate into a delectable drink. This recipe developed by Chef Michael features several variations that can change the taste of the hot chocolate to suit one's palate.

Mexican Hot Chocolate

1. Combine all ingredients, except garnish, and heat in a saucepan over moderate heat; do not boil. Stir constantly until chocolate is melted.

2. Strain and pour into cups.

3. Garnish with a pinch of cinnamon before serving.

Variations

1. Add 1 cup white sugar.

2. Add 1 chilli pepper.

Serves: 4

1 quart skim milk
8 ounces unsweetened chocolate
1 tablespoon vanilla extract
4 cinnamon sticks
1 teaspoon whole cloves
ground cinnamon for garnish

*This sweet bread pudding, developed by Chef Michael, was
used in his bread-pudding cooking demonstration at The Grove
in February 2006.*

Black Forest Bread Pudding

1. Preheat oven to 350 degrees (F).

2. Add pumpernickel and chocolate to a bowl.

3. In a saucepan, scald milk, cream, and butter over medium heat.

4. In a separate bowl, beat egg yolks, vanilla, and sugar until lemony
   in color. Add cocoa powder; whisk until blended. Temper ½ cup
   of milk mixture into egg yolk mixture, whisking constantly. Pour
   egg mixture into remaining milk mixture, blending well. Cool.
   Add reserved maraschino cherry juice.

5. Pour milk mixture over bread/chocolate mixture. Allow to sit
   until bread has absorbed all liquid.

6. Pour into greased 12 x 6-inch pan or individual ramekins; bake
   in preheated oven 35 - 40 minutes, less for individual portions,
   or until set. Serve with warm kirsch sauce (recipe on page 106).

*Cherries can be used for garnishing, if desired.

Serves: 12

12 cups stale pumpernickel bread,
   cut into cubes
10 ounces bittersweet chocolate chips
10 ounces milk chocolate chips
¾ cup milk
3 cups heavy cream
2 tablespoons butter
10 egg yolks
1 tablespoon vanilla extract
1 cup white sugar
3 tablespoons cocoa powder
1 16-ounce jar maraschino cherries,
   drained and juice reserved•

Chef Josef based this recipe on one developed by Chef Michael. The recipe for the Grand Marnier glaze, which goes so well with the pudding, is a Chef Michael creation.

White Chocolate Cranberry Bread Pudding with Grand Marnier Glaze

1. In saucepan, scald milk, cream, and butter over medium heat.

2. Preheat oven to 350 degrees (F).

3. In a separate bowl, whisk egg yolks with sugar until lemony in color. Slowly add ½ cup milk/butter mixture, whisking continuously. Pour egg mixture, a little at a time, into remaining milk/butter mixture, whisking constantly. Add vanilla; let cool.

4. Pour custard mixture over bread; let sit until bread has absorbed liquid. Add chocolate chips and cranberries.

5. Bake in a 12 x 6-inch pan in preheated oven for 30 minutes.

6. Remove pan; turn oven to broil.

7. Pour Grand Marnier glaze over top of bread pudding; put back in oven on lowest rack. Cook until bread begins to toast on top, about 5 minutes.

Serves: 12

1 ½ cups milk
3 cups heavy cream
2 ounces unsalted butter
10 egg yolks
1 ½ cups white sugar
1 tablespoon vanilla extract
2 medium loaves French bread,
    cut into cubes and left out to get stale
1 11-ounce bag white chocolate chips
1 12-ounce bag dried cranberries
Grand Marnier glaze (recipe below)

Grand Marnier Glaze

1. Combine all ingredients except butter in a saucepan; cook over medium-high heat until syrupy, about 10 - 15 minutes.

2. Remove from heat; whip in butter.

3. Serve as a sauce with desserts in addition to using as a glaze for white chocolate cranberry bread pudding (recipe above).

Yield: about 1¾ cups

1 cup Grand Marnier liqueur
½ cup brown sugar
2 tablespoons champagne vinegar
½ cup European-style orange
    marmalade
2 tablespoons butter

Pound cake continues to be one of the most popular desserts and most likely has been served at the president's home numerous times. Preparing this Chef Josef recipe results in a rich dessert that goes well with ice cream or berries—or as a stand-alone treat.

Pound Cake

1. Preheat oven to 350 degrees (F). Butter and flour a 9 x 5-inch loaf pan; set it aside.

2. Mix butter and sugar thoroughly, until mixture is light in color and sugar has dissolved. Scrape down the sides of the bowl. Add eggs, one at a time, beating completely and scraping the sides and bottom of the bowl after each addition. Add vanilla and lemon rind. Mix 1 minute on slow speed.

3. In a separate bowl, combine flour and baking powder; gradually add to batter, mixing on low speed about ½ minute or until well mixed.

4. Pour into prepared loaf pan. Bake in middle of preheated oven 50 - 60 minutes or until a clean wooden toothpick inserted in center of cake comes out clean. The cake should be golden brown.

5. Turn the cake out onto a wire rack to cool. To store, wrap cake in plastic wrap, and refrigerate for up to 3 days.

Serves: 18 (½-inch slices)

¾ cup unsalted butter, room temperature
1 cup white sugar
5 large eggs, room temperature
½ teaspoon vanilla extract
½ lemon rind, grated
1 ½ cups all-purpose flour
½ teaspoon baking powder

Chef Michael developed this recipe for a cooking class he taught for hotel and tourism management students at Virginia Tech. He later used the recipe as part of a cooking demonstration on bread pudding for the Faculty Women's Club. He created the recipe as an illustration of how to prepare bread pudding that is not, he says, "just your raisin and rum dish of old."

White Chocolate Bread Pudding

1. Preheat oven to 350 degrees (F).

2. Place brioche in a bowl; add white chocolate.

3. In a saucepan, scald milk, cream, and butter over medium heat.

4. In a separate bowl, whisk egg yolks and sugar until lemony in color. Temper ½ cup of milk mixture into egg yolk/sugar mixture, whisking constantly. Pour egg mixture, a little at a time, into remaining milk mixture, whisking constantly. Add vanilla. Cool.

5. Pour custard mixture over brioche and white chocolate; allow to sit until liquid is absorbed.

6. Pack into greased 12 x 6-inch pan or individual-portion cups; bake in preheated oven 35 - 40 minutes, less time if cooking individual portions.

7. Serve with amaretto sauce (recipe on page 104).

Serves: 12

12 cups stale brioche bread, cubed
11 ounces white chocolate chips
1 ½ cups milk
3 cups heavy cream
2 ounces butter
10 egg yolks
1 ½ cups white sugar
2 tablespoons vanilla extract

A Southern-style recipe, this soufflé may have been served at The Grove during the 1940s. The recipe is Chef Josef's revision of one he uncovered while conducting research for this book.

Rhubarb Soufflé

1. Preheat oven to 375 degrees (F).

2. Beat whites of eggs to stiff froth, add baking powder, and then fold into rhubarb mixture. Pour into a well-greased baking dish. Cover with crumbs.

3. Set baking dish in a pan of hot water; bake in preheated oven about 30 minutes or until firm, well puffed up, and delicately browned on top.

4. Serve hot with crème anglaise (recipe on page 104).

*In preparing rhubarb and many other fruit sauces, the use of all-phosphate baking powder makes it possible to use about half the usual amount of sugar and also neutralizes acidity.

Serves: 6

3 egg whites
½ teaspoon all-phosphate baking powder*
3 cups thick-stewed rhubarb (recipe below)
1 cupcake or macaroon crumbs
water

Thick-stewed Rhubarb

1. Wash rhubarb, cut into small pieces, and place in a saucepan. Add a small amount of water, and cook on low temperature. Add additional water as necessary so rhubarb does not dry out; cook until fibers are broken down, about 1 - 2 hours.

2. To the stewed rhubarb, add sugar, butter, and egg yolks. Cook slightly.

Yield: about 3 cups

1 ½ pounds rhubarb
water
1 cup white sugar
3 tablespoons butter, melted
3 egg yolks, well beaten

This white version of the brownie is one of Chef Michael's popular sweets served at receptions.

Blondies

1. Preheat oven to 325 degrees (F). Butter bottom of 12 x 9-inch baking dish. Line bottom with parchment paper.

2. In a bowl, combine white chocolate, butter, and vanilla; place over pot of simmering water. Stir until butter and chocolate are melted. Remove; allow to cool slightly.

3. In a separate bowl, whisk eggs and sugar until mixture becomes a lemony color and ribbons form off whisk. Gradually whisk chocolate mixture into eggs.

4. In another bowl, combine flour, baking powder, and salt. Pour flour mixture over chocolate mixture; stir to combine. Pour batter into baking dish; rap dish lightly on table a few times to even out batter.

5. Bake in preheated oven for about 45 minutes or until a toothpick inserted in the mixture comes out clean. For more chewy blondies, bake for less time.

Yield: 24

8 ounces fine white chocolate, chopped
8 ounces butter
1 tablespoon vanilla extract
4 eggs
1 ½ cups white sugar
2 ½ cups all-purpose flour
1 tablespoon baking powder
1 teaspoon salt
parchment paper

Chef Michael often prepares his brownies for receptions, and since they are so tasty, he sometimes uses them as a dessert, topped with a sweet sauce and garnished with fresh berries.

Brownies

1. Preheat oven to 325 degrees (F). Butter bottom of 12 x 6-inch baking dish; line with parchment paper.

2. Melt butter in a pot until butter foams and milk fat browns on bottom of pot. Remove from heat; stir in cocoa powder. Allow to cool somewhat. Whisk in chocolate.

3. In a separate bowl, whisk eggs, sugar, and vanilla until lemony in color and ribbons come from whisk. Gradually whisk chocolate mixture into egg mixture.

4. In another bowl, combine flour, baking powder, and salt. Pour flour mixture over chocolate mixture; stir flour in. Pour batter into prepared baking dish.

5. Bake in preheated oven for 45 minutes or until a toothpick inserted into the mixture comes out clean. For more chewy brownies, bake for less time.

Yield: 24

8 ounces butter
1 tablespoon cocoa powder
8 ounces bittersweet chocolate
   (60 - 70 percent cocoa)
4 eggs
2 cups white sugar
1 tablespoon vanilla extract
1 ¾ cups all-purpose flour
1 tablespoon baking powder
½ teaspoon salt
parchment paper

Guests at The Grove have made Chef Michael's crème brûlée a popular dessert, and he serves it often.

Crème Brûlée

Custard

1. Preheat oven to 325 degrees (F).

2. In a saucepot, combine cream, vanilla bean, and ½ cup sugar. Heat until sugar is dissolved into cream.

3. Remove from heat; let sit for 15 - 30 minutes. Remove vanilla bean; reserve.

4. Temper* cream mixture into egg yolks. Stir in salt. Strain through sieve to remove any eggs that solidified.

5. Pour custard mixture into ramekins; place in shallow baking dish. Pour enough boiling water into baking dish to come half way up the outsides of the ramekins. Cover dish with aluminum foil; bake in preheated oven until set, about 35 - 40 minutes.

6. Chill at least 3 hours in refrigerator.

7. Remove brûlées from refrigerator at least 15 minutes before serving. Top each with vanilla sugar; use blowtorch to caramelize sugar before serving.

*Whisk cream gradually into egg yolks so that the yolks are not cooked into solids.

Vanilla Sugar

1. Pat reserved bean dry with paper towel.

2. Place sugar and bean into food processor. Process for about 5 minutes; strain through a mesh sieve.

3. Use 1/3 cup of mixture with custard; save remaining sugar for other uses, such as replacing regular sugar in dessert recipes to add a vanilla flavor.

Serves: 6 (6-ounce servings)

2 cups heavy cream
1 vanilla bean, cut open and scraped
½ cup white sugar
4 egg yolks
¼ teaspoon salt
⅓ cup vanilla sugar (recipe below)

Yield: 2 cups

vanilla bean reserved from recipe above
2 cups white sugar

Chef Michael prepares this dessert as an after-dinner treat.

Crème Caramel

Custard

1. Preheat oven to 325 degrees (F).

2. In a saucepot over medium heat, combine cream, vanilla bean and seeds, and sugar. Heat to dissolve sugar into cream.

3. Remove from heat; temper into egg yolks. Stir in salt. Strain through sieve; reserve.

4. Prepare caramel (recipe below). Spoon caramel into ramekins just enough to cover bottoms of ramekins.

5. Pour custard mixture into ramekins over top of caramel; place in shallow baking dish. Pour enough boiling water into baking dish to cover ramekins half way up the outsides of the ramekins. Cover dish with aluminum foil; bake in preheated oven until set, about 35 - 40 minutes.

6. Serve in ramekins, or unmold and garnish with berries.

Serves: 7 (6-ounce servings)

2 cups heavy cream
1 vanilla bean, cut open and seeded
½ cup white sugar
6 egg yolks
¼ teaspoon salt

Caramel

Combine sugar and water in a saucepot. Cook over medium heat until sugar dissolves. Bring to a boil, using a pastry brush and cold water to brush down crystals that form on pan sides. Allow sugar to boil until it becomes a dark golden brown. Sugar will cook quickly from the time it begins to brown, so be careful not to burn. When ready, briefly dip bottom of pan into cold water to stop cooking.

⅓ cup white sugar
⅔ cup water

Menus from The Grove

Over the years, guests at The Grove have enjoyed a variety of events that were accompanied by a diversity of foods. The menus that follow are representative of the eras in which they were used, and when possible, the guests and specific dates of the events are included. Some of the menus contain generic names without identifying what comprised the particular dish, while others contain dishes for which this book provides no recipes. The menus are presented here solely for informational purposes for readers who are interested in what combinations of food items were put together for dinners, luncheons, breakfasts, teas, and receptions held at Virginia Tech's residence for its presidents.

A Menu from the Burruss Administration

Banquet at VPI
(probably not in the President's Home)
in 1933 – 1934
Chicken with dressing and gravy
Cranberry sauce, stuffed eggs, pickles
Fancy sweet potatoes
Green stringless beans
Corn pudding
Combination salad
Hot rolls, butter
Iced tea, coffee
Strawberry shortcake

Menus from the Newman Administration
(taken from Mrs. Newman's handwritten notes)

Saturday night
Chicken salad
Ham
Butter beans
Rolls
Tomatoes on lettuce
Pickled peach
Celery, carrots, olives
Pie

Sunday dinner
Fried chicken
Rice
Peas
Corn pudding
Sliced tomato salad
Ice cream
Cake
Tea or coffee

Dinner
Fried chicken
Gravy
Diced potatoes
Beets
Asparagus
Celery
Hot rolls
Coffee
2nd course—heart lettuce with dressing
3rd course—chocolate pie

Afternoon tea
Chicken salad
Sliced ham
Large pickled peach
Hot biscuits
Iced tea
[illegible] in shell shape or fan shape holding
strawberry ice cream and whipped cream on top
2 kinds of small square cakes
candy

Class of 1905 at 1955 homecoming
Sandwiches
Chicken salad
Olive and cream cheese
Cream cheese seasoned with Worcestershire
Ham biscuits
Potato chips
Celery, olives, and carrots,
Coffee
Yellow mints

Menus from the McComas Administration

**Luncheon for homecoming king and queen
candidates on September 20, 1989**
Citrus/avocado salad
Chicken breast with lemon sauce
Rice pilaf
Carrots and dill pickles
Rolls
Ice cream with sauce

**Buffet Dinner for Bob Edwards,
host of "Morning Edition" on National Public
Radio, on February 15, 1990**
Tomato juice cocktail
Tossed salad
Salmon fillets with hollandaise (glazed)
with a little tomato paste for color
Broiled tomatoes with cheese
Rice pilaf
Sesame chicken
Rolls and butter
Kentucky or chocolate pie
Ice cream

**Luncheon for board of visitors' spouses
on February 5, 1990**
Tossed salad with vinegar and oil
and French mustard vinaigrette
Ravioli with tomato sauce and Parmesan cheese
Scallops au gratin
Parsley broiled potato
Fresh vegetables
Croissants
Chiffon pie
Lemon ice cream
Peach parfait

**Tea for mothers of university faculty members
on March 5, 1990**
Punch
Coffee
Meringue cookies
Brownies
Minted butter with lamb loin canapés
Butter and radish tea sandwiches
Butter and watercress sandwiches
Short bread
Butter mints

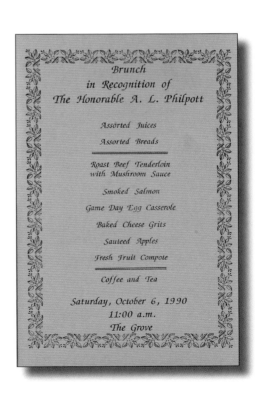

Brunch
in Recognition of
The Honorable A. L. Philpott

Assorted Juices

Assorted Breads

Roast Beef Tenderloin
with Mushroom Sauce

Smoked Salmon

Game Day Egg Casserole

Baked Cheese Grits

Sauteed Apples

Fresh Fruit Compote

Coffee and Tea

Saturday, October 6, 1990
11:00 a.m.
The Grove

**Breakfast for special English visitors
on March 20, 1990**
Cheese omelet (pear and braised lettuce)
Fresh fruit (grapes, strawberries, pear)
Cinnamon toast
Fresh orange juice
Pecan sticky buns
Coffee and tea

**Buffet dinner for National Merit Scholars
on March 22, 1990**
Tossed salad with Ranch dressing
Seafood Newburg
Beef tenderloin pepper steak
Rice pilaf
Croissants
Zucchini and summer squash sauté
Plain cheesecake with a variety of toppings

**Reception for Ut Prosim members
on April 7, 1990**
Shrimp mold with crackers
Egg rolls
Scallop ceviche
Stuffed mushrooms
Chicken mousse
Shrimp cocktail
Artichoke Parmesan pizza
Cashews and peanuts
California sushi roll
Bacon-wrapped scallops
Baked brie
Lamb mint canapés
Ham and white asparagus canapés
Prosciutto ham and melon

**Dinner for Alexander Gerasimov,
USSR press secretary, on April 17, 1990**
Fresh strawberries
Vegetable salad of cauliflower, broccoli,
carrots, and onions
Beef bourguignon
Seafood Newburg
Rice pilaf
Croissants
Petit fours
French pastry

Menus from the Torgersen Administration

**Deli buffet luncheon for track, field,
and wrestling teams and coaches
on February 8, 1996**
Beef
Turkey
Ham
American and Swiss cheeses
Potato salad
Broccoli salad
Relish tray of sweet and dill pickles, olives
Mayonnaise
Mustard (yellow and Dijon)
Cookies
Brownies
Lemon Squares

**Dinner for dignitaries
at ceremony announcing formation
of the Virginia Tech Corps of Cadets Center
for Leader Development on April 25, 1996**
Sautéed shrimp Florentine with sauce Mornay
Grilled beef tenderloin with sauce Bercy
Sautéed fresh mixed garden vegetables
Potato pancakes
Blueberry yogurt torte
Assorted breads (Parmesan biscuits; Italian,
olive breads; bacon rolls; corn muffins)

Let's get together for dinner!
"Old" and "New" Deans
Thursday, September 10th
6:30 .m., at The Grove
R.S.V.P.:
231-7525   *Paul and Dot Torgersen*

Menus from the Steger Administration

Dinner for Ron Brown Scholar Applicants on April 14, 2006
Caesar salad with garlic croutons
Chicken Marsala with mushrooms and crabmeat
Saffron rice pilaf
Asparagus
Brownie with chocolate sauce and fresh berries

Dinner for new diverse faculty and staff on September 24, 2008
Spinach salad with lump crab, avocado,
hard-boiled egg, and pistachio vinaigrette
Seared beef tenderloin with roasted tomatoes
and burgundy wine sauce
-or-
Pesto-crusted halibut with creamed fennel
and roasted tomatoes
-or-
Vegetarian: nothern bean Wellington
with purple basil, pine nuts, roasted tomatoes,
and puréed eggplant
Whipped potatoes with caramelized shallots
Fresh vegetable
Fudge brownie with caramel and chocolate sauces
and fresh berries

Dinner for board of visitors on May 31, 2009
Smoked king salmon with dilled new potatoes,
capers, and micro greens
Grilled veal chops with morels
and red wine demi-glace
Rosemary roasted fingerling potatoes
and braised fennel
Ricotta cheesecake with Marsala wine
and strawberries with balsamic syrup

Dinner for students in undergraduate honors seminar, taught by President Steger and Professor Paul Knox, on May 4, 2010
Batavian and frisée lettuce, lemon Stilton, and
grape relish with raspberry Dijon vinaigrette
Crab cake with avocado mousse
Inca red quinoa pilaf
Pink and purple asparagus
Baby carrots
Blondie with peach ice cream

Dinner in Honor of Ginney Fowler and Nikki Giovanni on May 29. 2010
Batavian and frisée lettuce
Grilled pink and purple asparagus
Sungold tomotoes and herb vinaigrette
Beef tenderloin
Adirondack blue potatoes
Roasted root vegetables
Hen of the woods mushrooms
Chocolate soufflé cake
Vanilla ice cream

Reception for Faculty Women's Club on September 14, 2011
Fruit punch
Heirloom tomato, smoked eggplant,
and basil finger sandwiches
Cucumber and watercress sandwiches
Grilled vegetables
Brownies
Blondies
Fruit
Raspberry crumble bars
Brie en croute with blackberries
Blueberry cream cheese coffee cake
Avocado and crab terrine
Apple fennel slaw
Dill new potato salad
Jerk chicken salad with charred corn
and black beans

Janet Steger selects flowers to use in one of her floral arrangements for an event in The Grove.

Recipes from First Ladies

This delicious, yet simple recipe was used by Eleanor Hutcheson, VPI's first post-World War II first lady. It was printed in a cookbook published by the Blacksburg Woman's Club more than half a century ago. The first lady is pictured below right.

Charlotte Russo*

1. In a small bowl, soak gelatin until soft in ½ cup water. Pour in ¼ cup hot water.

2. In a mixing bowl, whip cream until stiff. Sweeten to taste.

3. After gelatin is thoroughly dissolved, pour it into whipped cream; stir with a fork. Pour into a mold; refrigerate for at least 1 hour.

4. If desired, can be served with whipped cream.

*Also called Charlotte Russe and including 1 teaspoon vanilla extract, this concoction was often poured over a 1-quart mold lined with lady fingers before it was refrigerated, turned out on a platter, and served. The dessert was popular in the 1930s, 1940s, and 1950s.

½ box gelatin
½ cup water
¼ cup hot water
1 quart good cream
sugar to taste

Eleanor Hutcheson's recipe for boiled custard has been updated by her daughter-in-law, Ivis Hutcheson, who provided the first lady's recipes for this book. Although the recipe most likely carried a different name when Eleanor Hutcheson used it, her descendants have christened it with a name that reflects its origin in the family.

Gran's Custard*

1. Remove top pan of double boiler from bottom pan. Heat water in bottom pan of double boiler over medium heat.

2. Meanwhile, in the top pan, add sugar, flour, and eggs; beat together. Place back over bottom pan, maintaining heat on medium. Add milk. Boil and stir until mixture gradually thickens to desired consistency.

*Eleanor Hutcheson's grandchildren called her "Gran."

¾ cup sugar
1 teaspoon flour for thickness (use more if needed)
3 large or 4 medium eggs, beaten
1 quart milk

The following recipes for punch were found in notes kept by LizOtey Newman, who can be seen on the far right in the photograph with President Walter S. Newman and their great nieces and in the portrait on the left, which hangs in the Holtzman Alumni Center on campus.

Photo on right courtesy of Alice Dekker

Punch

1 quart to 20 people. Can get 5 quarts from 1 quart of frozen juice. 3 gallons of punch for 75 people

Serves: 125

8 quarts of orange and lemon ice
   (mixed without egg or milk)
9 quarts of orange juice, unsweetened
5 small cans of lemon juice
6 quarts of ginger ale—add last

Makes 3 pints of juice—Add 3 parts of water and 3 parts ginger ale.

24 lemons
12 oranges
2 pounds sugar
1 pint pineapple syrup

Punch

Put some juice in punch bowl first.
2 quarts of ice to 1 punch bowl

Serves: 200

12 cans of quart frozen orange juice
40 quarts of water
6 cans lemon juice
12 quarts of frozen orange and lemon ice

This recipe, provided by Alice Dekker, a great niece of first lady LizOtey Newman, was written in Mrs. Newman's handwriting (see bottom right). Alease Cardwell cooked for the Newmans, and her recipe for buckwheat cakes produced a favorite meal for the Newman family.

Alease Cardwell's Buck Wheat Cakes

1. Mix first 3 ingredients together. Crumble yeast cake into the mixture. Set to rise over night.

2. Next morning, add remaining ingredients after dissolving last 2 ingredients in 1 tablespoon of warm water.

3. Fry in hot griddle.

1 cup buck wheat
2 tablespoons flour
1 cup warm water
½ yeast cake
½ teaspoon salt
3 tablespoons Brer Rabbit molasses
½ teaspoon baking powder
½ teaspoon soda

Alease Cardwell, pictured on the right in the photograph, was the first family's cook. Her recipe for buckwheat cakes was popular with the Newmans. Photo courtesy of Alice Dekker

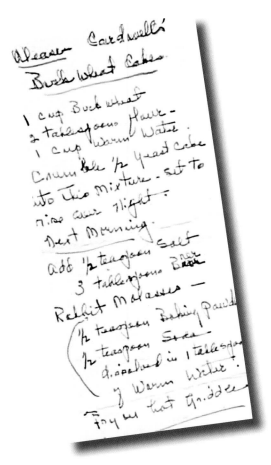

This recipe of the late first lady Peggy Hahn continues to be a family favorite and is often served with ham. It is a particular favorite of her grandson, Shane McKelvy, who is a sous chef at Preston's at The Inn at Virginia Tech.

Sweet Potato Biscuits

1. Preheat oven to 425 degrees (F).

2. In a large bowl, combine first 3 ingredients. Cut Crisco and butter into flour mixture. Add sweet potatoes and milk; stir until dry ingredients are moistened.

3. Knead 3 or 4 times. Roll to ½-inch thickness. Cut with 2-inch cutter.

4. Place on greased baking pan. Bake in preheated oven until golden brown, about 18 - 20 minutes.

2 cups self-rising flour
¼ cup sugar
¼ teaspoon cinnamon
3 tablespoons Crisco shortening
2 tablespoons butter
1 cup sweet potatoes, mashed
⅓ cup milk

Peggy Hahn's personal collection of recipes included the one below, which also features sweet potatoes.

Sweet Potato Muffins

1. Preheat oven to 400 degrees (F). Grease muffin tins.

2. In a mixing bowl, cream butter and sugar. Add eggs and mix well. Blend in sweet potatoes.

3. In another bowl, sift flour with baking powder, salt, cinnamon, and nutmeg. Add to sweet potato mixture, alternately with milk. Do not over-mix. Fold in nuts and raisins.

4. Fill muffin tins ⅔ full, and bake 25 minutes.

Yield: 24

½ cup butter
1 ¼ cups sugar
2 eggs
1 ¼ cups mashed sweet potatoes
1 ½ cups all-purpose flour
2 teaspoons baking powder
¼ teaspoon salt
1 teaspoon cinnamon
¼ teaspoon nutmeg
1 cup milk
¼ cup chopped pecans or walnuts
½ cup raisins, chopped (optional)

This recipe was copied from one in Peggy Hahn's collection.

Zucchini Bread

1. Preheat oven to 325 degrees (F).

2. In a large bowl, beat eggs; add sugar, oil, zucchini, and vanilla.

3. In another bowl, combine flour, salt, baking soda, baking powder, and cinnamon. Add to egg/zucchini mixture; blend. Add nuts.

4. Pour into 2 loaf pans. Bake in preheated oven for 1 hour.

Yield: 2 loaves

3 eggs
2 cups sugar
1 cup vegetable oil
2 cups raw zucchini, grated
3 teaspoons vanilla extract
3 cups all-purpose flour
1 teaspoon salt
1 teaspoon baking soda
¼ teaspoon baking powder
3 teaspoons cinnamon
1 cup nuts

According to Betty Hahn, daughter of Peggy Hahn, her mother grew up on a dairy farm, and everyone in her family was "crazy about ice cream." Betty says that her mother used to make vanilla ice cream or add different fruits that were in season. Both strawberry and peach were favorite flavors of the first family, who would "gather together and take turns turning the crank on the ice cream freezer."

My Homemade Ice Cream*

1. Beat eggs in top of double boiler; add sugar, cream, half-and-half, and vanilla. Cook over hot water until custard mixture thickens. Chill.

2. Add fruit to chilled custard. Place mixture in canister of 6-quart ice cream freezer. Add ice and rock salt around canister; turn crank until it meets resistance, which generally means that the ice cream has frozen. If it is too soft, shut the freezer, and begin cranking again. If desired consistency cannot be reached, put the canister in the freezer to let the ice cream get harder.

*A note Mrs. Hahn wrote on the recipe card says that instead of cream and half-and-half, homogenized milk can be used, but "it will not be as rich."

6 eggs
2 - 3 cups sugar
4 ½ pints whipping cream
2 quarts half-and-half
2 ½ teaspoons vanilla extract
2 big boxes frozen strawberries
   or 4 cups fresh peaches, mashed
   or puréed

Peggy Hahn made this chowder in large batches, increasing the ingredient amounts in the recipe below by four.

Manhattan Clam Chowder

1. Cook bacon in a large frying pan. Cook celery and onion in bacon fat.

2. Drain clams, reserving liquid. Add water to liquid to make 4 cups. Add to bacon, celery, and onion. Add other ingredients except clams, flour, and water. Cover and simmer for 35 minutes.

3. Blend flour with water to make a paste. Add to chowder, and stir until soup boils. Add clams.

3 slices bacon
1 cup celery, diced
1 cup onion, chopped
2 7-ounce cans clams
water
1 1-pound can diced tomatoes
1 cup carrots, diced
1 ½ teaspoons salt
¼ teaspoon thyme
dash of pepper
2 tablespoons flour
2 tablespoons water

Peggy Hahn and President T. Marshall Hahn play croquet on the front lawn of the president's home. Photo courtesy of Special Collections, University Libraries, Virginia Tech

Peggy Hahn's lemon chess pies were a great favorite of her family, and her daughters continue to follow her recipe.

Peggy's Lemon Chess Pie

Filling

1. Preheat oven to 325 degrees (F).

2. Sift together sugar and cornmeal.

3. Add milk to beaten egg yolks; add melted butter. Pour milk mixture into sugar mixture, stir, and add lemon juice.

4. Beat egg whites until fluffy; fold in.

5. Pour into two 9-inch pie shells (recipe below). Bake 50 minutes in preheated oven.

Serves: 14 - 16

1 ½ cups sugar
1 tablespoon cornmeal
1 cup milk
4 eggs, separated and yellows beaten
¼ cup butter, melted
½ cup lemon juice

Standard Pastry

1. Sift flour, salt, sugar, and baking powder.

2. Using a pastry blender (or 2 knives), cut in half of the shortening thoroughly or until mixture resembles coarse cornmeal. Cut in remaining shortening until particles are about the size of peas.

3. Sprinkle water, 1 tablespoon at a time, over small portions of the mixture. With a fork, press the flour particles together as they absorb the water; do not stir. Toss aside pieces of dough as formed, and sprinkle remaining water over dry portions. Use only enough water to hold the pastry together.*

4. Press all dough together lightly with fingers, or wrap dough in waxed paper and press together gently. Bear in mind that the less the dough is handled, the more tender and flakey the pastry will be. Chill dough.

5. Roll out on floured board, and put into pie pans.

*Dough should not be wet or slippery.

2 cups flour
1 teaspoon salt
1 teaspoon sugar
1 teaspoon baking powder
⅔ cup shortening, chilled
6 tablespoons cold water

Betty Hahn provided this sampling of her mother's handwritten recipes.

This cake recipe comes from the wide-ranging recipe collection of Peggy Hahn.

Chocolate Pound Cake

1. In a medium bowl, sift flour with cocoa, baking powder, and salt. Set aside.

2. Grease and flour a 10-inch tube pan. Preheat oven to 350 degrees (F).

3. In a large bowl, beat butter, shortening, and sugar until light and fluffy, about 5 minutes. Add eggs, one at a time, beating well after each addition. Beat in flour/cocoa mixture in 4 additions, alternating with milk in 3 additions, beginning and ending with flour mixture. Add grated chocolate and vanilla, mixing well.

4. Turn batter into prepared pan. Bake in preheated oven for 1 hour and 15 - 20 minutes.

5. Remove cake from oven and place, still in pan, on a wire rack; cool for 10 minutes. Turn cake out of pan; let cool completely on rack.

6. If desired, serve with whipped cream and shaved chocolate.

3 cups all-purpose flour, sifted
½ cup unsweetened cocoa
½ teaspoon baking powder
¼ teaspoon salt
1 cup butter or margarine, softened
½ cup Crisco shortening
3 cups sugar
5 eggs
1 ¼ cups milk
2 tablespoons unsweetened chocolate, grated
1 teaspoon vanilla extract

Peggy Hahn made the following simple, yet delicious, chicken salad, which she served at receptions and for light meals at the Grove and later at events held in the president's home on Rainbow Ridge.

Mrs. Hahn's Legendary Chicken Salad

1. In a large bowl, mix ingredients until well blended.

2. Serve as a salad with crackers on the side, spread on bread rounds,* or use as the filler for sandwiches.

*Slice bread; cut slices into crustless round shapes with canapé or biscuit cutters. Toast lightly, if desired, before using.

Yield: approximately 2 cups

1 pound chicken, boiled and cubed
1 cup celery, including leaves, chopped
1 sprig fresh dill, chopped
¼ cup mayonnaise
salt and pepper to taste

"This is one of my mother's simplest, most delicious, and enduring recipes," says Betty Hahn, daughter of first lady Peggy Hahn. Betty uses the recipe frequently for "an easy but fabulous dessert."

Mama's Apple Crisp

1. Preheat oven to 350 degrees (F).

2. Mix first 4 ingredients until well blended. Press on top of peeled and sliced apples in baking dish.

3. Bake in preheated oven until crust is browned and apples are juicy and cooked.

Serves: 6 - 8

1 stick butter, softened
1 cup flour
1 cup brown sugar, packed
1 cup oats
apples, peeled and sliced

Peggy Lavery's recipe for this seafood dish was in the Virginia Tech Faculty Women's Club's 1984 cookbook, Culinary Contentment, *and is reprinted here with the club's permission. The first lady, who never lived in The Grove but set in motion the renovation that returned it to its original purpose, is pictured at right.*

Travis House Oysters

1. Preheat oven to 400 degrees (F). Grease a 3-quart casserole dish.

2. In a large skillet, melt butter over medium heat.

3. Remove from heat; add flour, stirring until smooth.

4. Return to heat; cook, stirring constantly, for 5 minutes or until light brown. Add paprika, salt, pepper, cayenne, garlic, onion, and green pepper. Cook 3 - 5 minutes, stirring constantly. Add oysters and their liquid, lemon juice, and Worcestershire. Stir well.

5. Pour into prepared casserole dish. Sprinkle with cracker crumbs. Bake for 20 minutes.

Serves: 6 - 8

½ cup butter
½ cup all-purpose flour
1 ½ teaspoons paprika
½ teaspoon salt
¼ teaspoon pepper
dash of cayenne
½ garlic clove, minced
1 medium onion, chopped
½ medium green pepper, chopped
2 quarts fresh oysters
1 tablespoon lemon juice
2 teaspoons Worcestershire sauce
¼ cup cracker crumbs

Peggy Lavery's recipe for this dessert appeared in Culinary Contentment, *the 1984 cookbook published by the Virginia Tech Faculty Women's Club, and is reprinted here with the club's permission.*

Best Ever Cobbler

1. Preheat oven to 375 degrees (F).

2. Lightly grease a 9-inch pan. Cover bottom of pan with fruit.

3. In a medium-size bowl, cream ¾ cup sugar and butter.

4. Sift together flour, baking powder, and ¼ teaspoon of salt.

5. Add flour mixture and milk alternately to creamed mixture, stirring after each addition until blended. Pour batter over fruit.

6. Mix together 1 cup sugar, ¼ teaspoon salt, and cornstarch. Sprinkle over top of batter. Cover with boiling water; bake for 45 minutes.

Serves: 8

4 cups fresh fruit, cut into bite-size pieces
1 ¾ cups sugar, divided
3 tablespoons butter
1 cup flour
1 teaspoon baking powder
½ teaspoon salt, divided
½ cup milk
1 tablespoon cornstarch
1 cup boiling water

Peggy Lavery's recipe for this salad was also printed in Culinary Contentment, *the 1984 cookbook published by the Virginia Tech Faculty Women's Club, and is reprinted here with the club's permission.*

Creamy Spinach Salad

1. In a small bowl, blend sour cream and French dressing.

2. In a large bowl, combine spinach, oranges, cucumber, cheese, walnuts, and onion.* Pour sour cream mixture over greens. Toss lightly.

*Note: This part of the recipe can be prepared in advance.

Serves: 8

½ cup sour cream
¼ - ⅓ cup creamy French dressing
1 10-ounce bag fresh spinach, torn into bite-size pieces
1 11-ounce can mandarin oranges, chilled and drained
1 small cucumber, sliced
1 cup sharp cheddar cheese, shredded
½ cup walnuts, chopped (optional)
1 medium red onion, sliced and rings separated (optional)

Adele McComas White's recipe for this salad first appeared in Food for Thought, *the 1993 cookbook published by the Virginia Tech Faculty Women's Club, and is reprinted here with the club's permission.*

 Apple Salad with Fruit Dressing

Apple Salad

1. Core and cut apples into bite-size pieces, leaving skin on.

2. Toss apples with grapes, celery, raisins, and nuts. Cover with fruit dressing (recipe below); stir gently until fruit is coated.

*Although she originally made the recipe with raisins, the first lady now leaves them out.

Fruit Dressing

Combine mayonnaise, orange juice, sugar, and honey; stir until smooth. Fold in whipped cream.

Yield: about 7 cups

2 medium red apples
2 medium yellow apples
2 cups seedless grapes
1 cup celery, diced
¼ cup raisins (optional)*
¼ cup pecans or walnuts, chopped

½ cup mayonnaise
¼ cup orange juice
1 tablespoon sugar
1 tablespoon honey
½ cup whipping cream, whipped

Adele McComas White's recipe for chili con queso also appeared in Food for Thought, *the 1993 cookbook published by the Virginia Tech Faculty Women's Club, and is used here with the club's permission. Since publication of the recipe, she has made a few adjustments, particularly in the amount of cheese, and the following recipe is the one she now uses. The recipe, she says, originated in Las Cruces, New Mexico.*

Chili Con Queso

1. In a frying pan, melt butter over medium heat. Add onion and garlic; sauté. Add tomatoes, chilis, salt, and pepper. Reduce heat to simmer. Add cubed cheese, stirring until cheese melts.* Add Worcestershire and paprika, mixing well. Simmer for 15 minutes.

2. Serve with tortilla chips.

*Mixture can be thinned with cream, if desired.

Yield: about 1 ½ quarts

1 tablespoon butter
1 medium onion, chopped
2 garlic cloves, chopped
2 cans Rotel tomatoes with chilis
2 4-ounce cans chopped green chilis
salt and pepper to taste
1 2-pound Velveeta cheese, cubed
1 teaspoon Worcestershire sauce
1 teaspoon paprika

First lady Adele McComas White's recipe for this salad was published in Food for Thought, *the Virginia Tech Faculty Women's Club's 1993 cookbook, and is reprinted here with the club's permission. "It was my mother's favorite salad recipe, and she always made it when we had company," says the first lady, who likes to use it for women's luncheons.*

Pineapple Cream Cheese Salad

1. In a saucepan over high heat, cook pineapple liquid to boiling. Pour hot liquid over gelatin. Stir until dissolved; cool to room temperature. Add cream cheese; stir until dissolved. Chill in refrigerator.

2. When gelatin begins to set, add pineapple and celery, followed by whipped cream and nuts, blending well.

3. Pour into mold; place in refrigerator. After gelatin has completely set, unmold before serving.

Yield: approximately 8 cups

liquid from 1 can of pineapple plus
   enough water to equal 1 pint
1 6-ounce package lemon-flavor gelatin
6 ounces cream cheese, softened
1 20-ounce can crushed pineapple,
   drained and liquid reserved
1 cup celery, finely chopped
1 cup whipping cream, whipped stiff
½ cup pecans or walnuts, chopped

Adele McComas White receives numerous requests for the following recipe, which she acquired from a friend at Kansas State University.

Lynn's Pecan Tarts

Dough

1. In a bowl, combine 3 ingredients until well blended.

2. Form into small balls; place in mini-muffin pans. Press along sides and bottom to form each shell. Set aside without baking.

Yield: about 60 small tarts

2 3-ounce packages Philadelphia
   cream cheese
2 sticks margarine
2 cups flour

Filling

1. Preheat oven to 350 degrees (F).

2. In a bowl, mix sugars and margarine until well blended. Add other ingredients, mixing well.

3. Place filling in shells.*

4. Bake in preheated oven 20 - 25 minutes.

5. Remove from oven; serve warm or at room temperature.

*Mrs. White notes that she usually has more dough than filling.

1 cup brown sugar
½ cup granulated sugar
1 stick margarine, melted
1 tablespoon flour
2 eggs
2 tablespoons milk
1 teaspoon vanilla extract
1 cup pecans, chopped

Adele McComas White's recipe for this entrée first appeared in Food for Thought, *the 1993 cookbook published by the Virginia Tech Faculty Women's Club, and is reprinted here with the club's permission. The recipe came from her German grandmother. "It took her so little time to put it together," she says. "I find it takes me less time with practice—especially working with the dough."*

Beef Strudels

1. Prepare dough (recipe below) and filling (recipe below).

2. In a large pot over high heat, bring broth to boil.

3. After filling dough with meat mixture, prepare edges by pinching dough tightly together over and around meat filling. Drop into boiling broth; boil at least 15 minutes or until filling is cooked.

4. Remove strudels from pot; drain before serving.

*The first lady has used canned beef broth but prefers to make the broth herself by boiling a rib-eye steak—with fat—and adding water for the desired amount of broth.

Yield: 20 - 25 strudels

2 - 3 quarts beef broth*

Dough

1. In a mixing bowl, beat egg and yolks together until light; beat in water and salt. Stir in flour to make dough; set aside.

2. Prepare filling (recipe below).

3. On lightly floured board, roll dough into thin sheet; cut into 3- or 4-inch squares. Place a large tablespoon of filling (meat) on each dough square; fold dough over meat.

1 egg plus 3 egg yolks
3 tablespoons cold water
1 teaspoon salt
1 ½ cups all-purpose flour

Filling

In bowl, mix beef, breadcrumbs, salt, egg, and onions until well blended. Add beef broth; mix well.

1 pound lean ground beef
½ cup breadcrumbs
1 teaspoon salt
1 egg, well beaten
1 teaspoon onions, minced
2 - 3 tablespoons beef broth

For an Italian-themed dinner entrée for large groups, try the following recipe provided by Adele McComas White. The first lady found the original version of the recipe in her favorite cookbook, Betty Crocker's Hostess Cookbook, *which was published in 1967 and is now out of print. She continues to use the recipe.*

Baked Lasagna

Serves 8 - 10

1. For sauce, combine beef, pork, onion, and garlic in a large frying pan. Cook over medium heat until meat is browned and onion is tender. Drain excess fat. Add tomatoes, tomato sauce, 1 ½ tablespoons parsley, sugar, 1 teaspoon salt, and basil. Simmer uncovered over low heat for 1 hour or until mixture thickens. Remove from heat; set aside.

2. Preheat oven to 350 degrees (F).

3. For cheese mixture, combine cottage cheese, ½ cup Parmesan, 1 tablespoon parsley, 1 teaspoon salt, and oregano in a medium bowl. Set aside.

4. In a 13 ½ x 9 x 2-inch baking dish, layer half each of noodles, sauce, mozzarella cheese, and cheese mixture. Repeat, reserving enough sauce to spread a thin layer on top. Sprinkle with ½ cup Parmesan.

5. Bake uncovered in preheated oven for 45 - 55 minutes or until cheese is bubbly in center. Remove from oven; let stand 15 minutes. Cut into squares to serve.

1 ½ pounds ground beef
½ pound ground lean pork
1 cup onion, chopped
1 garlic clove, crushed
1 pound and 12 ounces canned diced tomatoes
15 ounces canned tomato sauce
2 ½ tablespoons parsley flakes, divided
1 ½ tablespoons sugar
2 teaspoons salt, divided
1 teaspoon basil leaves, crushed
2 pounds creamy large-curd cottage cheese
1 cup Parmesan cheese, grated and divided
1 teaspoon oregano leaves, crushed
8 ounces lasagna noodles, cooked and well drained
¾ pound mozzarella cheese, shredded

Adele McComas White, pictured here, was first lady of Virginia Tech from 1988 to 1994.

Adele McComas White's original recipe for these popular cookies was included in Food for Thought, *the 1993 cookbook published by the Virginia Tech Faculty Women's Club, and is reprinted here with the club's permission. According to the first lady, "This was my German grandmother's recipe—she probably made it with lard—and then my mother's. Grandma always had a 'cookie jar' filled with cookies made from this recipe. My mother was a fourth-grade teacher for 35 years, and it was a time when she could make these for school parties—with each student's name on one." Mrs. White has made some minor changes to the recipe since its publication that she believes result in better cookies.*

Old Fashioned Sugar Cookies

1. Preheat oven to 350 degrees (F).

2. In a large mixing bowl, cream sugar, Crisco and butter until well blended; add eggs, beating until creamy. Add vanilla; blend well.

3. In another bowl, add sifted flour, salt, baking soda, and baking powder; sift together. Add alternately with buttermilk to Crisco mixture, beating well after each addition.

4. Drop about 1 tablespoon of dough at a time onto greased cookie sheet, leaving enough space between dough drops for cookies to spread out without touching. Bake in preheated oven for 12 minutes or until edges brown slightly.

5. Cool at room temperature.

Yield: about 50 1-ounce cookies

2 cups light brown sugar, lightly packed
½ cup Crisco shortening
½ cup butter, softened
2 eggs
1 teaspoon vanilla extract
3 cups all-purpose flour, sifted
¼ teaspoon salt
1 teaspoon baking soda
1 teaspoon baking powder
1 cup buttermilk

This holiday dessert recipe of Adele McComas White was in Food for Thought, *the 1993 cookbook published by the Virginia Tech Faculty Women's Club, and is reprinted here with the club's permission. The first lady acquired the recipe from the mother of President James D. McComas, whose family lived on a dairy farm. According to Mrs. White, her mother-in-law insisted on churning her own butter and making her own buttermilk to use in the recipe.*

Christmas Fruitcake with Orange and Coconut Topping

Christmas Fruitcake

1. Preheat oven to 350 degrees (F).

2. In a large bowl, cream butter and sugar; add vanilla, orange juice, salt, and orange rind; mix well. Beat in eggs, one at a time.

3. Sift together 2 cups of flour and soda; add to butter mixture alternately with buttermilk.

4. Toss dates with 1 cup flour. Fold dates, cherries, nuts, and pineapple into batter; pour into well-greased large tube pan. Bake in preheated oven for 80 minutes.

5. Remove from oven; cool. Invert pan and remove cake; place on serving plate. Cover with orange and coconut topping (recipe below) before serving.

Serves: about 16

1 cup butter, softened
1 ¾ cups sugar
1 teaspoon vanilla extract
1 tablespoon orange juice
1 teaspoon salt
1 tablespoon orange rind, grated
3 eggs
3 cups cake flour, sifted and divided
1 ½ teaspoons baking soda
1 cup buttermilk
1 pound dates, chopped
1 8-ounce bottle maraschino cherries, drained and chopped
2 cups pecans, chopped
½ cup crushed pineapple, drained

Orange and Coconut Topping

1. In a pot over medium-high heat, combine orange juice, sugar, and rind; blend well. Bring to a bubbling boil; remove from heat.

2. Cool to room temperature. Add coconut to cooled juice mixture; stir until blended.

1 cup orange juice
1 cup sugar
1 teaspoon orange rind, grated
½ cup coconut, shredded

The following sugar cookie recipe was acquired by Adele McComas White from Mary Kay Warwick, manager of The Grove during the McComas administration. Warwick prepared the cookies to serve at events held at the president's home during the winter holidays.

Mary Kay's Holiday Cookies

Holiday Cookies

1. Preheat oven to 375 degrees (F). Grease 3 baking sheets.

2. In a medium bowl, thoroughly combine flour, baking powder, and salt; set aside.

3. Place butter in a large mixing bowl; using an electric mixer, beat on medium speed until light in color and smooth in texture. Add sugar; beat on medium speed until fluffy. Add eggs and vanilla; continue beating until thoroughly blended and smooth. Gradually beat in about half the flour/baking powder/salt mixture.

4. Remove from mixer. Using a large wooden spoon, add remaining flour/baking powder/salt mixture, stirring until well blended.

5. Divide dough into thirds. Place ⅓ of dough between large sheets of waxed paper; roll out until dough is ⅛-inch thick, periodically checking bottom of dough and smoothing out any wrinkles. Slide waxed-paper-covered dough onto baking sheet; refrigerate for about 15 minutes or until chilled and slightly stiffened. Follow same procedure for two remaining dough balls.

6. Remove first sheet of dough from refrigerator. Turn over so underside faces up. Peel off waxed paper; loosely replace it. Turn dough right side up; peel off and discard waxed paper. Using assorted 2- to 3 ½-inch cookie cutters, cut out dough; remove waxed paper from bottom. Transfer cookies to prepared baking sheet, placing them 1 ½ inches apart. Repeat process for second and third sheets of dough.

7. Save dough scraps, re-roll between sheets of waxed paper, and follow same procedure as above, including chilling.

8. If desired, colored sugar or nonpareils can be added at this point if cookies will not be iced.

9. Place baking sheets in center of preheated oven; bake for 7 - 10 minutes or until cookies are just beginning to turn brown around the edges. Remove from oven. Using a spatula, transfer cookies from baking sheets to wire racks to cool.

10. If desired, decorate with icing (recipe on facing page).

Yield: 3 - 4 dozen, depending on size

3 ¾ cups all-purpose flour
2 ¾ teaspoons baking powder
¼ teaspoon salt
1 cup unsalted butter, slightly softened
1 ⅔ cups sugar
2 large eggs
2 ½ teaspoons vanilla extract

Icing

1. In a small bowl, sift powdered sugar. Add corn syrup, vanilla, and water; stir until thoroughly blended and smooth. If desired, add food coloring. Sugar mixture can be divided into several parts so that a different food color can be added to each part.

2. Icing can be spread on cookies with a spreading knife (add water if too thick or sugar if too thin) or placed in a pastry bag with a fine writing tip (again adding water if too thick or sugar if too thin) and piped through the tips as outlines.

1 ⅔ cups powdered sugar
½ teaspoon light corn syrup
¼ teaspoon vanilla extract
2 ½ teaspoons water
food coloring (optional)

Virginia Tech's Student Ambassadors

The holiday cards of President and Mrs. James D. McComas (see above) featured a photograph of Virginia Tech's Student Ambassadors decorating the holiday tree at The Grove.

Dot Torgersen's recipe for this appetizer appeared in Culinary Contentment, *the 1984 cookbook published by the Virginia Tech Faculty Women's Club and is reprinted here with the club's permission. The first lady is pictured at right.*

Ham Balls with Pineapple Sauce

Ham Balls

1. Preheat oven to 350 degrees (F).

2. In a large bowl, mix ingredients until fully blended. Form into small balls.

3. Place on a cookie sheet with sides; bake in preheated oven for about 25 minutes or until brown. Reserve liquid for sauce (recipe below).

4. Put ham balls in a very large container; cover with sauce.

5. If making ahead of time, cover pan with heavy foil; freeze. Remove from freezer on day of use; place in 300-degree (F) oven for about 4 hours to warm before serving.

Yield: about 280 cocktail-size balls

3 pounds ground ham, smoked,
   or half regular and half Smithfield
2 pounds ground lean pork
2 eggs
½ teaspoon pepper
2 cups breadcrumbs
2 cups milk
1 tablespoon salt
1 tablespoon dry minced onion
1 can water chestnuts, finely chopped
½ cup almonds, finely chopped

Pineapple Sauce

In a large saucepan, combine all ingredients except flour; boil for 30 minutes. Add enough flour to thicken to the consistency of sauce.

2 large cans crushed pineapple
1 cup vinegar
juice of 1 lemon
2 cups pineapple juice
3 pounds dark brown sugar
1 teaspoon dry mustard
2 cups applesauce
1 teaspoon prepared mustard
⅛ teaspoon ground cloves
⅛ teaspoon allspice
⅛ teaspoon ginger
1 teaspoon dry onion flakes
liquid from ham balls (see above)
Wondra flour

Dot Torgersen's recipe for this appetizer was published in Food for Thought, *the Virginia Tech Faculty Women's Club's 1993 cookbook, and is reprinted here with the club's permission.*

Microwaved Bacon-wrapped Water Chestnuts

1. Arrange bacon in 12 x 7 ½-inch or 9-inch round glass baking dish. Cook bacon in microwave oven on high setting for 4 - 5 minutes or until partially cooked; drain. Cut bacon into 2 halves. Wrap each half-slice around a water chestnut, secure with a wooden toothpick, and arrange in baking dish.

2. Combine remaining ingredients, pour over bacon-wrapped chestnuts, and refrigerate several hours. Remove from refrigerator; drain, reserving marinade in refrigerator for reuse if desired.

3. Place a non-metal rack in baking dish, and arrange wrapped chestnuts on rack. Cover with a paper towel; cook in microwave on high for 1 ½ - 3 minutes. Rotate baking dish; cook on high for 3 additional minutes. Serve hot.

Yield: 16 appetizers

8 slices bacon, cut in half
1 8 ½- ounce can whole water
   chestnuts, drained
¼ cup soy sauce
½ teaspoon ground ginger
½ teaspoon garlic salt

Dot Torgersen's recipe for this salad was included in Culinary Contentment, *the 1984 cookbook published by the Virginia Tech Faculty Women's Club, and is reprinted here with the club's permission.*

Lisa's Caesar Salad

1. Soak garlic in olive oil for 24 hours.

2. Place French bread cubes in bowl; cover with 2 tablespoons of the garlic-olive oil mixture.

3. Place lettuce in salad bowl; sprinkle with salt, mustard, and pepper. Add red wine and 6 tablespoons garlic-olive oil mixture. Break raw egg* into salad. Add bread cubes and Parmesan cheese. Toss.

* Use shell eggs that have been treated to destroy disease-causing bacteria, such as salmonella, since raw eggs may harbor such bacteria.

Serves: 4

1 clove garlic
½ cup olive oil
1 loaf French bread, cut into cubes
   and toasted
2 heads romaine lettuce, torn into
   bite-size pieces
1 ½ teaspoons salt
¼ teaspoon dry mustard
black pepper to taste
2 tablespoons red wine
1 egg
Parmesan cheese to taste

This salad from Dot Torgersen was published in the Virginia Tech Faculty Women's Club's 1984 cookbook, Culinary Contentment, *and is reprinted here with the club's permission.*

Potato Salad

1. Cook potatoes, in jackets, in boiling water until slightly soft; remove from water; peel and dice. Add celery, sliced eggs, and onion. Toss lightly; set aside.

2. Fry bacon until crisp; reserve in drippings.

3. In a large bowl, beat 2 raw eggs; add sugar, salt, pepper, mustard, vinegar, and ½ cup water. Mix well. Pour mixture into hot bacon drippings; stir about 10 minutes or until mixture thickens. Pour over potato mixture; toss lightly to mix thoroughly.

4. Chill several hours in refrigerator. Remove from refrigerator; garnish with parsley.

Serves: 8 - 10

8 medium potatoes
water
1 stalk celery
4 eggs, 2 hard cooked and sliced, 2 raw
1 onion, minced
4 slices bacon, diced
1 cup sugar
1 ½ teaspoons salt
¼ teaspoon pepper
¼ teaspoon dry mustard
½ cup cider vinegar
½ cup water
1 tablespoon parsley, minced

A favorite recipe of Janet Steger is this sorbet, which she bases on one from Greg Patent's Patently Easy Food Processor Cooking. *Her version of the recipe, which calls for fewer ingredients, is very easy to prepare—and it is one enjoyed by her family.*

Strawberry Sorbet

1. Allow berries to partially thaw; cut larger berries into halves or quarters.

2. Put all ingredients in bowl of food processor, pulse 4 -5 times, and then pureé until smooth. If berries were thawed just the right amount, sorbet is ready to eat. If it is a little soft, freeze until semi-firm. Or store in freezer, and then allow to soften about 20 minutes in refrigerator before serving.

*A sweet, red liqueur made from black currants.

Yield: 1 quart

1 quart frozen strawberries, unsweetened
½ cup sugar
2 tablespoons crème de cassis*
1 tablespoon lemon juice

Janet Steger's good friend, Emily Stuart, who was active in the Blacksburg community for many years, gave her this recipe for banana bread, and it has become a favorite of the Steger family. Banana bread is always served at The Grove for breakfast and often at teas.

Banana Bread

1. Preheat oven to 325 degrees (F).

2. In mixer bowl, combine sugar and oil. Add other ingredients except for bananas and nuts in order given, mixing well between additions. Stir in bananas and walnuts.

3. Grease 2 standard loaf pans; pour batter into pans. Bake in preheated oven for 1 hour. If using small pans, approximately 4 x 8 inches, grease pans; pour batter into pans. Bake in preheated oven for 45 minutes.

4. Allow to rest in pans for several minutes, then remove, and wrap immediately while still quite warm. The banana bread should be served at room temperature, never served freshly baked or re-heated. Flavor "develops" and is much better the day after baking.

*Important: bananas must be quite soft and really over-ripe for best flavor.

Yield: 2 standard loaves (4 x 8 inches)

1 ½ cups sugar
½ cup canola oil
2 eggs
3 cups unbleached flour
¾ cup sour milk (to 1 tablespoon vinegar, add enough skim milk to make ¾ cup)
1 ½ teaspoons soda, added to sour milk
pinch of salt
3 very soft, over-ripe bananas, mashed*
½ cup walnuts, chopped

Janet Steger found the inspiration for this recipe, which has her own special touch, in Patently Easy Food Processor Cooking *by Greg Patent, published in 1985. She serves the light soup as a first course for dinners or with sandwiches for lunches.*

Lettuce Soup

1. Slice onion thinly; cut into strips about 2 inches long.

2. Heat oil in pot over medium heat, add onions, and cook until translucent. Add tomatoes and their liquid, chicken stock, salt, pepper, then lettuce. Simmer until lettuce is just wilted.

3. Serve garnished with freshly grated Parmesan cheese and chopped fresh parsley.

Yield: about 1 ½ quarts (serves 6)

1 medium onion
1 tablespoon canola oil
1 15-ounce can petite diced tomatoes, undrained
4 cups chicken stock
½ teaspoon salt
black pepper to taste
4 cups leaf lettuce, chopped
Parmesan cheese, freshly grated
fresh parsley, chopped

Janet Steger developed this recipe for Brunswick stew when her sons were in elementary school and her husband was dean of architecture and urban studies. Like her other recipes, she prepares it in the kitchen of the first family's private quarters on the second floor of The Grove. She serves the stew with green Tabasco sauce.

Brunswick Stew

1. In a slow cooker, combine chicken, water, onion, ham, potatoes, limas, and celery. Cook covered on low for 4 - 5 hours until chicken is done.

2. Remove chicken; shred. Return chicken to the pot; add remaining ingredients. Cook covered on high for at least 1 hour. Reduce heat; simmer until ready to serve.

Yield: 4 quarts

1 ½ pounds boneless, skinless chicken breast
1 quart water
1 onion, chopped
¼ - ½ cup country ham or lean bacon, chopped
3 potatoes, diced
1 10-ounce package frozen baby lima beans
1 cup celery, chopped
10 ounces frozen white corn
1 28-ounce can crushed tomatoes
1 teaspoon seasoned salt
1 teaspoon sugar
½ teaspoon black pepper
3 tablespoons Worcestershire sauce
1 teaspoon Tabasco sauce
3 tablespoons vinegar
½ teaspoon marjoram
11 ounces canned tomato juice (2 small cans)
liquid smoke (just a few drops) to taste

First lady Janet Steger pauses before guests begin to arrive for a formal dinner.

Janet Steger found this recipe, which she has slightly modified, in the 1960 Time/Life series Foods of the World: The Cooking of Spain and Portugal. *It is a dish that her family particularly likes, especially when garnished with homemade croutons. She always doubles the recipe when she prepares it.*

Gazpacho with Homemade Croutons

Gazpacho

1. Combine all ingredients except cold water in a large bowl; place small amounts of mixture at a time in a blender or food processor; purée. Return to bowl, and stir in cold water.

2. Refrigerate for at least 2 hours or until thoroughly chilled.

3. Stir well before serving. Offer garnishes (suggestions below) separately.

Garnishes

½ cup onions, finely chopped
½ cup green peppers, finely chopped
½ cup cucumbers, peeled and finely chopped
2 - 4 cups homemade croutons (recipe below)

Homemade Croutons

Cut bread into ¼-inch cubes. Add enough olive oil to a large skillet to cover the bottom; add bread cubes. Sauté over medium heat until golden brown and crisp, stirring frequently.

*If the bread is too fresh, dry it out in the oven before using.

Serves: 6 - 8

2 medium cucumbers, peeled and coarsely chopped
5 medium tomatoes, skinned and coarsely chopped (canned tomatoes can be substituted)
1 large onion, coarsely chopped
1 medium green pepper, seeded and coarsely chopped
2 teaspoons garlic, finely chopped
4 cups French or Italian bread, coarsely crumbled or torn
¼ cup red wine vinegar
3 teaspoons salt
1 tablespoon tomato paste
1 small (14 ½ ounces) can diced tomatoes
4 cups cold water

1 loaf day-old French or Italian bread,* sliced
olive oil

Another favorite recipe of Janet Steger is this healthy version of the Southern classic peanut soup that comes from Jane Brody's Good Food Book, *published in 1985. The first lady, who has altered the original version, always doubles the recipe when making this tasty main-course soup.*

Peanut Soup

1. In a large pan, sauté onion and garlic in peanut oil, stirring until onions are translucent. Add celery, carrots, potatoes, leeks, and broth. Bring to a boil, reduce heat, and simmer covered until tender, about 15 minutes. Stir in cayenne, pepper, salt, and peanut butter.

2. Purée, small amounts at a time, in a blender or food processor.

3. Serve hot, garnished with chopped scallions.

Serves: 4 - 6

1 large onion, diced (1 cup)
1 large garlic clove, minced (1 teaspoon)
1 tablespoon peanut oil
1 stalk celery, diced
2 carrots, diced
2 cups potatoes, peeled and diced
2 leeks, white part only, diced (optional, or add more onion)
4 cups chicken or vegetable broth
¼ teaspoon cayenne
¼ teaspoon black pepper
¼ teaspoon salt
½ cup smooth peanut butter
scallions, chopped for garnish

This delicious cookie recipe of Marie Livermore, shown here with Janet Steger's slight alterations, appeared in Smithfield Bakes *in the 1980s. Enjoying these cookies during the holidays has become a family tradition for the Stegers.*

Cranberry Cookies

1. Preheat oven to 375 degrees (F).

2. In a bowl, cream butter and sugars. Beat in milk, orange juice, and egg.

3. In another bowl, sift together flour, baking powder, salt, and baking soda; blend well with butter mixture. Stir in nuts and cranberries.

4. Drop by teaspoonfuls onto greased baking sheet. Bake in preheated oven for 10 - 15 minutes until golden brown. Cool on wire rack.

Yield: approximately 10 dozen

½ cup butter, softened
1 cup sugar
¾ cup brown sugar
¼ cup skim milk
2 tablespoons orange juice
1 egg
3 cups unbleached flour
1 teaspoon baking powder
½ teaspoon salt
¼ teaspoon baking soda
1 cup nuts, chopped
2 ½ cups fresh cranberries, halved or coarsely chopped

*Janet Steger found the original recipe for this ratatouille in
a Jane Brody cookbook and has adapted it to suit her family's tastes.*

Ratatouille

1. Cut eggplant into ¾-inch cubes, salt, and allow to drain in a colander for 30 minutes.

2. Meanwhile, heat 1 tablespoon olive oil in a large, heavy skillet or Dutch oven. Add onions and red and green peppers; sauté until onions are translucent. Add garlic and tomatoes; cook and stir for a few more minutes. Remove onion/pepper mixture from skillet to a large bowl.

3. Heat 1 tablespoon olive oil in the same large skillet. Add zucchini; sauté for about 10 minutes. Remove zucchini from pan to same large bowl with onions and peppers.

4. Rinse, drain, and dry eggplant.

5. Add 2 tablespoons olive oil to the large skillet. Add eggplant; sauté for about 10 minutes. Return other vegetables to the skillet; stir to combine. Add thyme, oregano, basil, black pepper, salt, cayenne, and parsley; stir. Simmer 30 - 60 minutes to desired consistency and tenderness.

6. Serve hot or at room temperature.

Yield: about 2 ½ quarts

1 ½ pounds eggplant (preferably 2 small eggplants), unpeeled
salt
4 tablespoons olive oil, divided
2 large onions, thickly sliced
1 large sweet red pepper, cut into strips ¼ inch x 2 inches
1 large green pepper, cut into strips ¼ inch x 2 inches
1 tablespoon garlic, finely minced
2 ½ pounds tomatoes, skinned and chopped (canned tomatoes can be substituted)
1 ½ pounds zucchini, halved lengthwise and cut into ½-inch slices
½ teaspoon dried thyme
½ teaspoon dried oregano
2 teaspoons fresh basil (or ½ teaspoon dried basil)
½ teaspoon ground black pepper
¼ teaspoon salt
⅛ teaspoon cayenne
2 tablespoons fresh parsley, minced

*Janet Steger's mother always made this corn pudding for family
occasions, and the first lady continues the tradition for holiday dinners,
where it is enjoyed by the Stegers' extended families.*

Corn Pudding

1. Preheat oven to 400 degrees (F).

2. Add flour to beaten eggs, and whisk well to eliminate lumps. Add milk, sugar, and salt; mix well. Stir in cream-style corn and baking powder, again making sure to eliminate lumps. Pour into a buttered baking dish.

3. Bake in preheated oven for 1 hour until golden brown.

Serves: about 6

3 tablespoons flour
3 eggs, beaten
1 ½ cups skim milk
¼ cup sugar
pinch of salt
1 can cream-style corn
1 teaspoon baking powder

Index for Recipes

Herbed Bread Pudding with Sage
and Toasted Walnuts, 159
Marbled Rye Bread Pudding with
Black Forest Ham, 125
Mornay Sauce, 91

mushroom(s)
Chicken Marsala with Fontina
Cheese, 136
Classic Risotto alla Milanese, 145
Grilled Vegetables, 50
Mushroom Strudel with Fresh
Thyme, 55
Newburg Sauce, 92
Sauce Chasseur, 102

N

napa cabbage, see cabbage

nectarines
Roasted Fall Fruit, 168

O

oil, truffle
Roasted White Asparagus with
Truffle Oil and Fresh Thyme, 158
Truffle Potato Dumplings with Brown
Butter, 155

onion(s)
French Onion Soup, 84
Grilled Romaine Lettuce with
Grilled Vegetables, 66
Grilled Vegetables, 50
Mâche with Charred Tomatoes,
Vidalia Onion, and Avocado, 61
Parmesan, Cheddar Cheese, and
Onion Toast, 45
Roasted Tomatillo and Onion
Sauce, 137
Southern Chow Chow with Roasted
Corn, 149
Virginia Beef Stew, 82

oysters
Fillets of Sole with Shrimp and
Oysters, 117
Oyster Dressing, 158
Travis House Oysters, 192

P

pancetta (Italian bacon)
Heirloom Tomato Finger Sandwiches
with Pancetta and Basil, 47

panko
Breast of Chicken in the Style
of Kiev, 133
Panko and Wasabi-crusted Baked
Salmon, 115
Parmesan-crusted Fillets of Sole, 116

Parmesan cheese
Cheese Straws, 43
Classic Risotto alla Milanese, 145
Eggplant Lasagna, 141
French Onion Soup with Cheese
Croutons, 84
Fresh Asparagus Wrapped in
Prosciutto Ham and Baked in
Phyllo with Parmesan Cheese, 51
Parmesan and Chive Rolls, 76
Parmesan, Cheddar Cheese, and
Onion Toast, 45

parsley, fresh
Fried Parsley, 111

pasta
Baked Lasagna, 197
Eggplant Lasagna, 141

pâté
Chicken Liver Pâté, 42

peaches
Peach Salsa, 135

peanuts
Peanut Soup, 208

pear brandy
Roasted Grapes, 165

pears
Arugula with Poached Pears, Port
Syrup, Spicy Walnuts, and Stilton
Cheese Salad, 67
Caramelized Pears, 164
Poached Pears and Port Syrup, 67
Roasted Fall Fruit, 168

peas
Split Pea Soup with Virginia
Ham Hocks, 82

pecan(s)
Homemade Granola, 70
Lynn's Pecan Tarts, 195
Pecan Sweet Potato Salad, 60
Spicy Candied Pecans, 153
Sweet Potato Casserole with Pecan
Streusel Topping, 144
White Chocolate Pumpkin bars, 169

pepper(s)
Belgian Endive Leaves with Roasted
Yellow Pepper Hummus and
Whipped Boursin, 41
Chili with Black Beans, 120
Denver-style Chili, 130
Grilled Romaine Lettuce with Grilled
Vegetables, 66
Grilled Vegetables, 50
Red Pepper Butter Sauce, 98
Southern Chow Chow with Roasted
Corn, 149

peppers, poblano
Strawberry and Poblano Salad, 65

peppercorn(s)
Chicken Liver Pâté with Green
Peppercorns and Port Wine, 42
Cognac Peppercorn Sauce, 94
Currant and Pink Peppercorn
Sauce, 125

Y

Z

References for the History of The Grove

A first-person account of a visit to Virginia Agricultural and Mechanical College, *Richmond Times Dispatch,* Richmond, Va., January 17, 1904.

"Alleghany Chapter DAR Was Organized in 1911," *News Messenger,* Christiansburg, Va., July 1, 1976, p. 7D.

Allen, Nadine, "Three Homes for Tech Presidents," *News Messenger,* Christiansburg, Va., July 1, 1976, page 5F.

Anonymous, a photo album with text about The Grove, 1990, from files in The Grove, Virginia Tech, Blacksburg, Va.

Anonymous, note on an envelope that Stedman Oakey did the interior decorating for Mrs. Newman, per Courtney at the Stedman House, from files in The Grove, Virginia Tech, Blacksburg, Va., nd.

"Architects: H. H. Huggins Incorporated," advertisement in *Roanoke Times,* Roanoke, Va., December 10, 1912, p. 9.

"Blacksburg Social News," *Montgomery News Messenger,* Christiansburg, Va., July 26, 1951, p. 8.

Boynton■Rothschild■Rowland Architects, "Conditions Study and Report," 2000, from files in Office of University Planning – Architecture, Virginia Tech, Blacksburg, Va., na, np.

Brownell, Charles E., Calder Loth, William M. S. Rasmussen, and Richard Guy Wilson, *The Making of Virginia Architecture,* (Richmond, Va.: Virginia Museum of Fine Arts), 1992.

Cassell, S. K., letter to John R. Hutcheson, April 8, 1946, Records of the Office for the Vice President for Administration, Stuart K. Cassell (RG 6/1), Special Collections, University Libraries, Virginia Tech, Blacksburg, Va.

Cassell, S. K., letter to Louis Smithey, Smithey & Boynton, Roanoke, Va., June 17, 1950, Records of the Office for the Vice President for Administration, Stuart K. Cassell (RG 6/1), Special Collections, University Libraries, Virginia Tech, Blacksburg, Va.

Chenault, Jim, "The Grove," *News Messenger,* Christiansaburg, Va., April 13, 1989, p. 1A.

Chesapeake & Potomac Telephone Company of Virginia, telephone directories for Blacksburg, Christiansburg, Radford, and Shawsville, Va., 1946, 1947, 1948, 1949, and 1951, Special Collections, University Libraries, Virginia Tech, Blacksburg, Va.

Commonwealth Architects, "Historic Structure Report for The Grove at Virginia Polytechnic Institute and State University," Richmond, Va., draft, 2007.

Cox, Clara B., *Generations of Women Leaders at Virginia Tech* (Blacksburg, Va.: Virginia Tech), 1996.

Cox, Clara B. and Jenkins M. Robertson, *History and Historical Data of Virginia Tech,* an online history book, found at *www.uni-rel.vt.edu/history/,* (Blacksburg, Va.: University Relations, Virginia Tech), 2010.

Cox, Janet, "Virginia Tech president's home will be renovated," *Montgomery News Messenger*, Christiansburg, Va., March 29, 1987, page 5B.

Crawford, Courtney of the Stedman House, letter to Mary Kay Warwick, April 3, 1989, in files at The Grove, Virginia Tech, Blacksburg, Va.

Dekker, Alice, e-mail messages to Clara B. Cox, September 14, 2011; December 12, 2011.

Dekker, Louisa, letter to Adele McComas, December 22, 1989, in files at The Grove, Virginia Tech, Blacksburg, Va.

Eggleston, Joseph D., letter to Prof. R. E. Hunt, May 8, 1919, in files at The Grove, Virginia Tech, Blacksburg, Va.

Eichhorn, Lynn, interview in Office of University Planning - Architecture, Virginia Tech, Blacksburg, Va., October 27, 2011.

Engineering and Geographical Information Systems Department, Town of Blacksburg, Va., telephone interview, February 24, 2012.

"Faculty and Officers," *The Bugle 1903,* the student yearbook published at Virginia Agricultural and Mechanical College (today's Virginia Tech), Blacksburg, Va., p. 10.

"First President's House Is Now Infirmary," *News Messenger,* Virginia Tech Centennial Edition, Christiansburg, Va., March 16, 1972, p. 14B.

"Grove Tour Information Sheet," May 16, 2001, in files at The Grove, Virginia Tech, Blacksburg, Va., na, np.

Hahn, Betty, interview at The Grove, Virginia Tech, Blacksburg, Va., March 18, 2011.

Heffernan, Licia, "Former president's house to be renovated," *Collegiate Times,* Virginia Tech student newspaper, Blacksburg, Va., May 8, 1987, p. 1A.

"History of the Department," website of the Department of Economics in the College of Science, Virginia Tech, *http://www. econ.vt.edu/history.htm.*

Hoge Jr., James Otey, ed., *The Diaries of James Armistead Otey* (Blacksburg, Va.: Pocahontas Press), 2004.

Holmes, Martha, interview at The Grove, Virginia Tech, Blacksburg, Va., September 19, 2011.

"Huggins, Henry Hartwell (1864 - 1912)," in files in Virginia Room, Roanoke Public Libraries, Roanoke, Va., na, np, nd.

Hughes, Nancy, "Reviving The Grove," *Roanoke Times,* Roanoke, Va., July 6, 1989, p. NRV-1.

Hutcheson, Ivis R., telephone interviews, March 21, 2012, and April 2, 2012.

"Home to be Renovated," *Spectrum,* Virginia Tech faculty/staff newspaper, Blacksburg, Va., April 12, 1987, p. 1.

Hutcheson, John R., letter to S. K. Cassell and J. R. Abbitt, April 6, 1946, Rccords of the Office for the Vice President for Administration, Stuart K. Cassell (RG-41), Special Collections, University Libraries, Virginia Tech, Blacksburg, Va.

Kark, Warren, telephone interview, February 24, 2012.

Kinnear, D. Lyle, *The First 100 Years: A History of Virginia Polytechnic Institute and State University* (Blacksburg, Va.: Virginia Polytechnic Institute Foundation Inc.), 1972.

Lancaster, Paul, "Letter to the Editor," *Spectrum,* vol. 18, issue 10, October 26, 1995, online at *http://scholar.lib.vt.edu/vtpubs/spectrum/sp951026/3c.html.*

Lavery, Peggy, telephone interview, January 11, 2012.

Marshall Jr., Mrs. Frank, "Blacksburg Social News," *Montgomery News Messenger,* Christiansburg, Va., December 1, 1949, p. 12.

Matty, Gregory M., "Building 274," hand-printed article, nd but probably written as a student class assignment while The Grove was serving as office space for the Center for the Study of Public Choice, on file in the Office of University Planning – Architecture, Virginia Tech, Blacksburg, Va., np.

McComas, Adele and James McComas, letter to supporters of The Grove renovation and refurbishment, November 1990, on file in The Grove, Virginia Tech, Blacksburg, Va.

McNeil, R. H., "Dedication at VPI This Week Recalls Draper's Meadows Drama," *Roanoke Times,* Roanoke, Va., August 18, 1935.

Minutes of the Virginia Agricultural and Mechanical College and Polytechnic Institute Board of Visitors, 1899-1944, on file in Records Management, Virginia Tech, Blacksburg, Va.

Minutes of the Virginia Polytechnic Institute Board of Visitors, 1944-1951, on file in Records Management, Virginia Tech, Blacksburg, Va.

Misra, Shaya, "Tech's White House," *Collegiate Times,* Virginia Tech, Blacksburg, Va., April 18, 1989, p. 1B.

Newman, LizOtey, scans of handwritten notes provided by Alice Dekker to Janet Steger, files in The Grove, Virginia Tech, Blacksburg, Va.

Newman, LizOtey, scans of handwritten recipes and family photographs provided by Alice Dekker to Clara B. Cox, Blacksburg, Va., 2011-2012.

Newman, Walter S., letters to Louis Smithey, Smithey & Boynton, Roanoke, Va., November 27, 1951, to June 20, 1955, Smithey & Boynton Records, 1922-1977 (Ms1992-027), Special Collections, University Libraries, Virginia Tech, Blacksburg, Va.

Pilkenton, Laurie, "President's House to be Restored," *Collegiate Times,* Blacksburg, Va., June 3, 1986, p. 1.

Pointon, Philip L., "Building 274, the President's House, Virginia Polytechnic Institute and State University," a student paper for History 4102, taught by George Green Shackelford, June 5, 1986, Special Collections, University Libraries, Virginia Tech, Blacksburg, Va., np.

Randall, Eric, "Grove becomes a home again," *Roanoke Times,* Roanoke, Va., April 13, 1989, p. 3B.

Randall, Eric, "Tech to renovate home for president," *Roanoke Times,* Roanoke, Va., March 28, 1987, p. 3A.

Sleuss, Michael, "Tech's president's house to undergo renovation," *Roanoke Times*, Roanoke, Va., March 16, 2000, p. 3B.

Smithey & Boynton, "General Description," in "Alterations to President's House, VPI, Blacksburg, Va.," April 5, 1950, Smithey & Boynton Records, 1922-1977 (Ms1992-027), Special Collections, University Libraries, Virginia Tech, Blacksburg, Va.

Smithey, L. P., letters to Walter S. Newman, May 17, 1956 to November 16, 1956, Smithey & Boynton Records, 1922-1977 (Ms1992-027), Special Collections, University Libraries, Virginia Tech, Blacksburg, Va.

Smoot, Ray, telephone interview, March 23, 2011.

"Specifications No. 1755," Virginia Agricultural and Mechanical College and Polytechnic Institute, 1900, in files of the Office of the University Planning - Architecture, Virginia Tech, Blacksburg, Va.

Spinelli, Martin, "Tech's Own 'White House,'" *Collegiate Times,* Virginia Tech, Blacksburg, Va., November 4, 1988, page 6A.

Staff reports, "Renovation of The Grove has cost Tech more than $1 million," *News Messenger,* Christiansburg, Va., July 23, 1989, p. 1A.

Steger, Janet, interview at The Grove, Virginia Tech, Blacksburg, Va., January 18, 2012.

Strother, Warren, and Peter Wallenstein, *From VPI to State University: President T. Marshall Hahn Jr. and the Transformation of Virginia Tech, 1962-1974,* (Macon, Ga.: Mercer University Press), 2004.

"Sudden Death of Mr. H. H. Huggins," *Roanoke Times,* Roanoke, Va., December 8, 1912, p. 20.

"Tech president's home undergoing renovation," *Richmond Times-Dispatch,* Richmond, Va., March 21, 2000, p. 4B.

Temple, Harry Downing, *The Bugle's Echo: A Chronology of Cadet Life at the Military College at Blacksburg, Virginia, The Virginia Polytechnic Institute,* vols. I, II, III, IV, V, VI (Blacksburg, Va.: Virginia Tech Corps of Cadets Inc.), 1996-2001.

The Bugle 1910, the student yearbook at Virginia Agricultural and Mechanical College (today's Virginia Tech), Blacksburg, Va., p. 151.

The Gray Jacket, a student publication at Virginia Agricultural and Mechanical College (today's Virginia Tech), Blacksburg, Va., vol. X, nos. 1, 3, 4, 5, 6, 7, 8, 1901-1902.

The Gray Jacket, vol. XII, no. 1, November 1903, pp. 33-34.

The Gray Jacket, vol. XII, no. 3, March 1904, p. 168.

"The Grove," About Virginia Tech: Buildings, online information at *http://www.vt.edu/about/buildings/grove.html.*

"The Grove again to be president's home and heart of campus hospitality," *Virginia Tech Magazine,* Virginia Tech, Blacksburg, Va., summer 1987, pp. 25-26.

Thomas, Minnie King, "H. H. Huggins, Roanoke's Most Prominent Architect," student paper (school not listed), May 12, 1981, np, in files in the Virginia Room, Roanoke Public Libraries, Roanoke, Va.

Torgersen, Dorothea "Dot," interview at The Grove, Virginia Tech, Blacksburg, Va. September 20, 2011.

"View of a Glass House That Cost $68,949," *Norfolk Virginian Pilot,* Norfolk, Va., February 16, 1953.

Virginia School Reports, 1898 and 1899, and 1900 and 1901, Biennial Report of the Superintendent of Public Instruction of the Commonwealth of Virginia (Richmond, Va.: J. H. O'Bannon, Superintendent of Public Printing), 1899 and 1901.

Virginia Tech, the student newspaper at Virginia Agricultural and Mechanical College and Polytechnic Institute (today's Virginia Tech), Blacksburg, Va., 1908, 1909, 1913.

Virginia Tech Alumni Association Board of Directors, resolution, approved April 25, 1986, and presented to the Virginia Tech Board of Visitors, Blacksburg, Va., May 16, 1986.

"Virginia's Executive Mansion," online at *http://www.executivemansion.virginia.gov/History/architecture.cfm.*

"Walsh's Roanoke City Directory," 1900, 1909, 1910, 1911, cited in Minnie King Thomas, "H. H. Huggins, Roanoke's Most Prominent Architect," see Thomas, Minnie King.

Wells, John E. and Robert E. Dalton, *The Virginia Architect: A Biographical Dictionary,* (Richmond, Va.: New South Architectural Press), 1997.

White, Adele McComas, electronic communication, February 12, 2012.

White, Adele McComas, interview at The Grove, Virginia Tech, Blacksburg, Va., July 26, 2011.

White, Adele McComas, letter to Clara B. Cox, February 7, 2012.

White, Adele McComas, letter to Mr. and Mrs. Horace E. Alphin, January 27, 1989.

White, Adele McComas, written recollections on President and Mrs. McComas's move into The Grove, entertaining in The Grove, and living in The Grove, fall 2011, np.

Wieczynski, Jo, "Grace and efficiency combine," *News Messenger,* Christiansburg, Va., pp. 1C, 3C, August 14, 1988.
"William W. Gray [Obituary]," *Montgomery News Messenger,* Christiansburg, Va., vol. 10, no. 11, May 29, 1940, p. 1.

Witkege, David, "The Brilliant, Brief Life of Harrie Huggins," *The Roanoker,* Roanoke, Virginia, September/October 1997, pp. 34-39.

Worsham, Gibson, "Brief Historic Structure Report for the Porches at The Grove, The President's House, Virginia Polytechnic Institute, Blacksburg, Virginia," prepared for Virginia Polytechnic Institute and State University, February 6, 1998, in files of the Office of the University Planning - Architecture, Virginia Tech, Blacksburg, Va.

Worsham, Gibson, called The Grove "a dramatic piece of architecture up on the hill," and his quote, made to newspaper reporter Jo Wiecznski, appears in "Grace and efficiency combine," *News Messenger,* Christiansburg, Va., August 14, 1988, pp. 1C, 3C.

A rendering for a porch option when The Grove was designed.

Notes

Notes

Notes